# The Tragedy of the Late Gaspard de Coligny

*(La tragédie de feu
Gaspar de Colligny)*

*(1575)*

# The Guisiade

*(La Guisiade)*

*(1589)*

*Carleton Renaissance Plays in Translation / 40*

General Editors

Carleton Renaissance Plays in Translation

François de Chantelouve
# The Tragedy of the Late Gaspard de Coligny

and

Pierre Matthieu
# The Guisiade

Translated with Introduction and Notes
by
Richard Hillman

Dovehouse Editions Inc.
Ottawa, Canada
2005

This book has been published with the help of a grant from the Humanities and Social Sciences Federation of Canada, using funds provided by the Social Sciences and Humanities Research Council of Canada.

Library and Archives Canada Cataloguing in Publication
Chantelouve, François de
    The tragedy of the late Gaspard de Coligny / François de Chantelouve ; and, The guisiade / Pierre Matthieu ; translated with introduction and notes by Richard Hillman.

(Carleton Renaissance plays in translation ; 40)
Translations of: La tragédie de feu Gaspar de Colligny, and La
    Guisiade.
Includes bibliographical references.

ISBN 1-895537-86-X

1. Coligny, Gaspard de, seigneur de Châtillon, 1519–1572– Drama.    2.
Guise, Henri, duc de, 1550–1588–Drama.    3. Saint Bartholomew's Day,
Massacre of, France, 1572–Drama.    I. Hillman, Richard W., 1949–.
II. Matthieu, Pierre, 1563–1621. Guisiade.    III. Title. IV. Series.

PQ1607.C4T713 2005              842'.3              C2005-903927-2

For information and orders write to:

Dovehouse Editions Inc.
1890 Fairmeadow Cres.
Ottawa, Canada, K1H 7B9

For information on the series write to:

Carleton Renaissance Plays in Translation
c/o Department of English
Carleton University
1125 Colonel By Drive
Ottawa, Canada K1S 5B6

Cover art: Rembrandt, Portrait of Cornelis Ansto (detail), 1641. Berlin: Gemäldegalerie.

Typeset in Canada: Carleton Production Centre
Manufactured in Canada

*For A. P.*

*— with thanks for a rhyme*

# Table of Contents

# Acknowledgments

I am grateful to the Social Sciences and Humanities Research Council of Canada for assisting my work at an early stage through an internal research grant (2000–2001) awarded and administered by the University of Western Ontario. Professor Donald Beecher, friend, colleague, editor, and publisher, displayed faith in the project from beginning to end and supplied professional guidance throughout. M. le Professeur Denis Crouzet generously shared with me his enthusiasm and his expertise. Otherwise, my principal obligation is to the many helpful and highly professional librarians with whom I have had dealings in locations throughout France. Special thanks are also due to those colleagues and friends in Tours and Montpellier who took a true leap of faith to help test my hypothesis that the play of François de Chantelouve, whether intended for the stage or not, would have been quite at home there.

R.H.

# Introduction

## Preliminary Remarks

It makes a revealing commentary on modern ideas of literature that the two plays presented in this volume have never been critically canonized and, indeed, have rarely been accorded literary status. The standard histories of French drama mention them either glancingly (usually in derogatory terms) or not at all; thus Raymond Lebègue, who in 1929 had simply dismissed François de Chantelouve in a footnote as "bizarre,"[1] twenty-five years later rounded out his opinion magisterially, and extended it to Pierre Matthieu, in forbidding tones calculated to discourage serious attention:

> Dans le dernier tiers du XVI$^e$ siècle je ne vois pas de tragédies, en dehors de celles de Garnier, qui mériteraient d'être réimprimées. Aussi nous ne nous attarderons pas aux œuvres d'un Chantelouve ou d'un Matthieu; nous préférons retracer le développement en France du genre tragique.

> [In the last third of the sixteenth century I see no tragedies, with the exception of Garnier's, that would deserve to be reprinted. We shall not linger, therefore, over the works of the likes of Chantelouve or Matthieu; we prefer to trace the development in France of the tragic genre.][2]

Happily, despite such absolute consignment of these works, and others like them, to mere oblivion, they have recently come to

9

attract interest — especially, and indispensably, in the form of new editions. As for studies of English literature, mentions of Chantelouve or Matthieu are few indeed, despite compelling reasons, in my view, for accommodating them within our understanding of early modern English culture's engagement with European affairs, of the evolution of English dramatic practice, and of the dramatic production of Shakespeare and Marlowe in particular.

What may be more revealing in a deeper sense, because the point bears on Western culture's progressive image of itself, is the impression given by the standard histories that these works are to be dismissed not merely on artistic but also on moral grounds.[3] For their claim to literary status in their own time — and both plays made that claim, although neither of the playwrights was primarily devoted to letters as such — was accompanied by political and religious absolutism of a particularly violent kind. Their time was the era of the protracted and brutal French civil conflicts that history has labelled the Wars of Religion (1562–98), and their absolutism was a function of intense religious conviction and political engagement: *The Tragedy of the Late Gaspard de Coligny* (1575) is devoted, not merely to justifying the massacre of Protestants that began in Paris on Saint Bartholomew's day (24 August) 1572, but to celebrating it; *The Guisiade* (1589) amounts to a strident call for vengeance in response to Henri III's spectacular liquidation of Henri, Duke of Guise (b. 1550), and his brother Louis de Lorraine, Cardinal of Guise (b. 1555), during the Estates General at Blois in December 1588. On the moral issue, too, the critical climate may now be more accommodating, given the widespread contemporary interest in the ideological functioning of literature, but this is by no means a certainty: the question is a complex one, as I will be proposing more fully below, and the long view of literary history hardly justifies confident predictions.

In any case, the essence of these plays' resistance to canonical status (hence part, I would argue, of their claim to our attention) has been their resistance to generic categorization. This is clear from Lebègue's flat exclusion of them from "le genre tragique" — that is, from the mainstream flowing towards "tragédie régulière," which consecrates the structural rules mandated by French classical theory (notably the neo-Aristotelian concept of the unities of time, place, and action). Other criteria of aesthetic quality —

language, characterization, emotional impact, and the like — have perhaps been less influential, since they are both more subjective and easier to accommodate retrospectively within the taste of the times. The rules of representation, however, as a matter of pure convention, may be objectively applied, and although these plays are also very different from each other, both make, literally, unruly tragedies: taken together, they represent both a rare breed and a mixed breed.

Tragedy is also traditionally supposed to deal with grand moral and emotional verities, transcending its time and place. Accordingly, the frankly polemical orientation and occasional contingency of *Coligny* and *The Guisiade* have encouraged their dismissal as sub-literary and ephemeral. The printed propaganda associated with both the Catholic and Reform causes throughout the latter half of the sixteenth century was enormous, the vast majority of it in the form of topical pamphlets and discourses, which run the gamut from official proclamations and reports of military and political "news" to activist treatises, such as the *Vindiciae contra tyrannos*, that are now considered landmarks in political theory.[4] In the "literary" category, there were more-or-less distinguished poetical contributions by major figures such as Pierre de Ronsard (*La Franciade*, *Remonstrance au peuple de France*) and Agrippa d'Aubigné (*Les tragiques*). But there were also an indeterminate number of pointed dramatic interventions, whose surviving representatives have not generally been credited with much distinction or accorded generic legitimacy.[5] Arguably, this is to impose on the theatrical activity of the era distinctions and restrictions that had little meaning at the time.

It has perhaps been possible to do so because, with respect to French theatre in the 1500s, there is nothing like the extensive records, including the plethora of published play-texts, that exist for the following century — or, indeed, for Elizabethan London. Undoubtedly, as in England itself — and especially outside London — there were far more productions of plays than have been recorded. By no means all plays performed, moreover, were published, while of those that were, not all have survived. Plays intended for production in schools — an important site of theatrical activity in the period — infrequently made their way into print. (The best-known exception is the *Abraham sacrifiant* of Théodore de Bèze, performed and published in 1550; Matthieu's own *Esther* is another; a third is *L'histoire tragique de la Pucelle de Dom-Remy, aultrement d'Orléans*, on the subject of Jeanne d'Arc, by Fronton Du Duc [pub. 1581].)[6] Émile Faguet's nineteenth-century evocation of a vibrant and diverse theatrical scene in Paris and the provinces during this period — "très brillant, très animé [very brilliant, very animated]," with popular and learned audiences rubbing shoulders and medieval mysteries sharing the stage with neo-classical tragedies — appears in its time to have made little headway against the idea of the French dramatic tradition as overwhelmingly, and narrowly, classical.[7] Yet his view has essentially received the authoritative endorsement of Lebègue[8] (despite the latter's hostility to "the likes of Chantelouve or Matthieu"), while Madeleine Lazard, with specific reference to the school plays, observes that "les guerres de religion ouvrent une ère de liberté [the Wars of Religion initiated an era of liberty]"[9] — liberty officially, if imperfectly, repressed in 1598 under Henri IV. Especially to the point is her conclusion that "[e]n français ou en latin, le théâtre permet l'explosion de violentes polémiques religieuses, les collèges prenant parti pour ou contre la Réforme [In French and in Latin, the theatre allowed the explosion of violent religious polemics, the colleges taking sides for or against Reform]" (p. 82). The discernible debris of that "explosion" may lie thin on the ground today, but what remains connects the phenomenon, albeit in indefinite ways, not only with the two works presented here, but also with the relatively numerous surviving tragedies on biblical and classical themes.

It is debatable to what extent some specimens of this biblical and classical tragedy may be considered propagandistic, or even actively ideological (assuming that all texts may be considered passively so). There would hardly be room for doubt about the Protestant orientation of Bèze's play (especially given Satan's appearance as a monk), even apart from our knowledge of the author or the address to the reader introducing the printed version. Likewise self-evident are the political allegories of Matthieu's *Aman* (i.e., Haman) and *Vashti*, drawn from the Book of Esther — close dramatic precursors of *The Guisiade* from the heyday of the Holy League (the radical Catholic political organization headed by the

Guises and financed by Philip II of Spain).[10] But other cases remain more difficult to decide, at least from our current cultural distance. The recurrent theme of God's chosen people tyrannically oppressed but destined to be liberated and vindicated is eminently reversible: it was, indeed, the Huguenots who more actively identified themselves with the persecuted Jews of the Old Testament, and it was they who initiated not only the tendentious religious drama but the broad rhetoric of tyranny and vengeance that pervades it. A key non-dramatic text in this respect is *La Judit* of the Protestant Guillaume de Salluste, seigneur Du Bartas, like Chantelouve a native of Gascony. This poetic adaptation of the Book of Judith implicitly promoted, not just the general hopes of oppressed Huguenots for an ultimate (bloody) triumph, but the widely shared Protestant view of the 1563 assassination of François, Duke of Guise (the father of Henri), as an act of providentially abetted tyrannicide. Like several other vital intertexts for *Coligny*—I will be discussing *La Judit* below (pp. 46–49) and indicating more particular parallels in my notes to the play[11]—Du Bartas's epyllion appeared in 1574. With respect to the religious drama, Matthieu may well have known the *Aman* of the Protestant André de Rivaudeau (1566), as well as the Latin one of Claude Roillet (pub. 1558). So, too, probably, did Chantelouve, whose second play, *Pharaon* (1576), rates as the earliest of the Catholic biblical tragedies to have survived, just as his *Coligny* is the first specimen still extant of Catholic political theatre.[12] But specific allegorical intention or reception is not so clearly mandated by Rivaudeau's text as by Matthieu's, and any topical application remains indistinct to modern scholarly eyes.[13] Certainly, when it comes to *Les Juifves* (1583) by Robert Garnier, the latter's ultimate dramatic exploration of human cruelty in relation to divine retribution, the critical consensus favours a broad moral and religious reading, rather than a narrowly political one.[14] As for Chantelouve's *Pharaon*, its indistinctness extends, surprisingly, even to its religious partisanship in general, despite its dedication to Charles de Lorraine, Duke of Mayenne (1554–1611), the brother of Matthieu's martyr-hero, and the preserve of some tendentious discursive indicators (a point I will return to).

A similar elusiveness and ambiguity apply generally to the period's dramatizations of ancient Roman themes—not surprisingly, since, again, much the same rhetoric of tyranny and victimization, and of the horrors of civil war, was applied on both sides of the perennial French struggle. Recuperating contemporary readings of, say, *César*, by the Protestant Jacques Grévin (c. 1560), or *Cornélie* (pub. 1574), by the Catholic Garnier, depends more heavily on biographical and other historical knowledge than on the texts themselves, although there are undoubtedly more encoded differences than criticism has hitherto registered. Allegorical ambiguity and indirection, abstract moralizing, avoidance of overt political engagement—these were not only the stock-in-trade but the enabling conditions of much theatre, and other writing, of the period. By contrast, the two texts of the present volume represent events from an undisguisedly partisan position and, from that position, insist on a clear distinction between the righteous and the wicked, good and evil.

It is largely by way of such insistence, perceptibly a holdover from medieval thought and dramaturgy, that the plays' neo-classical affinities come under strain and their hybrid generic make-up emerges more clearly. The effect is more striking in *Coligny*, whose classical pretensions, being more ostentatious (indeed noisy—they extend to a Senecan ghost and furies), prove more brittle. Both works, however—the vexed issue of the unities aside—parade an organic allegiance to classical models, as filtered through humanist theatrical practice, which throws into relief their failures to toe the line. The motif of vengeance is itself part of this allegiance, especially as Matthieu develops it to incorporate, in his conclusion, the supremely classical notion of an accursed royal house. Both *Coligny* and *The Guisiade* feature scenes between kings and their counsellors and include the usual debate in stichomythia between mildness and harshness—a device with a notable model in the Senecan *Octavia* (and a new currency in the Renaissance, thanks largely to Machiavelli).[15] But both are most obviously neo-classical in expression, structure, and technique—in their formal versification (mainly Alexandrine couplets), their allusions to classical mythology, their five-act structures, their use of choruses, and their eschewing of on-stage action in favour of lengthy monologues and the reports of messengers.

It is natural, then, that Matthieu apologizes for breaking decorum by bringing on stage the "low" personage of the Duke of Épernon, Henri III's widely hated "minion," who, as in much extreme Catholic propaganda, is caricatured in diabolical terms. At the same time, the apology is pointedly ironic, and the gusto with which Matthieu develops the caricature has a distinct medieval whiff. As for Chantelouve, the trappings of Senecan revenge drama palpably serve him, almost as they will later serve Thomas Kyd in *The Spanish Tragedy* (c. 1587), as an excuse for a neo-medieval sensationalism in the handling of the supernatural— here not only the diabolical variety, but also the divine. From a variety of intersecting generic perspectives, then, one may speculate with some confidence as to why these texts have not found comfortable lodging within the generally well-ordered edifice of early modern French literary history.

Let me return to the more elusive question of the resistance they pose to the moral imperatives of literary history. The basic point may be made succinctly, and with reference to the more technically accomplished of the two playwrights. Matthieu's style may not have won him wide admiration among critics, but he was an accomplished orator, capable of pulling out the rhetorical stops so as to engage and excite his audience. This was, moreover, practically the sole means of doing so in a drama that privileged declamation over dynamic encounters of a Shakespearean kind. It is very much to Matthieu's "literary" credit, then, that he can evoke, say, religious ecstasy with an almost hypnotic fervour (not wholly lost, I hope, in translation):

> On that day when we are pleasing in Heaven's sight,
> God will make us giddy with a flood of delight,
> And in the sweet sugar of those pleasures that nourish,
> His hand shall candy us, with rich savours to flourish,
> Our hearts with nectar fill brim-full, by His grace given;
> He shall open wide our eyes, our breasts shall be riven:
> Then this proud heart of stone from our sides shall He tear
> And give us instead one of tender flesh to wear.
>
> (*The Guisiade*, ll. 1447–54)[16]

What risks discomfiting modern sensibilities is the realization that this lyrical evocation of the sublimation of humanity through the union of God and man is intended as an incitement to mass murder. For at this historical moment, as Denis Crouzet resonantly puts it, "le Dieu de châtiment est aussi Dieu d'immanence amoureuse [the God of punishment is also God of loving inward presence]."[17]

Matthieu's inspirational words are given to the People of France, who at this point are addressing the King through their spokesman at the Estates General, and this outpouring of divine grace will tenderize their hearts, they inform him, if he dedicates himself to the slaughter of their Huguenot fellow citizens — instead of which, he treacherously arranges the "massacre" of the People's, and the Church's, champions. The model Henri is urged to follow is the 1572 massacre of Saint Bartholomew effected by Henri III's brother and predecessor, Charles IX, with the support of the Guises — a reminder that Matthieu is himself following in the line of Chantelouve. Given its importance to both playwrights, it is worth recapitulating that event here, although it remains in many ways mysterious — the mystery itself being, for Chantelouve and Matthieu, a sign of the presence of God.[18]

What is certain is that, following a bungled assassination attempt on the Huguenot leader, Gaspard de Coligny, Admiral of France (22 August 1572), a decision was made at the highest levels to liquidate the principal Protestants then in Paris (on the occasion of the reconciliatory wedding of the Protestant Henri, King of Navarre, with the French king's sister, Marguerite). A prominent, if not the dominant, role was played in the planning and execution by Henri, Duke of Guise, whose religious zeal doubtless contained an admixture of both political ambition and personal desire for vengeance. (Coligny had been accused of sponsoring the murder of the Duke's father François in 1563.) The mob violence that followed either did or did not get out of hand, depending on conflicting accounts of the event. In any case, on Sunday, 24 August 1572, several thousand Huguenots were surprised and slaughtered (estimates differ widely, but perhaps between two and four thousand), and, by royal order, "aftershock" massacres followed immediately in the principal cities of France. For Chantelouve, as in both Catholic and Protestant (including English) imaginations for years afterwards, the massacre occupies centre stage.[19]

For Matthieu, it remains in the wings as an essential and positive reference point, both historical and spiritual.

It seems fair to say that, despite plenty of instances to the contrary, including much more recent ones, criticism still clings to the post-Romantic notion that aesthetic and, more generally, intellectual inclinations go hand-in-hand with broad-mindedness and humanity. Paradoxically, this propensity persists within the very critical schools — those associated with post-modern literary and cultural studies — which insist that such a notion is untenable. The ideological "work" done by texts of all kinds has been increasingly recognized, and the very category of "literature" has been subjected to rigorous deconstruction. Scholars of the Renaissance, in particular, have cultivated a critical habit of exposing post-Romantic myths about the period, beginning with the term "Renaissance" itself. Yet the presumption of greater affinity with the present implied by the New Historicist label "early modern" often seems contradicted in practice. Perhaps because scholars inevitably remain imprisoned within the myths they reject (as Derrida has not only demonstrated but exemplified), a perspective that might be expected to represent the inhabitants of Europe in the period, not as reborn avatars of Antiquity but as very much our own ancestors, has in effect tended to put the emphasis on the *early*, and to distance them from "us." It turns out with remarkable regularity that what early modern literary texts chiefly lacked, despite their formal accomplishments, was varieties of moral enlightenment presumed to be the common property of Western intellectuals today. Such enlightenment projects itself as scrupulous sensitivity to questions of gender, race, class, and, not least, religious difference. Looming behind it, perhaps somewhat nostalgically, is a revolutionary, and Romantic, republicanism: *liberté*, *égalité*, and *fraternité* remain, after all, surprisingly durable rubrics.

The plays presented here belong unequivocally to the *Ancien Régime* — with a vengeance. Indeed, vengeance was a pervasive dramatic theme in the period precisely because the idea was deeply embedded in the political and religious ethos. By their very reactionary energy, *Coligny* and *The Guisiade* testify to the pressure being put, in late sixteenth-century France and Europe generally, on unitary modes of thinking about religion, politics, and society. They are tragedies, ultimately, of the fear of difference. A truly "early modern" approach, therefore, might mean that their time has come — hardly as landmarks of high culture, but as richly revealing objects of study.

To be realistic, however, it is also in the nature of literary study to shun the excessive, the overstated, the banal. This tendency may be a residue of the obsolete value of "good taste," but it also exists, one suspects, simply because researchers like to make discoveries. There is obvious satisfaction to be derived from disclosing the biases of texts that have passed for neutral, exposing the blind spots of authors who have been deemed enlightened, supplying the historical specificity of what has been reputed timeless. Thus the monumental *œuvre* of Shakespeare, most notably, continues to dominate criticism of early modern English literature in part because it offers an unparalleled abundance of fault-lines and fissures. The texts in the present volume, by comparison, present a forbiddingly monolithic face and provide only a slippery foothold to deconstructionist approaches, precisely because they so crudely and openly take sides.

They take, moreover — though in a sense that goes beyond antiquated partisanship — the wrong side, by lining up behind those now generally regarded as persecutors, hence against those classed as victims. Of course, these categories are contingent on point of view, and to allow the Saint Bartholomew massacre to fix them in place is to substitute an historical snapshot for history's motion picture, whose reversals and repetitions confirm the interdependence of victimization and vengeance. Certainly, in the context of the Wars of Religion, the discourse of each implies the other. That point may pertinently be illustrated from Marlowe's dramatic survey of major French political events from the Saint Bartholomew massacre to the assassination of Henri III — that is, over the exact span covered by the two French plays (for *The Guisiade* at least prophesies the latter event and, in its third edition, implicitly acknowledges it).

Although Marlowe's *The Massacre at Paris* is not, in several respects, a particularly coherent text (especially, no doubt, in the imperfect version of it that has survived), contemporary criticism reveals its own incoherence, and lack of historicity, insofar as it resists the play's rhetoric of just retribution. The full original title, after all, adds "*With the Death of the Duke of Guise,*" and that death, when performed by King Henry, is tied, by way of the title's key term, to the crime of sixteen years before: "Surcharged with guilt of thousand massacres, / Monsieur of Lorraine, sink away to hell!" (xxi.93–94).[20] The King may make a tainted instrument of divine justice, but he nonetheless fulfils the prophecy made by the impeccably pious and Protestant Henry of Navarre on that occasion:

> He that sits and rules above the clouds
> Doth hear and see the prayers of the just,
> And will revenge the blood of innocents
> That Guise hath slain by treason of his heart
> And brought by murder to their timeless ends. (i.41–45)

The same rhetoric heralds Navarre's battlefield defeat of the Catholics at Coutras (20 October 1587):

> The power of vengeance now encamps itself
> Upon the haughty mountains of my breast—
> Plays with her gory colours of revenge. (xvi.20–22)

Such language has a right to be excessive, since, like Navarre's victorious strength itself, it comes from God: "Thus God, we see, doth ever guide the right, / To make his glory great upon the earth" (xviii.3–4).[21] This is recognizably the vindictive style that *Coligny* and *The Guisiade* apply to the slaughter of Huguenots—almost never, it should be noted, under the name of "massacre."[22] That term is reserved by Chantelouve for the persecutions of Catholics by Protestants, while Matthieu uses it insistently for Henri III's assassination of the Guises. Marlowe, then, was simply (re)turning the discursive tables.

The fact is that subsequent history has broadly come down on the side of the Huguenots as victims in early modern France. This is not just a matter of body-counting, and it is arguably one that transcends questions of religion and nationality. It is morally more acceptable in modern Western culture generally to accommodate the excesses of protest, revolution, and reform than those of repression and counter-reform, and it proves particularly unsettling when the latter are defended articulately. (Allowances can always

be made, tacitly or not, for the collective excesses of popular igno-
rance — anti-foreign riots in Elizabethan London, for instance —
which may be seen as expressing displaced revolutionary senti-
ment, or playing into the hands of cynical authorities, or both.)
Thus we look for (and inevitably find) ambivalence, if not irony,
when Thomas Nashe, in *The Unfortunate Traveller* (1594), makes
his narrator revel in the slaughter of the Münster Anabaptists.[23]
The author, we tell ourselves, surely cannot be engaged in what
he is saying so engagingly.

One of the historical points which the plays at hand can usefully keep current for us is that the disciplining and punishing
(to invoke Foucault) of socially disruptive religious dissidents in
early modern Europe was not confined to witch-hunting, at one
extreme, or the censoring of unruly intellectuals (Galileo, Bruno),
at the other. Sophisticated and learned Renaissance Catholics (or
Anglicans, like Nashe) could take heresy very seriously, whether
or not they called it by that name. The French Catholics whose
point of view is enacted in these plays were far from shying away
from either the concept or the name, and both carried a potent
emotional charge. Heresy, in this perspective, is not merely deviant belief but a profound offence against the divine creation,
hence against God himself; it represents, in Robert M. Kingdon's
terms, "pollution," "contamination" (p. 39), and mere toleration
of it attracts the taint of sinful complicity.

No doubt, the unabashed, unapologetic rhetoric of justice, punishment, and vengeance that permeates these texts — for Matthieu
is by no means ironic (nor discernibly ambivalent) when he makes
his Nobility swear fidelity to the anti-heretic cause "By the tortures
and irons, the stakes and the prisons / Of the Princes of the Faith"
(*The Guisiade*, ll. 1245–46)[24] — served narrowly partisan ends and
ambitious personal interests. So did the non-dramatic propaganda
that provided the discursive climate; the *prédicateurs* (preachers)
who inflamed congregations into mobs, the pamphleteers whose
vitriol and lies (e.g., concerning the black magic of Épernon, hence
*The Guisiade*, Act III, Scene i) poured from the presses of the League,
well knew that concrete political interests were at stake, whether
or not they were prepared to see Spain ultimately in control of
France. Moreover, there were numerous and important French
Catholics, such as Montaigne and, more broadly, the faction of

so-called "Politiques," who shunned such fanaticism: hence, in the end, the remarkable success of Henri IV in uniting and pacifying France (though on the ineluctable condition of renouncing "heresy" himself). Nevertheless, recuperating an authentically historical context for these plays means giving full value to the sense of menace to divinely mandated order with which Protestantism inspired most devout Catholics in early modern France.

It was a double-edged menace, whose two aspects are not only developed in these plays but shown to be connected. First, there was the fear of real disorder, chaos, and violence: after all, the Huguenots, underdogs as they were, not only provoked the horrors of war, of which civilians were regularly the victims, but themselves committed numerous massacres fully worthy of that term. Then, there was the overlay (or underpinning) of spiritual fear. Insofar as the Huguenots militated against the institutions, representatives, and material manifestations of God, they found themselves identified with the diabolical enemies of God. Iconoclasm, in particular, of which there were recurrent violent outbreaks, touched a raw socio-cultural nerve. A venerable medieval Catholic tradition existed—and enjoyed dramatic expression, as in the fourteenth-century *Miracles de Nostre Dame par personnages*[25]—of representing human and demonic evil in unholy alliance within a dynamic mechanism of divine retribution whereby, in effect, the abused icons triumphantly restore themselves. The liveliest scenes in *Coligny* and *The Guisiade* (the liveliness being chiefly verbal, of course, despite the former's supernatural interventions) are those that develop the connections between the villains and their diabolical (if classically tricked out) supporters. The danger of destruction these allied forces represent is exuberantly evoked precisely so that its energy may be recuperated in the cause of retributive re-creation; that denouement, inevitably, breaks the alliance, enlisting the demonic in the divine cause of eternal reward and punishment.

I shall conclude these preliminary remarks by returning briefly to the "English connection" of the plays in question—part of their claim to attention from the Anglophone scholarly community. I have elsewhere made an extensive case for incorporating these texts within the same "discursive space" in which the historical drama of Shakespeare and Marlowe was produced and received during the 1590s.[26] An active imaginative engagement with French political and religious questions on the part of English theatre-goers may legitimately be inferred from the energetic English involvement in French civil war propaganda,[27] indeed in the wars themselves, as well as from related political issues ranging from the Spanish-English conflict to the activities of English Catholics in France, the "problem" of Mary Queen of Scots (whose mother was a Guise and whose first husband was François II), and the prospective French marriage(s) of Elizabeth. Such an engagement may reasonably be supposed, in turn, to have inflected perceptions of themes such as civil war, problematic succession, and effective monarchy, even when such matters were presented in "purely" English terms — or, indeed, in Roman ones, especially given the French precedents for using Roman material in such a way. But the engagement would presumably have been most active when English plays dealt with material already charged with such meanings. This was the case, as I have argued, with a number of major dramatic texts ranging from *Edward II* (Marlowe) to *Henry V* (Shakespeare). The "overlap" between the present texts and Marlowe's *The Massacre at Paris* is of a particularly provocative kind, since the radically dichotomous structure of the English play, by yoking the Saint Bartholomew murders with those of the Guises, effectively combines the subjects of Chantelouve's and Matthieu's tragedies.

It cannot be proven that Marlowe, much less Shakespeare, was directly familiar with either of the French plays in question. Such familiarity is by no means impossible, however, since those plays had, after all, been published (Matthieu's quite recently, and in multiple editions). There are a number of striking points of textual continuity — and, indeed, of discontinuity. (These have been largely presented in my previous work but will be supplemented here.) The case is strengthened by circumstantial evidence, including a "professional" factor: given what we know of the working habits of Elizabethan dramatists, it seems likely that, regardless of the non-dramatic sources that demonstrably furnished Shakespeare and Marlowe with their primary raw material, the English playwrights would have sought out previous dramatic treatments, insofar as such were known. Certainly, not only would such treatments have stood out as rarities within the "discursive space" in question, but, to the extent that both Shakespeare and Marlowe were (re)staging French themes from an English point of view, the French plays would have comprised their most direct ideological "competition." The interest of the latter for students of early modern English drama does not depend, however, on such possibilities and probabilities. It is, I believe, sufficient to read the texts of Chantelouve and Matthieu alongside those of Marlowe and Shakespeare — and as manifestations of the more general discursive "opposition" of which the English playwrights, and their audiences, could not have been unconscious — in order to guarantee that, at the very least, *The Massacre at Paris* can never again be treated as an isolated or abstract literary exercise in the representation of "exotic" material.

## The Tragedy of the Late Gaspard de Coligny

### The Author

Little is known personally about François de Chantelouve, seigneur de Grossombre (near Libourne on the estuarial Dordogne in Gascony).[28] What we do know suggests — and if there is a paradox, given his anti-Huguenot ferocity, it is only a superficial one — that he was thoroughly committed to early modern literary ideals and to literature itself. Strong evidence for this is the only other volume of his work that survives (pub. 1577), which, in addition to the less directly political tragedy, *Pharaon*, contains some accomplished verse, at once witty and serious, which shows a keen awareness of the latest poetical fashions (broadly speaking, those of the Pléiade).[29] The poems, which have never been republished, include "hymns" addressed to the Mascaret, the estuarial tidal phenomenon of Chantelouve's native region (see *Coligny*, l. 785 and n. 110), and to the flea — a witty encomium following the erotic lead of a well-known Latin poem wrongly ascribed to Ovid.[30] There is also a substantial Petrarchan sonnet sequence, punctuated by "chansons," which chronicles the poet's sufferings (indeed, he gives the impression of being genuinely melancholic), hopes, and fantasies (again, erotically tinged) with regard to a typical stony-hearted beauty, "Angélique."

Finally, this volume offers, scattered in the poet's own verses and in others addressed to him, a few tantalizing scraps of biographical information, certainly sufficient to confirm that *Coligny* (licensed for publication in 1574 and published in the following year) was a young man's production. Moreover, Chantelouve died a young man, presuming that the Bibliothèque Nationale's date of 1581 — offered with a question mark — is roughly accurate. He was only around twenty when he wrote his sonnets, since in one of them he accuses Angélique of being likely to cause his death "Sur les vingt-ans [At around the age of twenty years]," while another obligingly provides a *terminus a quo* for its composition by chronicling (complete with date) the exceptionally harsh winter of 1573, when, in January, he was able to walk on the frozen sea near Libourne.[31] His birthday was evidently the first of March, and he was born in a gloomy stone tower not far from a raging ocean.[32] We may also gather that he made the most of a stay in Paris, where he had business to discharge, by pursuing intellectual interests and acquaintances — so writes a young monk from Libourne who had himself been studying in the capital[33] — and that he dedicated himself to poetry when he was not engaged on the battlefield.[34]

For the salient fact known about Chantelouve is that he was a Knight of the Order of Saint John of Jerusalem (otherwise known as the Knights of Malta or Hospitallers), that prestigious and elite international body (noble birth being a prerequisite) of heirs to the crusading tradition. That tradition was revivified during the Wars of Religion, when domestic infidels rather than foreign ones were constituted as the immediate enemy, and it forms an underlying link between the plays in this volume. It was the stock-in-trade of the Guises (and, more generally, of the House of Lorraine to which they belonged), though it was far from being their exclusive property: there exists a particularly vivid account from Toulouse (also a hot-bed of Protestantism, and not far from Chantelouve's native region) of the public proclamation of a crusade in September 1568; Catholics were enjoined to distinguish themselves by wearing white crosses (as was the case during the Saint Bartholomew massacre itself).[35] Such was, in numerous localities, the sectarian tension preceding the third War of Religion (August 1568–August 1570), which in turn provided, as *Coligny* makes clear, the backdrop for the massacre two years later.

At least one literary text, moreover, which I will have further occasion to cite for specific parallels, invokes the crusading past against the same target as Chantelouve and in support of a similar view of the civil wars. For, likewise in 1568, a certain Pierre Du Rosier, "Gentilhomme bolnoys" (i.e., from Beaune), about whom nothing seems to be known, produced a verse-pamphlet entitled *Déploration de la France*, in which he pleaded with the Reform rebels to return to the example of their forefathers, who gained eternal glory in the Holy Land:

> Retirés vostre fer de vos propres entrailles
> Et coisés sur le Turc comme ce grand Billon
> Eternisés l'honneur de votre Chastillon.

> [Withdraw your sword from your own bowels and, as crusaders against the Turk like the great Bouillon, eternalize the honour of your Châtillon.][36]

The very rhyme encapsulates an opposition between the Catholic militancy epitomized by the legendary Godefroi de Bouillon, that Duke of Lorraine ("ce grand Prince Lorrain" [sig. Cii$^r$]) who made himself King of Jerusalem in the First Crusade (1099), and the apostate family whose most notorious member was Gaspard de Coligny.

By virtual definition, then, Chantelouve was, in the most literal sense, a militant in the Catholic cause, and his poetry vividly evokes his own experiences of battle—especially, it would seem, while serving under Henri d'Anjou (Charles IX's brother, the future Henri III) at the murderous and futile siege of La Rochelle in the first half of 1573[37]—in terms that mingle the aggressive partisanship of *Coligny* with revulsion at the horror of civil conflict:

> I'ay bien souuent, durant l'ardeur mutine,
> Des Citoyens l'vn sur l'autre irrités,
> Et au combat fierement incitez,
> Par le iargon des ministres indine,
> I'ay pour mon prince hazardé ma poitrine,
> Au plomp poudreux des Canons enragés,
> Soit quand les murs rebelles assiegés
> Sentoient d'Henry la fureur herculine,
> Soit quand l'ardeur de deux forts ennemis,
> Eut le voisin contre son voisin mis,

Soit a la bresche, ou soit a la bataille . . .

[Very often I have, in the heat of civil strife—when countrymen
were angered against each other, and incited to fierce combat
by the unworthy rhetoric of ministers—I have, for my prince,
exposed my breast to the powder-charged lead of raging can-
nons, whether when the rebellious walls, besieged, felt the
Herculean fury of Henri, or when the passion of two strong
enemies had pitted neighbour against neighbour, whether in
the breech or in pitched battle . . .][38]

Typically, the point of the sonnet is its conclusion that the poet was
never in such danger of being wounded as when his glance caught
the beautiful eye of his mistress, which ignites him like a piece of
straw ("Et si n'ay peu si tost estre blessé, / Que pour auoir l'œil
seulement passé, / Sur ce bel œil, qui m'ard comme vne paille").

Throughout his verse, Chantelouve's ethos and postures are
conventional enough—perhaps even his juxtaposition (if not fusion) of amorous avocation and spiritual vocation. (Knights of
the Order swore a vow of chastity, but then Rabelais had been,
amongst other things, a monk, while Ronsard himself had taken
minor orders.) Ultimately more useful as a guide to appreciating
*Coligny*, which in isolation risks seeming a mere jumble of literary
scraps thrown together in a spasm of hate, is the proof that Chantelouve nourished his craft with wide classical and contemporary
reading and that he conceived of it at once seriously and playfully;
he seems to have been temperamentally drawn to the combining
of intense feeling, however conventionalized, with comic effects.
A number of the same curious rhetorical flourishes and mytholog-
ical allusions are found in *Coligny* and in the non-dramatic verse
(I will be pointing to some of them), where, if they are not always
employed convincingly, they are never deployed casually. This
context adds a grain of salt to the apology for his Gascon rusticity
of language included in the conventionally humble dedication of
*Pharaon* to Charles, Duke of Mayenne, "tres haut tres magnanime,
& Catholique Prince."[39] Matthieu, more than incidentally, would
dedicate *The Guisiade* to the same Charles, who took up the mantle
of his slain brother Henri as leader of the Holy League.

Chantelouve's membership in the Order of Saint John of Jerusalem would have given him a particular sympathy and connection

with the House of Lorraine, which actively capitalized on that heritage of defending the faith in general, and crusading in particular, which it traced back to Godefroi of Bouillon and Charlemagne.[40] (The duchy of Lorraine, it should be noted, was not part of the kingdom of France until the eighteenth century.) The link with the struggle against heresy was resoundingly confirmed in 1525 by the triumph that followed the bloody suppression of the Protestant-inspired German peasants known as the "Rustauds" by Antoine, Duke of Lorraine, and his brother Claude de Guise. The renewed link with the medieval crusades was a key element of the mythology with which Antoine's son, Duke Charles III of Lorraine, surrounded himself,[41] and it was reinforced by the presence of the Order, which was entrusted with guarding sacred places.

François de Lorraine (1534–63), one of the younger sons of Claude, first Duke of Guise (1496–1550),[42] had been Grand Prieur of the Order and commander of the French galleys during Chantelouve's youth; indeed he must have loomed for Chantelouve as a veritable "mighty opposite" of the Admiral Coligny, having both vanquished the Turks at sea (near Rhodes in 1557) and helped to defeat Coligny himself at Dreux in 1562 — a battle that Chantelouve makes the latter recall with bitter shame (ll. 73–74). Brief as it seems to have been, moreover, Chantelouve's own military career overlapped with the lengthy one of the first Duke of Guise's grandson Claude, chevalier d'Aumale, abbé du Bec (1536–91), likewise commander of the galleys for the Order, who was killed at Saint Denis fighting for the League.[43] The latter's father, Claude de Lorraine, Duke of Aumale, who had been a prominent actor in the Saint Bartholomew massacre, was killed by a cannon-shot at the siege of La Rochelle on 14 March 1573, when Chantelouve might well have been present. Indeed, it adds to the picture of the interlocking aristocratic circles served by the strain of theatrical propaganda in question to know that the sons of the slain Duke of Aumale were subsequently placed by Charles, Cardinal of Lorraine, in the institution he had recently founded, the Jesuit university at Pont-à-Mousson in Lorraine, near Nancy.[44] There they might well have been taught, some four years later, by a young professor of rhetoric, Fronton Du Duc, and, two years after that, may have been present at, or even taken part in, the performance of his play about another crusading figure from Lorraine, *La Pucelle*.

Needless to say, Chantelouve's Order was anathema to Huguenots, its establishments obvious targets; Keith Cameron, in the illuminating introduction to his edition of *Coligny*, pertinently cites the evidence (from the peace treaty of 1576) that the Order's commanderies had been subject to seizure during the uprisings in the Southwest that followed the Saint Bartholomew massacre.[45] The Admiral's previous depredations in Saintonge, singled out in the play (ll. 284, 447), must also have seemed, for Chantelouve, particularly close to home. (That province corresponds to the present Charente and Charente–Maritime, having Saintes, roughly halfway between Bordeaux and La Rochelle, as its principal city.) The singularly virulent treatment reserved in the play for Armand de Clermont, baron de Piles, a prominent victim of the massacre, also conceivably reflects personal animosity. Piles, like the Admiral himself, had become a figure of heroic martyrdom for Protestants, and he had become so in counterpoise to a discourse of vilification. There was a particular focus for such attacks, for he was associated with a violent affront upon Catholics perpetrated at Saint-Jean d'Angély.[46] That town in Saintonge, very close to La Rochelle, was taken by the Protestants in 1568. It was the site of an ancient and important abbey, which owed its stature to a relic of the saint commemorated in the town's name. The abbey was ravaged and the relic destroyed; this may well have seemed a matter of personal honour to a knight of the Order of Saint John.

Chantelouve's dedication of *Pharaon* to the Duke of Mayenne has certainly been invoked to suggest that play's probable application, with its lesson on royal tyranny and divine vengeance, to the emerging struggle between Henri III and the radical Catholic faction headed by the House of Lorraine.[47] Still, the political points remain behind the biblical scenes, and the play's only modern editor manages to consider it a pro-royalist expression of political moderation.[48] But while it is true that the League discourse labelling Henri III as a Pharaoh-like tyrant, Henri, Duke of Guise, as Moses, was not yet widespread in 1576 — it would become insistant and explicit over the next ten years or so, as Matthieu's use of it confirms[49] — this was precisely the period when the cause of the

Guises, and the rhetoric supporting it, were in active formation.[50] Chantelouve would seem to have been both ideally placed and willingly inclined to contribute to this process.

This is not the place to present the case at length, but *Pharaon* does indeed adapt and supplement its biblical material in keeping with such a supposition. In so doing, it arrogates, essentially like *Coligny* but in a lower key, a dramaturgical liberty more suggestive of medieval miracle plays than of humanist theatrical ideals, and the miracle-working Moses, chosen by God as saviour of his people, emerges as a warrior-hero, such as young Henri of Guise had become after his victory at Dormans in 1575.[51] That victory, at which an army of the infamous German mercenary cavalry known as the *reîtres* (Ger. *Reiter*) was virtually annihilated, initiated the mythology of Guise as a heaven-sent purifier of France, resented by a jealous and ungrateful monarch.[52] Precisely such an idea is attached by Chantelouve to Moses (prominently seconded, it should be noted, by his brother Aaron, as was Guise by the Duke of Mayenne), who is actually called upon by the desperate Egyptians to deal with invading Ethiopians:

> Ils m'élisent pour chef, and mes robustes doigts,
> A l'aide du Tonnant, loin des murs égyptois
> Chassent le noir soldat. J'égorge, j'extermine
> Tout ce que je rencontre, et la dextre divine
> Foudroie par ma main l'Ethiope brûlé.
> Je nettoie l'Egypte et vainqueur suis allé,
> Battant l'ost ennemi par maints endroits pénibles,
> Endroits mortellement de fiers serpents horribles,
> Endroits où je portais des cigognes afin
> De défendre mon camp de maint hydre malin.
> Bref, Dieu réchauffe tant de mon ost le courage,
> Me donne tant de cœur que le sanglant orage
> De mes bras massacrants moissonne fièrement.

[They choose me for their leader, and my powerful grip, with the aid of the Thunderer, chases the black soldiery far from Egypt's walls. I cut throats, I exterminate all I encounter, and the divine right hand, through my hand, strikes with thunder the burnt Ethiopian. I cleansed Egypt and went forth a conqueror, defeating the enemy force in many harsh places, places of deadly horror with fierce snakes, places where I carried

storks in order to protect my camp from all the evil serpents.[53]
In short, God so enkindled the hearts of my army, and gave me
such courage, that the bloody storm of my massacring arms
reaped a terrible harvest.][54]

As both plays in this volume amply confirm, this passage is
replete with the language and imagery, including the link between the slaughter of enemies and the killing of "serpents,"
that were attached by radical Catholics to their mystical struggle
against Huguenots. The nearly final words of Matthieu's Guise
(ll. 1853–56) furnish an especially close echo. (The word "massacre" can be used by Moses, perhaps, because the Huguenots
are not directly in question.) There is an intimation, moreover,
of the crusading ideal: once the (demonically black) foreign enemies are driven out of Egypt, the campaign extends beyond. The
envious fear attributed by Chantelouve to the tyrant-king, who
is convinced by a wicked counsellor that the young Moses will
take his crown, vividly anticipates League propaganda, as does,
of course, the divine vengeance ultimately wrought upon him, of
which Moses is the instrument. Then there is Pharaoh's daughter,
Térinisse, who loves and protects Moses as best she can, yet is torn
by loyalty to her father: surely, she makes at least as plausible a
stand-in for Catherine de Medici as does Matthieu's Esther.

All in all, Chantelouve's piece enacts, in a remarkably comprehensive fashion, the installation of the basic discursive elements
that will become the staple of League propaganda over the next ten
years and that will be deployed directly, with no punches pulled,
in *The Guisiade*. These include very particular terminology that,
at least by initiates in 1576 and universally in 1589, would have
been understood as alluding to the French monarch. In rebuking
Pharaoh's tyrannous cruelty, as he thirsts for the destruction of
Moses, Térinisse exclaims,

> . . . Les Sarmates félons
> Près de toi sont humains! Les rougissantes plages
> Où sont horriblement les sanglantes androphages,
> La Scyte barbaresque est douce mille fois
> Plus que la fière Egypte où tigrident les rois!

[The murderous Sarmats, next to you, are human(e). The crim-
son beaches where the bloody cannibals are found, barbarous

Scythia, are a thousand times more gentle than fierce Egypt,
where kings act like tigers!]                    (ll. 318–22)

It is Catherine de Medici in her own person who, in *The Guisiade*,
first confronts her son with an image of himself as a tyrant with
"a Scythian or a Sarmat's heart" (ll. 250–51); at the end, it is the
mother of the Duke of Guise, the precise equivalent of Térinesse,
who, when her son has received the death that Pharoah intended
for Moses, applies the epithet "Sarmat" (l. 2095). If this is a commonplace, it has a particular application, for the Sarmats were
thought of as the ancestors of the Poles, and when Matthieu's
Henri, King of France and Poland, parades his grievances in soliloquy at the opening of Act II, Scene ii, he regrets having abandoned
the "sceptre of Sarmatia" ("sceptre Sarmatique") (l. 471). Agrippa
d'Aubigné also uses the term in *Les tragiques* to comment causti-
cally on the Poles' foolish offer of their crown to Henri d'Anjou.[55]
There seems to be little point in resisting the evidence, both internal and external, that Chantelouve concluded his brief dramatic
career in the same way he began it: as a committed propagandist.

## Date, Editions, Performance

As with Chantelouve's life, on these matters, too, facts are scant.
As previously mentioned, the play as published in 1575 (the only
known sixteenth-century edition)[56] contains an imprimatur from
the authorities of the Sorbonne; this is dated 23 October 1574. The
work was therefore composed within the two years following the
massacre. Cameron demonstrates, moreover, that it closely follows the official apologia commissioned from Guy Du Faur de
Pibrac, which first appeared in early 1573.[57] In contrast with the
distinctly unapologetic glee of many Catholics over what Camillo
Capilupi, for one, treated as Charles IX's "stratagem"[58] — a view
shared by most Protestants — Pibrac's version sought above all
to absolve the monarchy of responsibility and suspicion. (It was
apparently produced at the behest of Catherine de Medici, most
immediately to bolster Henri d'Anjou's prospects of election to
the throne of Poland.) The king, therefore, had to be represented
as naturally merciful and tolerant, and as having acted, with great
reluctance, only after discovering a murderous Huguenot conspiracy headed by the Admiral. This is certainly Chantelouve's line,

although the element of triumphant glee has by no means been expunged.

The caricature of Coligny as a villain matches more popular Catholic propaganda. As documented by Crouzet, accusations of boundless ambition, regicidal intentions, and ruthless Machiavelism had been levelled at Coligny as early as 1568: one text published in that year even gives him an imaginary monologue akin to the opening soliloquy of Chantelouve's character.[59] After Coligny's death, such a portrait would have served particularly to counteract Huguenot idealizations of him as a heroic martyr. Demands for the Admiral's official rehabilitation, in fact, were increasingly backed by armed action, especially in the Midi, and, as Cameron suggests, such events might well have provoked a vitriolic riposte in 1574 particularly.[60] For reasons to be explained below, I would propose, as further confirmation of this as the year of composition, the publication in the same year of Garnier's tragedy *Cornélie*. And I would add the suggestion that such an intervention might have seemed particularly apt during the politically unstable interval following the death of Charles IX on 30 May of that year.[61]

After what seems to have been its hurried initial printing, probably in Paris,[62] Chantelouve's play was ignored until the mid-eighteenth century, when there was a renewal of scholarly interest in Renaissance history. At that point *Coligny* received a careful (though disdainful) new edition, accompanied by a number of explanatory notes and textual emendations; this was printed once by itself and once together with Pierre de L'Estoile's *Journal de Henri III* (that treasure trove for historians).[63] This edition was taken into account by Cameron in producing his scholarly text of 1971, which remains definitive, despite the more recent version of Lisa Wollfe in the highly useful collection, Théâtre Français de la Renaissance.[64]

There would be nothing at all to say on the subject of stage history were it not for the extraordinary claim made by the early nineteenth-century historian Capefigue that the play had a major propaganda impact in its time by way of performances throughout France.[65] This assertion is not attributed or documented, unfortunately, and I have not seen it repeated elsewhere. Nor have I encountered confirmation of the tantalizing reference by Faguet, which would be very much to the point if verified, to performance of *Pharaon* in 1579 at the Hôtel de Bourgogne by the Confrères de la Passion.[66] (The latter was one of Paris's principal acting troupes, known — and this certainly fits the picture — for playing both neo-classical tragedy and the traditional medieval mysteries.) As for Capefigue's claim, Charles Mazouer, for one, considers it "plus que vraisemblable [more than probable]," given the play's obvious propagandistic orientation and potential theatrical appeal.[67] Nor is the notion incompatible with the work's official authorization and its probable printing in Paris despite the playwright's provincial base. It is not at all a difficult piece to mount: it would be stageable by a small number of actors, and one can readily imagine school performances of the sort mentioned by Lazard and recorded for some of Garnier's tragedies.[68] Indeed, by comparison with Garnier's works, *Coligny* seems virtually made for the stage. There are two original stage directions (following ll. 856 and 1008), as well as evidence that the author presumed a visual dimension — notably, Mercury's references to his (iconographically determined) costume and the probable appearances of the Admiral, first with a hangman's noose, then with his wounded arm in a sling. One fact, at any rate, is virtually certain: as with *The Guisiade*, there appear to have been no productions of *Coligny* between its time and ours.

## The Play

Despite its inevitable formal division into five acts, with choruses, *Coligny* is roughly half the length of *The Guisiade*. The latter, in this respect as in others, corresponds more closely to the norm for French neo-classical "recitative" tragedy of the period, as exemplified primarily by Garnier. *Coligny*'s relative concision, partly the result of shorter set-speeches, throws into relief the relative variety of its dramatic effects, which include abrupt transitions and interlocking ironies. In Act I, the Admiral's initial rage and frustration are given immediate political direction through dialogue with his chief henchman Montgomery. Act II shows the King and his Council believing that they can make peace with a wishful thinking that borders on naïveté (but only just). The assurance of God's watchful favour, however, is also put in place. Next, the cynical discussion of Briquemault and Cavagne confirms that the peaceful overtures of the Protestants are a sham, so that the Chorus's subsequent paean of peace is ironically undercut, although an intimation of treachery again redeems virtuous innocence from mere simplicity, while the prayer for divine aid implies the power of faith. Still, the third Act's shifting of the scene to the supernatural plane through Mercury (the conventional Messenger with a difference) presents a surprise answer to that prayer. The effect is to heighten at once reassurance and suspense, as well as to install a comprehensive irony for the final acts, where it is left entirely to the spectator to relate events to the unfolding of the divine will.

Act IV introduces the diabolical at first hand, roughly on the model of Seneca's *Thyestes*, through the ghost of Andelot and the Furies; the latter are rolled, like the Council, into a single speaking part, and their ghastly appearance (if we allow ourselves to think in terms of staging) makes an astounding contrast with their smooth-talking. Finally, the fifth Act presents the "proof" of the king's reasoned and reluctant actions, despite his righteous anger, by giving us the Informer, then the typical debate over mildness and harshness between the King and his Council, with the King notably inclined to mildness. This forms the prelude to a distanced account of the execution of justice (at once sanitized and sanctified), which is provided, as convention dictates, by the Messenger. Finally, the Chorus sets the seal on the blending of royal justice with divine vengeance, then ironically refocuses the tragedy on the person of the Admiral, pointing out the fitting end of his boundless ambition in the high place he now occupies on the gallows.

For an "actionless" play, all of this, within 1,200 lines, makes for a remarkably dynamic one, and this quality is further enhanced by more, and more frequent, variations in metre than are usual in the period. The contrast between Alexandrines (so-called "vers noble") and the varied line-lengths and rhyme patterns of the Choruses is, in itself, standard, though the Choruses of *Coligny* are freer in their technical variations than those of *The Guisiade*. But Chantelouve also makes use of ten-syllable couplets ("vers commun") for less formal dialogue, which is thereby injected with increased energy, while the octosyllabics of the pivotal monologue of Mercury strike a tonal balance between the lightness of motion appropriate to the personage and the deadly seriousness of his mission. Jupiter himself, as quoted in Mercury's account, makes a truly fatherly stand-in for God the Father — at once homely and majestical — in a way that harks back to medieval dramatic representations of the divine. At this point, the neo-classical overlay seems thin indeed, as it does when Coligny and Andelot dress up their diabolism in Senecan trappings. Yet in fact, Chantelouve's most distinctive "aesthetic" achievement is arguably to adapt his classicism so as to evoke, and complicate, the medieval theatrical representation of good and evil.

This elusive effect is easy to dismiss as naïve incoherence, confirming the author's imperfect mastery of his craft at every linguistic level — for Faguet's dismissal of his style as "ampoulé et métaphorique . . . souvent inintelligible [puffed up and full of metaphors . . . often unintelligible]" (p. 334) has not been disputed, as far as I know.[69] I would suggest, instead, an approach by way of the dominant model of humanist tragedy available to Chantelouve and his readers: that of Garnier. Garnier's drama, of course, is on a very different discursive level, and it has enjoyed a commensurately different afterlife as "high" literature. Aesthetics aside, this is possible, I think, because Garnier, although he was by profession a dispenser of the king's justice, resists categorization as a propagandist. If his work is universally acknowledged to reflect dismay over France's civil self-immolation, as he himself affirmed in his prefaces, he certainly never made theatre out of contemporary events, and the absence of aggressive partisanship in his classical and biblical tragedies has allowed his position to be deemed transcendentally humanistic, if not neutral.[70] Garnier briefly joined the League in 1588, two years before his death, but virtually all of his editors and critics have claimed him for the cause of moderation.[71] It is hardly my business here to dispute posterity's consensual reading of Garnier, but I propose that Chantelouve might have read him rather less abstractly and more tendentiously. And he might have been particularly alert to the shift between the two Roman plays, *Porcie* and *Cornélie*, in their representation of vengeance.

This distinction emerges most clearly against Chantelouve's analogous neo-Senecanism, if only we resist dismissing it as otiose. However indeterminate the question of influence, it is possible to draw a good many structural and rhetorical parallels between

Chantelouve's work and the three tragedies, all on classical themes (including *Hippolyte* [1573]), that Garnier had published before 1575. To take large matters first, Garnier's first tragedy, *Porcie*, first published in 1568 (but republished in 1574), proclaims its civil war theme through an opening invocation of discord by the Fury Mégère, whom we may connect both with the Fury in *Coligny*, Act IV, Scene ii, who helps stir the Admiral into action, and with the furious Admiral himself in the speech that begins the play. *Hippolyte* opens with a vengeful ghost rising from the underworld, as does Chantelouve's Act IV. The fact remains that the opening of Seneca's *Thyestes* (Act I), with the ghost of Tantalus egged on by a Fury, would have furnished a quite sufficient model for Chantelouve, although it is one, as I will argue, with especially telling differences. Most of the parallels between Chantelouve and Garnier — if not quite all the rhetorical ones, as will appear — are commonplaces, and for Cameron, notably, they do not establish more than an independent indebtedness on the part of both authors to Senecan tragedy, which was very much in fashion.[72]

It was in fashion, however, partly because it lent itself to moralization in Christian terms. Indeed, Seneca's plays had received a sort of unofficial imprimatur in France from Pierre Grognet's popular vernacular digest, first published in 1534, of "sentences et motz dorés de toutes les Tragedies du grant censeur, et Philosophe moral, Seneque [pithy sayings and golden words from all the tragedies of the great arbiter of conduct and moral philosopher, Seneca]" — paraphrases interspersed with edifying commentary and biblical parallels.[73] Underworld torments, worldly instability and vanity, divine retribution (the particular prerogative of Jupiter) — such stock motifs had already been fast-dyed with Christian significance. They had also proved adaptable to topical affairs, as, notably, in Du Rosier's 1568 *Déploration* (cf. *Coligny*, nn. 12, 57, 71, 95, 117, 118, 167). A French reader or auditor of the 1570s would hardly have been able to exclude current political or religious meanings from, say, the conventional "*clémence/rigueur*" debate, which closely echoes the often-staged medieval motif of the celestial confrontation between mercy and justice. The same principle would apply to contemporary readings of Garnier and arguably, according to the sensitive measures of the times, would have made *Porcie* and *Cornélie*, despite their multiple and substantial overlaps, appear to be poles apart.[74]

At one central point in the former tragedy, there is a debate over mildness and harshness between the philosopher Arée and the victorious Octave (Octavius Caesar), who has joined in the Triumvirate with Antoine (Mark Antony) and Lepide (Lepidus) to defeat the forces of Brute (Brutus) and Cassie (Cassius), the assassins of Julius Caesar. As Jondorf has observed, this exchange closely echoes the prime model of such debates—that passage in *Octavia* (then wrongly supposed to be a work by Seneca himself) where that philosopher is shown counselling mildness to the emperor Nero, who is otherwise inclined.[75] There is, however, a crucial difference: unlike Nero's, the language of Garnier's Octave, as from start to finish in the play, is that of revenge ("Nulle vengeance peut égaler leur offense [No vengeance can match their offence]" [Lebègue, ed., l. 844]), while the rebuttal of Arée — that the gods would use up their thunder if they punished all who offended (ll. 845–48)—anticipates the Christian New Law of mercy. Even one of the Triumvirs, Antoine, resists the idea of vengeance in unmistakably positive, though Aristotelian, terms ("mon magnanime cœur [my magnanimous heart]" [l. 1233]). After all, it is through the terrible cycle of vengeance that the Fury Mégère applies her baleful influence to foment civil war, with Octave her most conspicuous instrument. Bloodshed for the sake of vengeance is used as the primary marker of tyranny — to the point where even Porcie wishes that Julius Caesar had not been killed, for the sake of "le commun repos [general tranquillity]" (l. 554):

> J'affecte plustost voir nostre dolente Romme
> Serve des volontez de quelque Prince doux
> Qu'obeir aux fureurs de ces Scythiques Lous,
> De ces trois inhumains, qui n'ont en leur courage
> Que l'horreur et l'effroy, que le sang et la rage.

> [I would rather see our suffering Rome in servitude to the desires of some mild prince than obey the fury of these Scythian wolves, these three cruel monsters, who have nothing in their hearts but horror and fear, blood and rage.]    (ll. 564–68)

This is undoubtedly the authentic voice of Garnier in his earliest works. The argument exactly matches that of his 1567 "Hymne

de la Monarchie," where, prominent among the Roman examples
of civil war are, again, the ravages of "ces trois Tyrans, ces Tygres
affamés [these three tyrants, these famished tigers]."[76] The political point in both texts applies to the divisive tendencies widely
attributed by Catholic royalists, moderate or not, to the demands
of Huguenots, not only for religious freedom, but for places of
surety and local self-government. ("Inhumain" — at once "inhuman" and "inhumane" — is one of Chantelouve's key epithets for
Coligny.) And when Porcie goes on (ll. 573ff.) to predict that
new Hydra-heads of tyrannous ambition would proliferate even
if these were slain — so that a Hercules would be needed to eliminate them, if indeed one were strong enough — she further taps
into the discourse of fearful Catholics, a discourse that pervades
both *Coligny* and *The Guisiade*.

Porcie thus implicitly leaves room for a positive vengeance,
which would be divine, and which alone would be potent enough
to break the cycle of human retribution. That will become precisely, in post-Saint Bartholomew Catholic rhetoric, the Herculean
achievement of Charles, merciful by nature but, when necessary,
the instrument, not of a demonic Fury, but of God's unleashed
fury (cf. *Coligny*, ll. 632, 694 and n. 92). The king thereby realized, in effect, the full mirror image Garnier had held up to him
in the "Hymne," when he addressed the goddess Monarchie, "qui
consommes / Les tumultes ciuils qui bourrellent les hommes [you
who put an end to the civil tumults that torment mankind]": "Tu
as au côté droit la Justice sacrée, / Et de d'autre tu as la Clémence
succrée [You have on your right hand sacred Justice, and on your
left sweet Mercy]" (Chardon, ed., p. 269 [sig. Ciii^r]).

In 1574, *Cornélie* would necessarily have been received as a
post-Saint Bartholomew play, even if composed before the cataclysm itself.[77] It is significant from such a perspective that the later
work, in a sense, returns to the "original" tyranny, that of Julius
Caesar himself, and shifts its preoccupation with vengeance from
the infinitely destructive human variety to the apocalyptic divine
version. Ambition is no longer a side issue, but the keynote:
"Mechante Ambition, des courages plus hauts / Poison enraciné,
tu nous trames ces maux [Wicked Ambition, poison rooted in the
loftiest spirits, you weave these evils for us]" (ll. 23–24). So it is of

*Coligny*: "Ambition, to whom men's downfall is due, / Alas, how your final effects are dire" (Ternaux ed., ll. 1145–46).[78]

Garnier's religious and political affinities were hardly a secret: he was not only a Catholic with impeccable royalist credentials[79] but a close associate and protégé of Pibrac, to whom he had addressed "Hymne de la monarchie" — "A vous donq! (mon du Faur) de qui le cœur loyal / S'occupe iour et nuit pour le sceptre royal [To you, then, my Du Faur, whose loyal heart is busy night and day for the royal sceptre]" (p. 251 [sig. Aii[r]]) — and to whom he would dedicate his third and final Roman play, *Marc Antoine* (1578).[80] (Posterity has accorded Pibrac, too, a humanistic and moderate label, thanks in part to his own syncretic declaration of Christian Neo-stoic principles in *Quatrains*, and his exculpation of the monarchy for the Saint Bartholomew massacre, so closely followed by Chantelouve, is not necessarily incompatible with such an interpretation, when viewed in its context: it was precisely the kind of tissue of lies that might be justified by its author's conviction of a higher truth, a greater good[81] — or, as Garnier might have preferred to put it, the least of possible evils.) Garnier was also the third contributor (with Ronsard and Amadis Jamyn) to the collection of funeral verses for king Charles, *Le Tombeau du feu Roy Tres-Chrestien Charles IX, Prince tres-debonnaire, tres-vertueux & tres-eloquant*, which appeared (also, naturally, in 1574) from the press of F. Morel, the same (official) Parisian publisher who had published Pibrac's justificatory treatise. The common ideology of the contributors is clear, even if Garnier's poetical tributes lack the messianic fervour displayed by his colleagues, who praise Charles outright for his crusade against heresy.

All things considered, I suggest, from the point of view of Chantelouve and those like-minded, an identification of *Cornélie*'s bloody tyrant, Caesar, with Coligny must have appeared a virtual matter of course in 1574, regardless of Garnier's intention. *Cornélie* would thus have been taken to figure the more horrible sufferings that France would have endured had the Admiral not been eliminated; it would also have foreshadowed that elimination, as is insistently done regarding Caesar in terms of divine punishment, which may be deferred but not escaped. In sharp contrast to the clement philosopher of *Porcie*, *Cornélie*'s Cicero is a spokesman for this idea from the very first lines, where he prays that the gods, though angered against the entire nation — and the litany is taken up by the Chorus — may single out for punishment "les plus coupables testes [the guiltiest heads]" (Ternaux, ed., 1. 5). The collective punishment of the French nation for its sins was likewise evidence of God's righteous anger, according to much contemporary Catholic (and Protestant) discourse, but also a promise of ultimate redemption. The mechanism is figured in the familiar notion of the scourge of God, which is articulated in *Cornélie* by Philippes (anticipating the Council's interpretation of Huguenot successes in *Coligny*, ll. 441ff.):

> Le merité supplice
> Ne suit incontinent apres le maléfice,
> Et souvent les grands Dieux gardent expressément
> Les hommes scelerez pour nostre châtiment :
> Puis, s'en estans servis, rendent avec usure
> Le guerdon de leur crime et de leur forfaiture.

> [Deserved punishment does not follow immediately after the offence, and often the great gods purposely preserve crime-tainted men for our punishment, then, having made use of them, pay with interest what they have merited by their felony and evil-doing.] (Ternaux, ed., ll. 891–96) x

Faith in God's ultimate vengeance is one thing, human vindictiveness another. And Garnier's *La Troade* (1579) seems on balance to condemn the latter, even while, again, leaving plenty of scope for the former, and indeed for mortal impatience at delay.[82] Yet it is arguably part of the function of Cornélie as a vengeful victim to redeem vindictive desire from the stigma it carries from Seneca's and Garnier's own preceding pagan models, as well as from Christian teaching, which, after all, is much closer to Porcie's renunciation of all bloodshed. Cicero's prayers and hope for vengeance are relatively dispassionate; Cornélie invests hers with all the emotional force of righteous hatred, even as her language, too, shifts into the Christian register:

> J'espere que bien tost les Dieux, las de l'esclandre
> Qu'il fait journellement, broyront son corp en cendre,
> Si dans Rome trop lasche il ne se trouve aucun
> Qui vange d'un poignard le servage commun.

Non, je verray bien tost (Dieu m'en face la grace)
Son corps souillé de sang estendu dans la place,
Ouvert de mille coups, et le peuple à l'entour
Tressaillant d'allegresse en bénire le jour.

[I hope that soon the gods, weary of the outrage he daily com-
mits, will smash his body into ashes, if Rome is so cowardly
that no one may be found to avenge with a dagger the common
slavery.

No, I shall soon see (with God's grace) his body, fouled
with blood, stretched out in the public square, cut open by a
thousand blows, and the people round about bless the day,
jumping for joy.] (Ternaux, ed., ll. 899–906)

Cornélie's passion is obviously to be pitied, thanks in part to her
sex; her longing to see Caesar transformed to ashes echoes her
lament over her husband's ashes, which she has just received ("O
douce et chere cendre, ô cendre deplorable [O sweet, dear ashes,
O pitiful ashes]" [l. 855]). All round, she makes a far more appealing and respectable spokesperson for vengeance than Thyestes
or Atreus—and most certainly than Octave; she is thus the perfect vehicle for subtly modulating Senecan ghoulishness into the
sphere of Providence.

On precisely this ground, perhaps surprisingly, Cornélie joins
the Judith of Du Bartas's non-dramatic account, which represents
the divinely enabled decapitation of Holoferne (Holofernes) by
the Jewish heroine as inspiring a similar combination of jubilation
and vindictive mutilation. The head of the "tyran d'Assyrie" is
fixed on the wall and attacked by the populace of the rescued
Bethulia:

Là les peres, les fils, les pucelles, les vefves,
Tristes d'avoir perdu par les ethniques glaives
Leurs enfans, leurs parens, leurs amis, leurs espoux,
Esperdus de tristesse et fumantz de courroux,
Pellent son menton palle, esgratignent sa face,
Crachent dessus son front, arrachent de sa place
La langue qui souloit mesme outrager les cieux
Et d'un doigt courroucé luy pochent les deux yeux;
Car de cent torts receus la vive souvenance
Leur fait sur un corps mort prendre morte vengeance.

[There the fathers, sons, maidens, widows, grieved at the loss by the heathen swords of their children, parents, friends, spouses, wild with sorrow and boiling with rage, dig his pale chin, scratch his face, rip from its place the tongue that was accustomed to offend the very heavens, and with an angry finger gouge both his eyes: for the vivid remembrance of a hundred harms received makes them take dead vengeance on a dead body.][83]

Next, the wholesale slaughter of the pagans by the Israelite soldiers is triumphantly performed and gruesomely evoked, after which the non-combattants "Sortent pour contempler la vengeance que Dieu / A fait des ennemies de son cher peuple hebrieu [Come out to contemplate the vengeance that God has wrought upon the enemies of his dear Hebrew people]" (6.293-94). Finally, the rest of Holoferne's corpse, discovered during the customary pillage of the dead, undergoes a further, and definitive, mutilation: "... il n'a nerf, tendon, artere, veine, chair / Qui ne soit detranché par le sot populace / Et si son ire encor ne trouve assés l'espace [... there is no nerve, tendon, artery, vein, piece of flesh that is not sliced off by the foolish populace, and still its fury does not find enough scope]" (6.310–12).

There is no question of irony here; the very excess of the retribution on the human scale proves that it proceeds from God, the wrathful father, protecting his chosen people from the ambition of a tyrant:

> O Seigneur, le desir et du meurtre et du sac
> Fit venir ce payen dans le terroir d'Isac;
> Mais, au lieu qu'il voulait le sang d'Isac espandre,
> Ore il veut pour Isac le sien propre despandre
> Et ta clemence a fait que son ambition
> Produise effect contraire à son intention.

> [O Lord, the desire for both murder and pillage caused this pagan to enter the land of Isaac; but in the place where he wished to shed the blood of Isaac, for Isaac he is now willing to expend his own, and your mercy has caused his ambition to produce an effect opposite to his intention.]     (6.189–94)

For Catholic readers in 1574, the concluding prayer must have res-onated — perhaps with particular poignancy for a fellow-Gascon — as a provocative Protestant call to avenge the injury of Saint Bartholomew:

> Ainsi, ainsi, Seigneur, desormais puissions nous
> Te sentir non pour juge, ainçois pour pere doux;
> Ainsi les fiers tyrans de ton Eglise chere
> Te sentent desormais pour juge et non pour pere.
>
> [Thus, thus, Lord, hereafter may we feel you not as a
> judge, but as a mild father: thus may the fierce tyrants to your
> dear Church henceforth feel you as a judge, not as a father.]
> (6.357–60)

The provocation would have been rendered more pointed still by the generally understood identification of Du Bartas's Holoferne with François, Duke of Guise, whose assassination nine years ear-lier had been very much in the vengeful air in August 1572.[84] In celebrating the fulfilment of that vengeance, Chantelouve effec-tively substituted his own blasphemous and tyrannical villain for that of Du Bartas — and the notorious fact that Coligny's corpse was decapitated and otherwise multilated would have reinforced the reversal for contemporaries.

Not only does Chantelouve surround his would-be tyrant with language very close to Garnier's for Caesar, but he grafts onto his predecessor's nominally pagan discourse the Judæo–Christian justification of *La Judit*, appropriating its apocalyptic rhetoric for the Catholic side. What emerges intertextually is a pious demon-stration that Christian France has already experienced the pre-emptive intervention of the divine, working the miracle of the massacre to forestall the tragedy that befell Rome. Thus Chante-louve adapts, for his Jupiter's unabashed use, language that, in the mouth of the earthly tyrant Octave, is as self-condemning as the bellicose bluster of Du Bartas's Holoferne. When Octave is begged by Arée to relent, he hubristically spins out his "never" with cos-mic variations: "Plustost du jour flambant l'eternelle clairté / Se joindra sociable avec l'obscurité [Sooner the eternal brightness of the flaming light shall be joined in fellowship with darkness]" (*Por-cie*, ed. Lebègue, ll. 877–78). Jupiter, in *Coligny*, does likewise — speaking on his own impeccable authority:

> O such an end may well appall,
> Into my awful hand to fall,
> Great are my judgements downward sent
> Upon those men most eminent.
>> Sooner than my power shall cede,
>> Chaos's mingled mass shall breed
>> The elements some other way;
>> Night shall sooner become the day.
>>> And sooner shall this vaulted sky,
>>> Daughter of my hands, in ruins lie,
>>> Than the authors of crimes abhorred
>>> Shall fly the slicing of my sword.  (ll. 701–12)[85]

Since the relation between French and English perspectives on key French events, as played out discursively, is also in question here, it is pertinent to mention that Kyd, who translated *Cornélie* in late 1593 or early 1594 (evidently as a bid for noble patronage), seems implicitly to acknowledge its applicability to the events of August 1572. The latter had been recently dramatized, after all, by his erstwhile associate Marlowe (murdered on 1 June 1593 while the case against him for "atheism," in which Kyd was a key informant, was pending).[86] In order to justify his translation, Kyd would have needed at once to establish Garnier as a great author transcending French religious politics and to signal his own wary consciousness of Garnier's Catholicism. Hence, perhaps, a curious double move on the translator's part. On the one hand, Kyd softens (by substituting an allusion to Aesop's fable about nurturing a viper) the virtual justification, by Garnier's wise Cicero, of the preventive killing of such unnatural traitors as Caesar — or Coligny: "massacre" is actually the term used in the original.[87] This is to parry the direct ideological thrust of Garnier's text. On the other hand, Kyd varies the end of the same speech — and this can have been no mere lapse in translation (such as can be found elsewhere) — in such a way as to remind readers subtly of his original's ideological application. When Garnier's Cicero envisages divine revenge, he accurately (and with greater moderation than Cornélie) predicts the fall of Caesar in the Capitol: "ton corps, dechiré de cent poignars aigus [your body torn by a hundred sharp daggers]" (Ternaux, ed., ll. 829–30). Kyd substitutes an image that quite precisely evokes the mutilation and degradation of Coligny:

"And thy dismembred body (stab'd and torn) / Dragd through the streets, disdained to bee borne" (Boas, ed., III.ii.80–81)[88]

To define points of contact between Garnier's neo-classicism and that of Chantelouve is to throw into relief the radically divergent effects produced by the latter's simultaneous medievalism.  Particularly striking — and at first glance a crude breech of decorum in the common sense as well as the formal — is the self-discrediting comic exaggeration attached to the villainous Admiral and his henchmen.  The monologues of Coligny and Andelot are the key instances, but the technique extends even to the brief exchange between Montgomery and Piles (Act III, Scene ii) following the Admiral's wounding, when, with the willful blindness of stubborn sinners, they hysterically call obvious what we know to be untrue — the responsibility of the king and Guise: "It's him, with my Lords his brothers, and Guise, too — he's one: / A villain like me knows a villain when he sees one" (ll. 749–50).[89] Such grotesquery recalls the medieval mysteries and miracles with their comic devils and blustering tyrants — Herod or Pharaoh or Julian the Apostate (the last is especially to the point, as will become clear) — but a further dimension is contributed by the classical overlay, still another by the historical reality and political immediacy.  The multi-textured irony that results plays out, not only tonally but also epistemologically and arguably with profound implications, along the boundary between comedy and tragedy.

The classical element poses a particular interpretative challenge.  It is tempting for a modern reader (or translator) to enrol the more incongruous classical moments under the rubric of parody — when the unspeakably foul Admiral, for instance, mounts suddenly to poetical heights on Virgilian wings:[90]

> O daughter, you who from Tithonus' saffron bed
> Arise to show the gods the universe outspread
> By daylight, as the gate swings open and discloses
> All heaven with carnations deftly strewn, and roses,
> Have you ever perceived, using your watchful eyes,
> Brave men as unhappy as I beneath the skies?        (ll. 57–62)[91]

At the opposite extreme, but essentially of the same kind, is the bathetic recital by the ghost of Andelot of his varied underworld

punishments, which he abruptly elucidates by invoking the hero-
ics of Hercules:

> Now my neck is squeezed so hard by a strangling noose
> That I drivel scum and puke out poisonous juice.
> Thus the son of Alcmene, in his righteous fury,
> Of Pirithous' death to venge the injury,
> Bent Cerberus' inhuman throat to his strong rule,
> Till he perceived the putrid venom of his drool.     (ll. 875–80)[92]

In Andelot's case, the continuation leaves no doubt that the classicism is part of a grotesque, gargoyle-like decorative effect:

> If then to repose at my ease I should desire,
> I recline on a bed of coals glowing with fire.
> If I am cold, to warm me I have lots of — ice;
> And if I feel, in hell, that a meal would be nice,
> All of serpents and toads my prodigious collation
> Is made ready, which serves to keep me from starvation.
>                                           (ll. 881–86)[93]

Insofar as the character's self-consciousness, even wit, throws
such effects into (comic) relief, however, and itself becomes part of
the all-enfolding comic framework — God's thwarting and punishing of evil — we are dealing, not with parody (at least in the
modern sense), which would be didactically counterproductive,
but with a highly functional enlargement of medieval dramaturgy.
There the soul-hungry devils or doomed worldly tyrants *enact* the
futility of their evil, but are not generally felt to *act* it — that is, to
stage it to others. That is what happens here, and the acting takes
place on a rickety classical scaffold. By continually announcing
itself as a transparent fiction, the framework of pagan mythology
comically makes the point that the essential tragedy of Christian
damnation consists, not in imaginary proliferation of the tortures
of Tartarus *ad absurdum*, but in the knowledge, despite oneself,
of one's wilfully chosen evil, hence of God's justice and vengeful
power. Such cursed consciousness of the cursed self is the obverse
of the transcendent bliss associated with looking God in the face —
the privilege of the righteous and the martyred:

> And what angers me more is that all of those monklings,
> Those cardinals and priests, the whole rabble of churchlings

I went about killing, I did them so despise,
Free from death and pain are living in Paradise
And, filled with happiness, behold the divine face,
And among God's children have their appointed place.

(ll. 897–902)[94]

The sinners of *Coligny* are finally less blind than short-sighted, chief among them the Admiral: this is, after all, *his* tragedy. Even in the extraordinary self-disclosing soliloquy with which the play opens, his blustering atheism is bound up with a despair that presumes, not only the otherworldly torments that he, too, fantastically recounts, but their origin in a "juste punisseur [righteous punisher]" (l. 12):

Open up, make room for me, the labour is mine
Of that thieving Sisyphus, deceiving Ixion.
And if there is any God upon whom to call
(For in my foul heart I believe in none at all),
Let him show his power, and fling upon my pate,
Instead of some pointless rock, his thundering hate.

(ll. 13–18)[95]

To seek out hell, complete with torments, as his "natural" home is only superficially comic because it is implicitly to acknowledge his human nature, and so his status as God's creature.

I have elsewhere pointed out that the self-introductory soliloquy of Guise in Marlowe's *Massacre* provides a mirror image of Coligny's, complete with exposure of religious devotion as a hypocritical "cover" for regicidal ambition.[96] The English treatment sustains and pursues the inversion—and thereby also intertextually engages *The Guisiade*—by showing Guise finally dispatched (sixteen years later) by the unlikely instrument of his erstwhile accomplice, Henri III, now performing God's retributive justice. Yet Marlowe's arch-villain remains a shallow Machiavel in comparison to Chantelouve's, and a still more intriguing parallel may be drawn with *Doctor Faustus*, even if the comic elements are there mainly stripped from the tragic hero (only to be redeployed, perhaps, in the ancillary comic scenes). Faustus, like Coligny, is trapped between his better knowledge of God's omnipotent justice—the reality of hell—and his irresistible impulse to circumvent that knowledge by gaining illusory forms of power:

the Admiral's much-cited cunning is the equivalent of Faustus's magic. God is portrayed as allowing him free rein for a time, then bringing him up short. So much may be said of medieval dramatic tyrants in general, but through all the blustering crudity of the Admiral, which certainly evokes such models, the dimension of self-consciousness adds a touch of early modern, proto-Marlovian, complexity.

The parallel extends to the role of Andelot (ll. 857ff.), who functions as a virtual Mephistopheles. Chantelouve's dramaturgy is at its most flagrantly Senecan here — witness the vengeance-sowing ghosts of *Agamemnon* and *Thyestes* — but it swerves all the more conspicuously in a medieval direction, again with a psychological twist.[97] Although Andelot rises from hell, he is never "out of it," being avowedly tortured by alienation from "the face of God,"[98] even if he can appreciate his respite from his physical torments (ll. 909–12). Unlike the ghost of Tantalus in *Thyestes*, to whom he bears such a strong superficial resemblance — and Chantelouve is unlikely not to have noticed that "Andelot" is a near-anagram of "Tantale" — the Admiral's brother is complicit with the evil he has come to cause. For Tantalus, having to spread the spirit of vengeance among his family at the Fury's command is worse punishment than those he normally suffers, and he longs to return to them. For Andelot, what Seneca's Fury presents to Tantalus with sarcasm — "See, I am giving you a holiday" (*Thyestes*, ed. and trans. Watling, l. 61) — is literally true, and he makes the most of his time off, playing his part willingly.

Playing it, moreover, involves a dissembling strategy suggestive of diabolical seduction. Andelot takes psychological advantage of a vulnerable moment — "finding him thus blaspheming, with downcast mind, / I know that to my will he'll be the more inclined" (ll. 917–18)[99] — and gives his brother a vengeance-inducing pep-talk based on an appeal to pride but tinged with a reminder that the Admiral is responsible for Andelot's own fate ("... where your war sent me [... où m'envoya ta guerre]" [l. 926]). The Fury who seconds Andelot (ll. 971ff.), most unlike that of *Thyestes*, keeps her whips out of sight (even if, presumably, she cannot do much about her hair), and her discourse is a parodic masterpiece, joining to the rhetoric of honour both flattery and supplication. Andelot and the Fury are tacitly complicit in obscuring the horrors of the place to which they seek to lure their victim. The former's reticence goes well beyond that of the Ghost of Hamlet, who vividly evokes his tortures, even if he is "forbid / To tell the secrets of my prison-house (I.v.13–14).[100] Andelot evokes, indeed, a rather pacific locale, where swords are not permitted (ll. 965-68), while the Fury absurdly speaks of his soul as reposing (l. 1002). All in all, it is not easy to find, in the dramatic annals of the French or English Renaissance, a case that so thoroughly mingles classicism and Christianity in a supernatural intervention of the precise kind that Hamlet fears, when he suspects that the vindicative spirit of his father "[a]buses me to damn me" (II.ii.603).

Still more remarkable, perhaps, given the multiple intertextual resonances, is Chantelouve's fusion of the two traditions, classical and medieval, in the supernatural element that enfolds the Admiral's tragedy within the divine comedy: the intervention of Jupiter, by way of Mercury, at the opening of Act III. Here a Shakespearean is likely to think first of the reassuring apparition of Jupiter in *Cymbeline*, behind which lies a large body of dramatic romance inflected by the miracle pageants and saints plays of the late Middle Ages.[101] Cameron has identified several strands apparently intertwined in Chantelouve's device[102] — even including, perhaps, the usual appearance of a star in the sphere of Mercury in November 1572 — and I will tease out still others. In the deep background, for contemporaries, undoubtedly lay sequences in Virgil's *Aeneid* (4.198) and Ovid's *Metamorphoses* (1.675ff.) where Mercury undertakes earthly missions at Jove's command — respectively, the admonition of Aeneas to desert Dido and the decapitation of Argus (to free the suffering Io). Most immediately in the foreground would probably have been the pageant of the "Paradis d'Amour" staged as part of the wedding celebrations of Henri de Navarre and Marguerite de Valois shortly before the Admiral's wounding, which spoiled the party (cf. *Coligny*, ll. 817–22).

Despite its trappings of classical mythology, this pageant was laden with the symbolism of religious opposition, heaven and hell; it featured the descent and re-ascent of the divine messenger upon a cock. Such syncretic imagery, in the culture of mid-sixteenth century France, was far from merely decorative: it functioned within the symbolic system of Neo-platonic mystical philosophy. So Crouzet has effectively demonstrated, precisely in relation to

the Saint Bartholomew massacre as manifesting the "secrets" of
God, and his discussion of *La Franciade* of Ronsard, which happened to appear just after that event in 1572, focuses on the roles
attributed there to Jupiter and Mercury.[103] The latter has various
functions, among them, in an extension of his classical role of psy-
chopomp, to bring the souls, after their torturous purgation of
sins, to drink the regenerating waters of oblivion.[104] In its classical
decor, Chantelouve's underworld is reminiscent of Ronsard's (and
for that matter Du Rosier's).[105] His Mercury, however, has nothing to do with it, and his uncompromising traditional Catholicism
makes no concession to Neo-platonic fables of mystical regener-
ation. The souls that Chantelouve's King "sank deep into Styx's
gloomy channel [envoya souz les stiges flos]" (l. 1138) might as
well abandon all hope (see l. 888).

*La Franciade* seems more pertinent to *Coligny* for its adaptation
of the Virgilian model to figure divine protection and promotion of
French royalty. Ronsard's angry Jupiter calls upon the messenger
god to initiate the overdue mission of Francus, the son of Hector
rescued from the fall of Troy, who is destined to found the royal
line of France and renew Troy in Paris:

> . . . Mercure il appella:
> Pour obeïr Mercure s'en-alla,
> Prompt messager à la plante legere,
> Devant le thrône où l'appelloit son pere.
> Vole, mon fils, où Francus est nourri,
> Huche les vents: dy que je suis marri
> Contre sa mere et ceux qui sans louange
> Trompent son âge en une terre estrange.
> Je ne l'ay pas du massacre sauvé
> Pour estre oisif de paresse agravé.
> . . . . . .
> Pource desloge, et le fais en-aller.

[Mercury he summoned. Mercury came in obedience, the
prompt messenger, fleet of foot, before the throne where his father called him. Fly, my son, where Francus is being nurtured;
summon the winds. Say that I am put out with his mother
and those who abuse his age by keeping him ingloriously in
a foreign land. I did not preserve him from massacre for him
to rest idle in increasing laziness, a do-nothing in the flower of

his age. . . . So get moving and make him start out.]

(*La Franciade*, 1.163–79)

What follows is the fitting-out of Mercury with his traditional costume and caduceus, then a description of his swift flight and alighting. The sequence is closely imitated — including verbal echoes[106] — from the pivotal moment of Book 4 of the *Aeneid* where another Trojan refugee is instructed to place his divinely mandated destiny as the founder of Rome above his narrow (indeed illicit) human desires.

Ronsard's Mercury duly discharges his errand, first repeating the message word for word, then evoking, in a significantly abridged version, the future glory of the line to be inaugurated by Francus,

> Qui doit hausser la race Priamide,
> Doit abaisser la grandeur Æzonide,
> Doit veincre tout, et qui doit une fois
> Estre l'estoc de tant de Rois François,
> Et par sus tous d'un CHARLES, qui du monde
> Doit en la main porter la pomme ronde.

> [who is to raise up the race of Priam, humble the grandeur of
> Greece, who is to overcome all and one day serve as the stock
> of so many French kings, and above all of a Charles who in his
> hand shall bear the orb of the world.] (*La Franciade*, 1.245–50)

The same royal Charles is the object of Jupiter's special care in Chantelouve; his glorious palace represents the fulfilled promise of "une nouvelle Troye" (*La Franciade*, 1.178) and, indeed, contains a tapestry renewing the Golden Fleece (*Coligny*, l. 656), thereby implicitly humbling "la grandeur Æzonide" — that is, of Greece (Aeson was the father of Jason, who led the Greeks to obtain that emblem of sacred kingship).[107]

Given Chantelouve's intertextual engagement of *La Franciade*, a particularly resonant word in Jupiter's message according to Ronsard (a note sounded again when the message is repeated), is "massacre." (In Virgil, Jupiter says merely that Aeneas's mother, Venus, "vindicat armis [delivered him from the weapons]" [4.228] of the Greeks.) That highly charged term, after all, had been circulating in the French discursive climate well before the events of Saint Bartholomew's day. Certainly, *La Franciade* postdates the thwarted attempt of the Huguenots to surprise the royal family at Meaux (1567) — an event widely regarded by Catholics as an attempt on the life of the young king Charles.[108] However indirectly, Ronsard thereby encouraged the project of Chantelouve, which would also be that of Matthieu in *The Guisiade*, of (re)placing the label of "massacre" on the bloodthirsty enemies of the heroes of true religion and (however the point is hidden — not to say dis*guised* — in Matthieu's case) true royalty. In *Coligny*, "massacre" is what the Admiral, Montgomery, and their followers intend for Charles and his brother Henri (the word stands out in the French in ll. 130, 624, and 1126), as they seek to cut off the flourishing stock of Francus — a natural follow-up to Montgomery's killing of Henri II (ll. 127–32). The conspirators aim at nothing less than "to extirpate the royal line [la mort de la royale race]" (ll. 1119–20). Thus, for Charles to cut off the conspirators by anticipation (see l. 1135) goes beyond mere self-defence; his act reflects and reaffirms the glorious destiny of Francus's line according to the divine plan. A cosmic covenant underpins Charles's special relation with Jupiter:

> . . . I have taken him so well
> In charge, he may in safety dwell:
> His innocence and I protect him;
> My chosen king I do elect him.                    (ll. 617–20)[109]

If the dynamic of vengeance is mandated by that convenant, it does not enter into the Mercurian analogue in *La Franciade*. It does, however, have strong and specific warrant in another: the medieval tradition of Saint Mercurius ("Mercure"), the warrior saint. Cameron's citation of this tradition is particularly apt and well worth developing.[110] In the legend of Saint Basil the Great and the Emperor Julian, of which a dramatic version survives in the *Miracles de Nostre Dame par personnages*, Mercurius serves as Our Lady's hit-man. It is he who executes her decision to take vengeance (that note is clearly sounded several times) for the insults directed at herself and her son by the vainglorious and tyrannical Apostate (who, ironically enough, seeks to impose belief in Jupiter).[111] Mercurius thereby forestalls the harm with which Julian threatens Caesaria, a city of faithful Christians under Basil's protection. Instead of delivering the city into the hands of eagerly waiting devils, the latters' "grant maistre" (*L'Empereur Julien*, l. 666) is himself borne off to hell, body and soul. The essential situation and action bear an obvious resemblance to those of *Coligny*, the abominable Apostate making a natural model for the Admiral.

There are also technical similarities, beginning with the use of octosyllabic couplets, between Act III, Scene i, and the representation of Mercury's mission in the miracle play. The resemblance is close enough to suggest — and the idea is by no means improbable — a stage tradition with which Chantelouve was familiar. First, Our Lady, descending in great pomp from heaven on a throne, summons Mercurius by way of the angels Gabriel and Michael:

> Appellez moy sanz plus d'espace
> Mercure, mon bon chevalier.
> Je vueil qu'il me voise vengier
> De Julien, cel homme infame;
> Mon doulx fils et moy trop diffame,
> Si ne doit plus estre souffert:
> Vengée en veuil estre en appert.

> [Call to me Mercurius, my good knight, at once. I wish him to
> see to it that I am revenged upon Julian, that wretched man:
> my sweet son and me he defames excessively; he cannot be
> allowed to keep it up. I wished to be manifestly avenged for
> this.]                                                    (ll. 629–35)

Then, when Mercurius arrives, she gives him his instructions, sounding very much like Chantelouve's Jupiter:

> Mercure amis, sanz demourée
> Vaz me tost, vaz sanz dalaiance
> De Julien prendre venjance.
> Tu le doiz bien grever et nuire:
> Il a empensé de destruire
> Et de gaster ceste cité
> Et moi a yre a excité
>      Trop malement.

> [Friend Mercurius, do not linger, but go right away, go without
> delay, and take vengeance on Julian for me. You must cause

him great pain and harm: he has formed the intent of destroying and ruining this city and has aroused me to anger in a way
too evil.]                                              (ll. 645–51)

An auditor could hardly have avoided being impressed by this
speech, since it is subsequently cited — as Chantelouve's (as well
as Ronsard's) Jupiter is cited by Mercury — by those who have had
a vision of the supernatural intervention: first, Saint Basil himself
(" 'Vaz me tost, va sanz contredit / De Julien prendre venjance'
['Go at once, go without demur, and take vengeance on Julian
for me']" [ll. 863–64]), then Julian's steward Libanius (" 'Vaz me
de Julien vengier' ['Go and take vengeance on Julian for me']"
[l. 970]), who is converted on the spot.[112]

Yet for all the self-conscious medievalism of Chantelouve's device, its deceptively complex effect depends on its classicism, and
this, too, is reinforced intertextually. A whole series of allusions
to the *Aeneid*, especially in the Chorus concluding Act I, ensure
that the Virgilian model redeployed by Ronsard in *La Franciade* is
present directly, as well as indirectly. Coligny is thus cast, not just
as an anti-Francus, but as a perverse Aeneas, stubbornly resistant
to the divine will, in contrast to the Roman hero's legendary piety.
To the point here is the initiation of the sequence in Virgil by the
vengeful prayer against Aeneas and Dido intoned by the jealous
king Iarbus, whose offer of marriage the Carthaginian queen had
spurned.[113] He vividly evokes Jupiter's punishing thunderbolts.
Next come Jupiter's instruction to Mercury and the execution of
the latter's errand to Aeneas. Chantelouve's dramatic rework-
ing effectively transfers to Coligny himself the twisted personal
vindictiveness in Iarbus' appeal to Jupiter; the latter, in turn, is
invested with the transcendent benevolence of a deity essentially
different from Virgil's, or Ronsard's, pagan one. Chantelouve's
Jupiter exercises his vengeance belatedly, reluctantly, and for the
greater good — precisely to prevent the sort of human suffering
epitomized by the fate of Dido, betrayed by Aeneas. After all,
it is the Chorus of the People of France that, in admonishing the
Admiral, "No woman, surely, gave you suck, / But a tigress of
Hyrcania [Une femme ne t'a nourri, / Mais une Tygresse yrca-
nine]" (ll. 259–60), speaks with Dido's voice (cf. *Aeneid*, 4.367).

Finally, a tour of intertexts for Chantelouve's theatrical *tour de force* turns up a precedent even for the grim humour that tinges the deadly serious business of Jupiter and Mercury. The Prologue to *Le Quart Livre* of Rabelais depicts a council in heaven among the pagan gods, presided over by Jupiter (and prominently including Priapus).[114] Just after ordering Vulcan to have the Cyclops forge him a new supply of thunderbolts (cf. *Coligny*, ll. 713–16), Jupiter turns his attention to a poor woodsman, who has been noisily importuning the god because he has lost his axe, his means of livelihood. There follows a moral fable aimed against those who — in effect, like the Admiral and his followers — would abuse and cheat heaven in pursuit of their selfish desires. In a familiar style recalled by Chantelouve, Jupiter sends Mercury down, emblematically arrayed like the playwright's character,[115] to offer the woodsman his choice among three axes: his own poor one, a silver one, and a gold one. If he takes any but his own, Mercury is to cut his head off (a reminiscence of Mercury's decapitation of Argus in the *Metamorphoses*). The woodsman chooses honestly and is given the other two axes as a reward. These he carries to Chinon ("ville insigne, ville noble, ville antique [outstanding city, noble city, ancient city]" [*Le Quart Livre*, p. 27] — one thinks of Chantelouve's Jupiter presenting Paris, "Laquelle n'eut jamais de prix [City beyond all earthly price]" [*Coligny*, l. 605]) — and exchanges them for money.

The cautionary and serious point comes next: when the townspeople learn how the poor man became rich, they rush to imitate him, acquiring axes in order to lose them and ask Jupiter for a new one. But when offered the same choice, they invariably choose the golden axe, and Mercury cuts off their heads. The lesson is not only moral but religious: "Et de qui estez vous apprins ainsi discourir et parler de la puissance et prædestination de Dieu, paouvres gens? . . . humiliez vous davant sa sacrée face et recongnoissez vos imperfections [And who taught you thus to speak and speechify about the power and determinations of God, poor fools? . . . humble yourselves before his sacred face and acknowledge your imperfections]" (p. 31). The concluding moral of the play, with the Admiral decapitated and his desire to rise to a great height ironically fulfilled on the gallows, is quite compatible. One wonders whether Chantelouve, in intertextually invoking Rabelais here, was also, with something like a god's-eye-view, evoking an irony afforded by the passage of time. Rabelais's patron and protector when the revised version of *Le Quart Livre* was published (1552) was Odet de Coligny, Cardinal de Châtillon, who is addressed in the preface. He was the elder brother of Chantelouve's villain; without resigning his church office, he converted to Protestantism and married in 1564, then fled to England, where he died in 1571. Chantelouve places him squarely in hell (*Coligny*, ll. 10 and 893–94).

At the pivotal point of the play, then, as indeed from start to finish, Christian and classical intertexts combine to reinforce the distinction between Fortune and Providence that is summarized by the concluding Chorus, and symbolized by the play's central ironic image: the Admiral's boundless ambition, what the Fury presents (l. 972) as his thirst to enrol his name among the stars, has mockingly earned him, thanks to divine justice, the highest point on the public gallows. The irony, incarnated impressively for the crowds that flocked to the spectacle, was itself a commonplace at the time; it was deployed by, amongst many others, Ronsard in verses also published in 1575 (and addressed to Pibrac):

> Ce guerrier qui tantost
> Terre et mer d'un grand Ost
> Couvroit de tant de voiles,
> Court de teste et de nom
> Pendille à Mont-faucon:
> Ainsi vous plaist, Estoiles.

> [That warrior who recently covered land and sea with a great army, with so many sails, shortened by a head and in his name, dangles at Montfaucon: so it pleases you, Stars.][116]

The irony gains depth by inverting, and so refuting, the body politics of martyrdom. As has been recognized with regard to Renaissance execution practices in general, the public display and mockery of the mangled body grimly flirt with the paradigm of the crucified Christ. That paradigm had been multiply reenacted through the long line of martyrs who suffered similarly — a line given new impetus by the Reformation, as is clear from the martyrologies of John Foxe (1516–87) and his French counterpart, Jean

Crespin (1520–72). The project of *Coligny* includes not only fore-stalling the Admiral's legal rehabilitation but counteracting his quasi-hagiographical elevation in Protestant discourse. That process was already well underway among those of the Religion, and it was destined to reach large proportions: a flood of propaganda makes the point, including the widely diffused *Vita Colinii* — exactly contemporary with Chantelouve's play (written in 1574, published in 1575) — whose author (almost certainly François Hotman) reports the wounded Admiral's thanks to God for deeming him worthy to suffer for His sake.[117] To hang the Admiral upside-down, his head and hands cut off, castrated, with a calf's tail in his anus,[118] was to put him on display as the parody of a martyred saint.[119] Chantelouve evokes the image all the more effectively for knowing readers (and spectators?) by leaving the details to their imaginations. The Chorus is thereby freed to take the moralizing high road, merely gesturing towards the completed trajectory of the grotesque in the Admiral's portrayal. His ending bears corporal witness, not to a martyr's sacrifice, but to the fatal spiritual consequences of his only constant allegiance: "O ye shades of darkness in Hades pitiless— / O my dear companions . . ." (ll. 1–2).[120]

## The Guisiade

### The Author

About the relatively public life of Pierre Matthieu (1563–1621) there are few questions, except of the sort that only the man himself could answer.[121] He was born in Franche-Comté within the diocese of Basel and spent his early years in small towns in that region, where his father was a poor but respected schoolmaster and eventually a rector. After receiving an excellent general education under his father's supervision and obtaining a church benefice to finance his education, Matthieu chose to study law, first in Paris, then closer to home in Valence (Dauphiné). In his mid-twenties he embarked upon a legal career in Lyons. Matthieu was a jurist not only by training and profession, but also, it seems, by inclination. For one thing, his profession offered an entrée into political affairs. Not, apparently, that he particularly sought power for himself (or could readily have gained it, given his modest family origins), but he attached himself willingly and ably to those who did. In 1589, when he wrote *The Guisiade*, he was secretary to the Duke of Nemours, the half-brother of the Duke of Guise and governor of Lyons.[122] More fundamentally, however, Matthieu seems to have had a mind that relished gathering evidence, forming judgements, and arguing cases with passionate vigour; even where he is one-sided, he shows, like all good lawyers, a thorough understanding of the fundamental issues involved and of his adversary. (Hence, perhaps, the preoccupation of *The Guisiade* with the psychology of its villain, Henri III.)

Matthieu's long life is documented by dozens of publications, some of them lengthy, in a remarkable variety of forms.[123] These can be divided (very roughly) into two groups, corresponding to the two major political engagements of Matthieu's career. Those engagements were, first, with militant Catholic causes, latterly in flagrant opposition to Henri III, and, secondly, with the relatively inclusive and tolerant royal authority of Henri IV. It is this first youthful phase—from 1587, when Matthieu established himself as a lawyer in Lyons, to 1593—that provides the context for *The Guisiade*, the last of five tragedies that he wrote. This phase, which includes works of sacred poetry, biblical commentary, canon law, and casuistry, is characterized by an increasing intensity of religious fervour mingled with political radicalism. That potent and volatile mixture marks his participation in what Crouzet has persuasively labelled "les imaginaires eschatologiques de la Ligue [the eschatological imaginations of the League]"—an apocalyptic mentality attached to an idealization of the past, and to the House of Lorraine, through a renewal of the myth of crusade.[124]

In anticipation of the Estates at Blois in 1588, Matthieu put into print a direct profession of his political-religious faith, written in verse: *Stances svr l'hevreuse publication de la paix et saincte vnion. Avec un Hymne de même argument*.[125] This is an anticipation, too, of the moment in *The Guisiade* (ll. 1488ff.) when the Union (by which, effectively, the king was forced to accept the terms of the Guises) is joyously proclaimed and hailed by the people. This little poetic pamphlet reflects the current doubts about Henri's sincerity—not least in the title page device, which shows clasped hands with the motto "*Sine fravde, Bona fide*"—and there is a fitting irony, therefore, in Matthieu's recycling of several passages from it for the address of the Clergy to the King in Act III, Scene ii(b), of *The Guisiade*.[126] Six months after the murder of the Guises (16 June 1589), he delivered, then published, a funeral oration addressed to the Penitents of Lyons as the climactic event of a memorial organized by the local government — confirmation of the prominence he had attained, and also, unquestionably, of his oratorical abilities. Essentially the same political, religious, and emotional buttons are pushed as in *The Guisiade*, and in the peroration Matthieu himself addresses Henri in the prophetic voice of doom assigned to Madame de Nemours on stage. Yet the structure as a whole remains under impressive formal control, impeccably within the bounds of forensic discourse.[127]

The culminating (not to say crowning) publication in this virtual series was also, almost literally, a pivotal one: *Discours veritable, et sans passion. Sur la prinse des armes & changemens aduenus en la ville de Lyon, pour la conseruation d'icelle, sous l'obéissance de la S. Vnion & de la Coronne de France, le 18 septembre 1593, etc.*[128] The rhetoric of the Union in this title signals Matthieu's continuing League allegiance, and the crown mentioned is to be safeguarded by the Duke of Mayenne pending the arrival of "vn Roy vrayement Catholique, agréable à nostre sainct Pere, & aux Estats de ce Royaume [a king who is truly Catholic, acceptable to our Holy Father, and to the Estates of this realm]" (p. 15). The Duke of Nemours, however, was now definitively off the scene, having been expelled by the governing council for abuses of power; Matthieu not only signed the declaration to that effect (dated 23 September 1593) but, to justify the action, mustered the full rhetoric of Machiavellism and tyranny that he had previously reserved for the arch-villain Henri III.[129]

Meanwhile, Henri IV had been preparing himself to become, whether a "truly Catholic" king or not, at least a plausibly Catholic one, performing his ceremonial abjuration on 25 July 1593. This action would not immediately, in fact, earn him the Papal seal of approval, which was to come only in September 1595 after intensive diplomatic efforts. Its practical effect, however, was the rapid collapse of active opposition. Weary of war, the cities of France yielded in rapid succession to the king's persuasions (which included generous financial incentives).[130] In Lyons, too, the moderate Catholic faction ("Politiques") eventually prevailed, and on 8 February 1594, the gates were opened to the royal troops. The existing governing council was dismissed and a new one installed, to be kept under strict control.[131] A few voices still cried out in the wilderness, but Matthieu, in effect, had lost his calling.

Immediately, however, he found a new one with a much brighter future — astonishingly, as no less than the ex-apostate's historiographer. The post was officially available to him only in 1610,[132] but already in 1594 the first edition of his history of the recent troubles under Henri III and Henri IV saw the light, accompanied by a discourse on the "grands effects" of the latter's conversion (a subject, after all, in which he was particularly well versed). And so the second phase and still more prolific phase of Matthieu's authorial career was inaugurated — with, indeed, a sort of fanfare in the form of *L'entree de très-grand, très-chrestien très-magnanime et victorieux prince Henri IIII. Roy de France & de Nauarre en sa bonne ville de Lyon, le IIII septembre l'an MDXXXXV. de son regne le VII. de son aage le XLII. Contenant l'ordre & la description des magnificences dressees pour cette occasion.*[133] As is not unusual for the period, the title does indeed say it all.

But Matthieu, under Henri IV, proved to be far from a mere propagandist. His voluminous and ever more widely ranging histories are serious and remarkably untendentious works of scholarship — rather as if the advocate had become the judge. And the historian's, or judge's, perspective made it inevitable that he would finally find himself justifying the elimination of the Guises by Henri III.[134] It also lent a certain urgent sincerity to the major poetic achievement of his later career, the enormously popular *Tablettes de la vie et de la mort* — a work in the tradition of Pibrac's moralizing *Quatrains*, with the usual Neo-stoic clichés about the vanity of worldly pleasures (and ambitions) summoned up to make the usual case for death and eternity. In his last years, the wheel ironically came full circle, as Matthieu produced (though not in dramatic form, as Ben Jonson had done) a history of Sejanus directed against Concino Concini, marquis d'Ancre, the widely hated favourite of Marie de Medici.[135] In keeping with the precedent of Sejanus, this avatar of Matthieu's former *bête noire*, the Duke of Épernon, suffered the same fate as the heroic Duke of Guise: assassination on the orders of the king (Louis XIII); his wife was executed for witchcraft. (D'Épernon himself, incidentally, despite even his rumoured involvement in the 1610 assassination of Henri IV, lived until 1642 and died in his bed, aged almost ninety.)

Matthieu's career as a dramatist ended at a young age, but it had also begun unusually early.[136] When he was only about fifteen, by his own account, he composed his *Clytemnestre*, which was modelled closely (though not slavishly) on Garnier; this work was undoubtedly revised substantially before its eventual publication in 1589 (an *annus mirabilis* for Matthieu as a playwright, and otherwise). The model of Garnier seems to have served in life as well as in art, given Garnier's legal profession and official activities. It would have served, however, only up to a point, since, fellow Leaguer though he briefly was, Garnier kept his drama at a relative remove from religious and political partisanship. Only with *Les Juifves* did the latter move out of classical into biblical territory, and then he displayed a much more careful sense than Matthieu of the practical advantages of lament over critique. Before Matthieu arrived at his direct dramatic assault on a ruling monarch — a predictable correlative of the League's verbal violence in other forms but, it would seem, generically unprecedented — he, too, had taken to biblical tragedy. It bears witness to his precocity, literary ambition, and education (and perhaps to his budding religiosity as well) that he composed his *Esther* (pub. 1585) at around the age of twenty. (Although it is more than twice as long as *The Guisiade*, this is the only one of Matthieu's plays known to have been performed: it was staged at the school where his father, who apparently dabbled in playwriting himself, was rector.)[137]

Matthieu's initial treatment of Esther was not polemical, but the story certainly had such potential, for it recounts, within the familiar framework of the tribulations and ultimate triumph of God's chosen people (complete with bloody vengeance), the success of Queen Esther in protecting the Jews against the wicked counsellor Haman. Her father Mordecai is destined for execution by Haman, but, thanks to her intervention with the king, Ahasuerus, the two men are made to exchange places, and Haman is hanged on the gallows that had been built to hang her father. In fact, the story had already been made to yield politically loaded theatre, but from the Protestant point of view, in Rivaudeau's *Aman* (itself preceded by the Latin version of Roillet). Matthieu appears to have seized on the opportunity offered by the opening of the Estates General of Blois in 1588—the event that was to ratify the Union, hence the triumph of the League—in order to return to his material and rework it into two "pièces à clés":[138] *Aman* and *Vashti* (the latter being the queen who preceded Esther). Both these plays were also published in 1589, in the same volume as *Clytemnestre*. In Matthieu's new scenario, the Duke of Guise is clearly cast as Mordecai, the Duke of Épernon as Haman, Henri III as Ahasuerus, and Catherine de Medici as Esther. This was perhaps not her first apparence in the role. Ironically, such an identification had been possible for Protestants to make when Rivaudeau's play appeared some twenty years earlier. More ironically still—but then such irony is built into the circulating typologies of the times—the wicked counsellor and persecutor of God's people at that earlier period might well have been associated with François, the preceding Duke of Guise.[139]

Just before Christmas of 1588, the triumphal promise of the Estates, for Leaguers, turned to veritable tragedy with the king's definitive casting of the Guises as treacherous counsellors, deserving—and instantly consigned to—destruction. With that event, even transparent fiction became too indirect for Matthieu's purposes. In calling the characters of *The Guisiade* by their true names, and later in supplying (for the third edition) prose Arguments spelling out the reality of his persons and events, he reveals his conviction that all discursive masks must be put aside, lest they remain susceptible to ambiguity or re-appropriation. (After all, in the League view, the king, having dropped his mask by committing the murder, immediately put it on again by accusing the Guises of plotting a *coup d'état*.) The truth of scripture is claimed no less absolutely for *The Guisiade* than for its biblical precursors. Moreover, that truth is now fixed and established beyond all power to change its appearance. Fiction fuses with the ultimate verity, thereby confronting the murderous king, who sought to write the name of traitor in blood upon the mangled corpse of Guise, with the prophetic writing on the wall, which proclaims Guise a martyr and affixes the seal of Henri de Valois's imminent downfall. In the series of Matthew's interventions, theatrical and otherwise, in the tumultuous religious politics of the late 1580s,

*The Guisiade* convincingly arrogates the authority of the last word, and it is hard to imagine what he could have done for an encore.

The fact remains that he promised one: a statement appended to *The Guisiade* speaks of a sequel, to be called *Sacrilege*, which would give special attention to the second principal victim of Henri's actions, the Cardinal of Guise, but also include "the imprisonment of the Princes and other Lords, with a continuation of the history and all that happened since the cruel treatment of the dead bodies until the death of the Queen Mother." This last event occurred on 6 January 1589, barely two weeks after the murders. Still, the pressure placed on the neo-classical unities of time, place, and action would have been more acute than in the case of *The Guisiade*, and something closer to a chronicle method might have imposed itself. It would have been fascinating to see Matthieu's response to the technical challenge. Why this promise was never fulfilled we cannot be sure, but the fact is that within a few years, if not months, events took several turns Matthieu had not anticipated, confronting him, as both a politician and an author, with formidable challenges even to his impressive capacity for adaptation and survival.

### Date, Editions, Performance

*The Guisiade*'s date of composition can be determined within narrow limits: the murders at Blois occurred on 23 December 1588; the first edition of the play appeared anonymously in Lyons in May or June of the following year. The work was republished almost immediately; that the second edition was rushed into print is suggested by the lack of introductory matter, a fact that once caused it to be considered prior.[140] Finally, still a third edition saw the light before the end of the year. This last version names the author, refers to the League candidate for king ("Charles X," Cardinal of Bourbon, who died in 1590), and incorporates substantial revisions, mostly additions, to the dialogue, as well as to the ancillary matter. (Prefatory Arguments were added to each scene.) It is possible to relate some of these changes to the new imperatives evidently imposed by the assassination of Henri III on 1 August 1589. That spectacular development is reflected at once in a heightened apocalyptic perspective and in a defensiveness on specific points.

The multiple editions of 1589 and the relatively high number of copies still extant in various libraries bear witness to a design to diffuse the printed text widely as part of the League's enormous production of published propaganda. (Pallier documents 872 titles produced in Paris alone between 1585 and 1594.) Indeed, it is a highly suggestive fact, which appears to have gone unnoticed by scholars, that one of the copies of *The Guisiade* in the Bibliothèque Nationale bears a Toulouse imprint.[141] Yet the play's very topicality soon turned against it—Matthieu himself was hardly likely to wish it recalled to notice in later years—and it was not republished until, as with *Coligny*, Lenglet du Fresnoy produced a modernized version as a species of historical curiosity in 1744. In 1990, Louis Lobbes re-edited the work from the early texts to a high scholarly standard. He also admirably clarified the relation among the three early versions, basing his edition on the third but recording the variants. There are few textual difficulties, certainly by comparison with the poorly printed *Coligny*.

The League's campaign of printed propaganda was complemented by public manifestations and the rousing sermons of the *prédicateurs*, so it would not be surprising if performances of *The Guisiade* also took place. Indeed, the only other surviving propaganda play on the same theme, *Le Guysien* by Simon Belyard, published in Troyes in 1592 and analogous in broad outline to Matthieu's—except, most remarkably, that the Duke of Guise is killed on-stage—is introduced by a statement referring to its performance.[142] A related case would seem to be that of a tragedy on the subject of Chilperic II—one of several abusive models applied to Henry III—that was printed in 1590: the *Parlement* of Paris prevented it from being mounted there in 1594, and its author was arrested.[143] Still, there is nothing to indicate that *The Guisiade* was ever performed, and the same is true of Matthieu's other tragedies, with the exception of the school production of his youthful *Esther*. That exception, however, combines with the author's evident appreciation of rhetoric as public performance, as well as the theatrical references in his opening "Discourse" and concluding "Notice," to confirm at least that Matthieu conceived of his work very much in dramatic terms. Hence, too, the Arguments added to individual scenes in the third edition serve, not only to sharpen the ideological point of the dialogue, but imaginatively to set the stage; at times they constitute virtual stage directions, as if Matthieu were deliberately appropriating the power of the theatre to heighten and direct the response of his readers.

## The Play

If *The Guisiade* has attracted more attention from literary historians than has *Coligny*, one reason is doubtless its comparative amenability to critical analysis: "tragédie irrégulière" it may strictly be — the action, after all, follows historical events extending over six months or so — but less aggressively so, and (for better or worse) it presents relatively few compositional anomalies in need of elucidation. The smoother surface of the piece as a literary composition begins, arguably, with Matthieu's greater control of poetic language and expression. Although he has been accused of the same stylistic vices as Chantelouve,[144] and his sentences can be considerably more tortuous, his claim to produce "verse grave and flowing [un vers grave et coulant]" ("Discourse on the Subject of This Tragedy" — see below, p. 177) in the classical style is generally justified. His oratorical experience and rhetorical training make themselves felt throughout and are sometimes put functionally on display, as in his recreation of the speeches at the Estates. Also important, however, is the sense he communicates of conscious deference to the principles of humanist neo-classical theatre, with which he manages to render his historical content and propagandistic purpose remarkably harmonious. As the introductory "Discourse" confirms, Matthieu, in theory and spirit, as well as practice, was far closer than Chantelouve to those who set the taste for contemporary French tragedy in the high style. One need not go nearly so far afield, therefore, in attempting to explain the nature and form of Matthieu's project, which remains as readily accessible in its aesthetics as in its politics.

The key to Matthieu's success in maintaining a general impression of conformist classicism is his sustained stylistic decorum. Just how conscious he was of the question is shown by his clever means of capitalizing on a deviation from the norm. The scene of Épernon's conjuring that opens Act III is as close as the play comes to rehabilitating the sensational supernaturalism of *Coligny*, and Matthieu, in his Argument, presents the effect as imposed upon him by the breech in moral and religious decorum that is represented by the man himself:

> Against his will was the poet constrained to interpose amidst the majesty and grandeur of those who play this Tragedy a man of such slight value as Épernon. Yet the certain opinion which the entire people of France have regarding his behaviour, and the fact that he above all others enkindled the King's bloody deliberations against the House of Lorraine, have caused him to enter in this third Act, in the form of a desperate man, a sorcerer, with all his demonism.

The scene between the King and his wicked counsellors, whom Matthieu mysteriously (and mischievously) designates by the indecipherable rubric of "N.N.," "so as not to dishonour his poem with their names" (Act IV, Scene i, Argument), moves in a similar direction but evokes the diabolical more subtly. The pattern of demonic seduction is familiar enough; so too is the demonizing of Machiavelli's doctrines. The subtlety consists in presenting the King's interaction with the voice of temptation in a way that suggests an internal dialogue, hence a psychological process. This is, moreover, preparation for his extended dialogue with himself just before the murder (ll. 1959ff.), where the voice of the "N.N." has been thoroughly internalized.

This effect points to a real achievement of Matthieu's dramaturgy, one that is possible precisely because he restrains himself from melodramatics where the essential evil — that of Henri himself — is concerned. Many of the diatribes directed by the League against the king, even before the cataclysm at Blois and certainly after it, resort to forms of caricature: in the crudest possible terms he is labelled a debauchee (usually a homosexual one), a sorcerer, a butcher. There are elements of all these stereotypes circulating around Matthieu's Henri, but they are not simply applied as labels of monstrous inhumanity. No doubt the King finally looms as a monster through the bloody haze evoked by the Messenger and Madame de Nemours, but it is his deed that produces him in this shape, and the deed both issues from a complex network of psychological forces and finds its immediate punishment (albeit heaven-sent and prefiguring more tangible retribution) in the form of conscience:

Like a second Cain, you shall be dogged at your heels
By the ghost of my child, as you sit at your meals;
The blood of that noble Duke shall swell up your veins;
You shall be flayed alive, put to the utmost pains
Of relentless remorse; panic-terrors your head
Shall fill to overflowing with horror and dread —
And if, though a coward, you feign yourself undaunted,
Your pale conscience shall ever by vengeance be haunted.

(ll. 2145–52)[145]

Henri emerges as a remarkable anticipation of Shakespeare's Macbeth.

There is, then, in Matthieu's characterization a genuine sense of the enigma that Henri III presented for many contemporaries, and still does for historians — an enigma only deepened psychologically by the category of "envious jealousy" applied by Matthieu in his opening "Discourse." The riddle is played out, to considerable dramatic effect, across the verbal and mental games that Henri plays with others, and with himself. Discourse itself is the battlefield, in a sense, on which Matthieu self-consciously chooses to engage him, leaving it to the leaders of the League to pursue the struggle by more concrete means. Henri is shown to be deeply confused about his private and public representation of himself, and ultimately to be the most pathetic dupe of his own rhetorical skill, which the author at once appropriates, by reproducing it, and puts to shame. In this respect it is less Macbeth that Henri resembles than Richard II.[146] Technically, after all, he is not a usurper of royal power (whatever the claims of the line of Charlemagne), but a king who de-legitimizes himself and, in words and deeds, virtually asks for his deposition, from which death will necessarily ensue.

But if Matthieu avoids melodrama in depicting Henri, keeping him confined for the most part on the human level, he pulls out all the stops in conducting the main business of the play — the transformation of political assassination into martyrdom. The Duke of Guise must be established as the essence of purity of faith and selflessness, in direct rebuttal of the propaganda that Protestants (and "Politique" Catholics) had retailed at least since the Saint Bartholomew massacre, and that Henri himself (repeating Charles IX's tactic with regard to Coligny) now took over in order to justify himself. As part of this project, Guise must be seen to fall into Henri's trap out of innocence, rather than arrogance. The latter explanation of his vulnerability undoubtedly comes closer to the truth, and it is certainly the line taken up and extended by Protestant moralists, who portrayed Guise as the typical over-reaching Machiavel, blinded to imminent downfall by delusions of infallibility, if not invulnerability. Such is the vision of Marlowe in *The Massacre at Paris*, which effectively—uncannily, if Marlowe did not actually know Matthieu's work—rewrites *The Guisiade* so as to reintegrate the Duke within the cycle of divine vengeance, so that his murder is mandated as the fulfilment of his bloody actions of 1572.[147] Matthieu's archetypically tragic invocation of apocalypse, resounding at its conclusion with ominously inconclusive curses, is thus tidily enfolded into the divine comedy *à la huguenote*.

In the light of Chantelouve's *Coligny*, it is easier to see that Matthieu, too, fifteen years later, was writing against (hence necessarily within) the Protestant discourse that had developed around Saint Bartholomew's day. As with mythologized events in general, diverse reports of the last words of Guise and the behaviour of the king quickly proliferated. The version of Matthieu, as narrated by the Messenger (ll. 2031ff.), brings Guise's death especially close to that of one of Chantelouve's villains, Armand de Clerment, baron de Piles, as represented in Protestant martyrologies (the affirmation of fidelity to the king, the condemnation of treason, the treacherous blow).[148] If Chantelouve's vilifying portrayal of Piles was itself a response to such accounts, for Matthieu, the recapitulation is part of a wholesale appropriation and inversion of the myth of the 1572 massacre, beginning with the term itself and extending, implicitly, to the royal justification, with trumped-up accusations, that followed. Henri III has become the tyrant whom the Herculean Charles IX—and the image of Hercules pervades the play—effectively kept at bay for some years. Now the new Hercules has been, like the original one—indeed, like the Christ whom Hercules typologically prefigured—treacherously murdered ("ainsi mourut Alcide [in the same way died Alcides]" [l. 2090]). The forces of evil have temporarily prevailed, but God, as Madame de Nemours reminds us in intoning her curse, will surely revenge.

As it happened, however, the promised divine revenge, when Jacques Clément obligingly performed it, worked very much in favour of the surviving arch-apostate. This fact complicated Matthieu's position in preparing his third edition, as it complicated the political future of the Holy League itself. It was Henri IV who definitively appropriated—quite consciously—the role of Hercules. He even coopted the services of Matthieu himself in promoting it on the occasion of his royal entry into Lyons in 1595:

> Depvis de grand coup d'Estat, ceste viue et genereuse resolution que la ville de Lyon suyuit pour en s'affranchissant d'un seruitude estrangere, se remettre sous la iuste obeissance de celuy que Dieu, la Nature & la Loy auoient declaré Roy de France, elle n'eut plus grand desir au cœur, plus ferme pensee en l'ame, que l'heur, l'honneur & le contentement de voir cest Hercule des François, qu'elle ne reconnaissoit que par la viue image de sa bonté, les salutaires effects de sa clemence, & la reputation de sa valeur, n'attendant d'autre main que de la sienne le restablissement de ses ruines, le soulagement de ses Citoyens, la guerison de ses playes, ne se promettant que de sa presence l'eslongnement de ses ennemis, & la fin de ses miseres.

> [Since that great *coup d'état*, that spirited and noble resolution that the city of Lyons followed in order, in freeing itself from foreign servitude, to restore itself to just obedience to him whom God, Nature, and the Law had declared King of France, it has had no greater desire in its heart, no firmer thought in its soul, than the happiness, the honour, and the satisfaction of seeing that Hercules of the French whom it knew only by the lively image of his clemency and his reputation for valour, expecting from no other hand than his its restoration from its ruins, the relief of its citizens, the healing of its wounds, nor promising itself other than, by his presence, the distancing of its enemies and the end of its miseries.]                    (*L'entree*, p. 1)

Given this outcome, an ironic reading of the Duke of Guise's dialogue with Henri III in Act II, Scene ii, becomes possible—to the point of suggesting again that Matthieu, accomplished lawyer that he was, could not keep himself from doing justice to the arguments of his opponent. In this variation on the mildness/harshness debate, the Duke exhorts Henri to take a tough line in dealing with the rebellious heretics: "Comme un second Hercul honnoré vos conquestes, / Par l'immortel trophé de ce monstre à sept testes [You'll be a second Hercules in victory, / When of that seven-headed beast you've made a trophy]" (ll. 623–24). Henri is allowed to make a quite plausible case for the superior benefits of mildness — a lesson that his successor applied, with notable success, to Matthieu himself, among many more politically prominent figures. The audience knows, of course, that this king's mildness extends only to Huguenots, and that he will shortly be slaughtering the heroic Guises. It is not surprising, therefore, to hear Guise's own words perversely recycled in support of that treachery by Épernon: "A fin que nostre Roy, qui si bien dissimule, / Soit estimé par tout comme une second Hercule [That thereby our King, who dissembles with such ease, / May be esteemed by all a second Hercules]" (ll. 887–88). The irony is that Henri III's legacy, especially when he too was treacherously murdered, came close to proving the adage about the devil speaking truth. For if the House of Lorraine was itself a candidate, in the eyes of many, for the status of a Hydra, the sudden loss of two of its heads at Henri's supremely effective (if hardly heroic) single stroke proved quite sufficient in the circumstances to deal its ambitions a mortal blow. Dedicating *The Guisiade* to a third head, the Duke of Mayenne, proved a futile gesture towards reviving the beast, and one wonders whether Matthieu himself, even as he prepared the final edition in the euphoric but turbulent wake of his own prophecy's fulfilment — God's vengeance unleashed upon Henri — did not sense that apocalypse was petering out.

## A Note on the Translations

The present translation of *Coligny* is based on Cameron's edition and adopts his line numbering. For the reader's guidance I have supplied scene divisions, not present in the original, and some basic stage directions (nothing elaborate is required). I have also reviewed Cameron's treatment of the notes and variants printed by Lenglet du Fresnoy in 1744,[149] consulted the edition of Wollfe, and referred to the text of 1575 in all cases of difficulty. My notes record the few instances where I have preferred a reading different from Cameron's.

In the case of *The Guisiade*, the excellent recent edition by Lobbes renders recourse to the original texts unnecessary. I have therefore translated according to Lobbes's reproduction of the third 1589 edition and indicated in the notes those points where the variants among the early editions appear significant. Act and scene divisions are as indicated in Lobbes's text. There is even less need for stage directions (wholly absent from the original) than in *Coligny*, but I have signalled a few entrances where it would otherwise not be immediately clear who is on stage.

As in my rendition, for the same series, of *La Pucelle* by Fronton Du Duc, I employ hexameter couplets in a flexible iambic metre for the Alexandrine, which constitutes the basic metrical form of French drama in the period.[150] Apart from the Choruses, Matthieu's play is uniformly written in that metre. By contrast, Chantelouve makes resourceful use, as has been discussed, of varying verse-forms, and, as with the Choruses in both plays, I have attempted to approximate the varying forms of the original. Naturally, I have also aimed to convey stylistic and tonal features with the greatest possible fidelity, and this has often required making choices. Most notably, I sometimes lend a self-conscious humour to the "bizarre" and "bombastic" qualities that Lebègue condemned in Chantelouve. This reflects my judgement, hardly that the playwright was not being serious, but, on the contrary, that his seriousness was of so high a kind that the ridiculous found a natural, even an irresistible, place within it — essentially, the place of the gargoyle in relation to the cathedral.

# Notes to the Introduction

1 Raymond Lebègue, *La tragédie religieuse en France: les débuts (1514–1573)*, Bibliothèque Littéraire de la Renaissance, n.s., vol. 17 (Paris: H. Champion, 1929), p. 100, n. 2.

2 Raymond Lebègue, *La tragédie française de la Renaissance*, 2nd ed., Collections Lebègue et Nationale, 4th ser., no. 46 (Brussels: Office de Publicité, 1954), p. 65. Matthieu is barely mentioned by Lebègue even in a 1974 survey entitled "La Renaissance: théâtre et politique religieuse," in *Études sur le théâtre français*, 2 vols., vol. 1: Moyen Âge, Rennaissance, Baroque (Paris: Nizet, 1977); nor did his opinion of Chantelouve substantially evolve, to judge from his casual disparagement, in the latter essay, of *Coligny*'s style as "boursouflé [bombastic]," although he also acknowledges its free mingling of topicality and mythology as characteristic of contemporary practice (pp. 203–04). In 1973, a prominent English specialist in French literature was still sufficiently unacquainted with the *Guisiade* to be capable of describing it as an attack on the Catholic League (Geoffrey Brereton, *French Tragic Drama in the Sixteenth and Seventeenth Centuries* [London: Methuen, 1973], p. 40); Chantelouve does not even appear in his index.

3 Gillian Jondorf actually declares that she has omitted *Coligny* from her study, *French Renaissance Tragedy: The Dramatic Word*, Cambridge Studies in French (Cambridge: Cambridge University Press, 1990), because she is so "repelled" by it (p. 5); she does not mention Matthieu at all.

4  Hubert Languet (?) (also attrib. Philippe de Mornay; pseud. Stephanus Junius Brutus), *Vindiciae contra tyrannos: sive, De principis in populum, populique in principes, legitima potestae*, first pub. "Edinburgh" (Basel?), 1579. A good sense of the pamphlet phenomenon may be gained from Denis Pallier, *Recherches sur l'imprimerie à Paris pendant la Ligue (1585–1594)*, Centre de Recherches d'Histoire et de Philologie, 4ᵉ Section de l'École Pratique des Hautes Études, 6; Histoire et Civilisation du Livre, 9 (Geneva: Droz, 1975); Lisa Ferraro Parmelee usefully supplies an English dimension in *Good Newes from Fraunce: French Anti-League Propaganda in Late Elizabethan England* (Rochester, NY: University of Rochester Press, 1996). See also my book, *Shakespeare, Marlowe and the Politics of France* (Houndmills, Basingstoke, Hampshire: Palgrave, 2002), in which I seek to demonstrate the relevance of current French issues to English drama in the 1590s.

5  See Lebègue's survey, "La Renaissance : théâtre et politique religieuse," which is very useful on the subject generally.

6  See Fronton Du Duc, *The Tragic History of La Pucelle of Domrémy, Otherwise Known as the Maid of Orléans*, trans. with Introduction and Notes by Richard Hillman, Carleton Renaissance Plays in Translation, 39 (Ottawa: Dovehouse, 2005).

7  See Émile Faguet, *La tragédie française au XVIᵉ siècle (1550–1600)*, 2nd ed. (Paris: Fontemoing, 1912), esp. pp. 190–95.

8  See esp. Lebègue's essay, "La tragédie 'shakespearienne' en France au temps de Shakespeare," in *Études sur le théâtre français*, vol. 1, pp. 298–339, but also *La tragédie française à la Renaissance*, *passim*.

9  Madeleine Lazard, *Le théâtre en France au XVIᵉ siècle*, Littératures Modernes (Paris: Presses Universitaires de France, 1980), p. 83. The remarkable extent and variety of the French school theatre in this period have been well documented by Lebègue in *La tragédie religieuse en France*, pp. 143–56, and *La tragédie française de la Renaissance*, pp. 69–70.

10  Cf. Louis Lobbes, ed., *La Guisiade*, by Pierre Matthieu (Geneva: Droz, 1990): "La tragédie scolaire d'*Esther*, transformée en pièce à clés dans *Aman*, était devenue avec la *Guisiade* un pamphlet ligueur [The school tragedy *Esther*, transformed into a drama *à clef* in *Aman*, had become, with *The Guisiade*, a

League pamphlet]" (p. 12). The League was not a single nor a simple phenomenon: on the political-religious movements in their evolving historical context, see the invaluable reference work, *Histoire et dictionnaire des Guerres de Religion*, ed. Arlette Jouanna, Jacqueline Boucher et al. (Paris: Robert Laffont, 1998), pp. 305–89, 1042–44 ("Ligues").

11  See *Coligny*, ll. 499–500 and nn. 20, 75, 105, 164, 167, 170, 172. By a further intertextual twist, the play's insistence on the vanity of worldly ambition and vivid evocation of otherworldly retribution in pagan terms amount to a redeployment of elements prominent in a text on which Du Bartas himself seems to have drawn: Claudian, *In Rufinum [Against Rufinus]*, in *Claudian*, ed. and trans. Maurice Platnauer, 2 vols., Loeb Classical Library (Cambridge, MA: Harvard University Press; London: Heinemann, 1976), vol. 1; see *Coligny*, nn. 118, 167, 170.

12  See Lebègue, *La tragédie religieuse en France*, p. XIV, and "La Renaissance : théâtre et politique religieuse," p. 203.

13  See Elliott Forsyth, *La tragédie française de Jodelle à Corneille (1533–1640). Le thème de la vengeance*, Études et essais sur la Renaissance, 5 (1962; rpt. Paris: H. Champion, 1994), p. 161, and Keith Cameron, ed., *Aman: Tragédie sainte*, by André Rivaudeau (Geneva: Droz, 1969), pp. 32–35. In pointing out that the play's date of publication, not of composition, would have determined any political interpretation it received, Cameron here identifies a principle of great importance, which I will be applying to Garnier's *Cornélie*.

14  See, notably, Forsyth, pp. 210–15.

15  On what she terms the *"clémence/rigueur* [mildness/harshness]" debate, see Gillian Jondorf, *Robert Garnier and the Themes of Political Tragedy in the Sixteenth Century* (Cambridge: Cambridge University Press, 1969), pp. 105–13.

16      Lors nous aurons les cieux à nos desseins propices :
        Dieu nou enyvrera d'un torrent de delices,
        Et dans le succre doux des almes voluptez
        Sa main nous confira, versant de tous costez
        En nos cueurs un nectar de sa grace divine :
        Nous ouvrira les yeux, fendra nostre poictrine,
        Arrachant de nos flancs ce fier cueur de rocher,
        Et metra en sa place un coeur tendre et de chaire.

17  Denis Crouzet, *Les guerriers de Dieu. La violence au temps des troubles de religion (vers 1525–vers 1610)*, 2 vols. (Seyssel: Champ Vallon, 1990), vol. 2, p. 404. Crouzet is one of the most insightful and stimulating recent historians of the period, and his understanding of it has largely informed my own.

18  For a concise and objective account of the known facts, see *Histoire et dictionnaire des Guerres de Religion*, ed. Jouanna et al., pp. 194–204. For a thorough analysis of the discursive environment surrounding that event — essential context for *The Guisiade* as well as *Coligny* — see Denis Crouzet, *La nuit de la Saint-Barthélemy. Un rêve perdu de la Renaissance* (Paris: Fayard, 1994). Relevant works in English include Nicola Mary Sutherland, *The Massacre of St Bartholomew and the European Conflict 1559–1572* (London: Macmillan, 1973); Robert M. Kingdon, *Myths About the St. Bartholomew's Day Massacres 1572–1576* (Cambridge, MA: Harvard University Press, 1988); and Henri Noguères, *The Massacre of Saint Bartholomew*, trans. Claire-Éliane Engel (London: Allen and Unwin, 1962).

19  See Hillman, *Shakespeare, Marlowe and the Politics of France*, *passim*.

20  The text cited (by scene and line numbers) is Christopher Marlowe, *The Massacre at Paris*, in *Dido Queen of Carthage and The Massacre at Paris*, ed. H.J. Oliver, The Revels Plays (London: Methuen, 1968). I develop the point in question in *Shakespeare, Marlowe and the Politics of France*, pp. 75–82.

21  It is remarkable that some American critics, in particular, who find Navarre's rhetoric implausibly self-righteous and violent, seem not to have listened carefully to "The Battle Hymn of the Republic," much performed on patriotic occasions.

22  There is an exception in *The Guisiade* (l. 625) — an intriguing one, since the speaker is Henri III, represented as having secret sympathies with the Huguenots.

23  Thomas Nashe, *The Unfortunate Traveller*, in *The Works of Thomas Nashe*, ed. Ronald B. McKerrow, rev. F.P. Wilson, 5 vols. (Oxford: Blackwell, 1958), vol. 2, pp. 232–40. Cf. my discussion in *Shakespeare, Marlowe and the Politics of France*, pp. 42–44, where I make a comparison with the rhetoric of the French civil wars.

24  "Par les geines, les fers, les buchers, les prisons / Des Princes de la Foy."

25 *Miracles de Nostre Dame par personnages*, ed. Gaston Paris and Ulysse Robert, 8 vols. (Paris: Firmin Didot, 1876–83).

26 See Hillman, *Shakespeare, Marlowe and the Politics of France*.

27 See Parmelee and, again, Hillman, *Shakespeare, Marlowe and the Politics of France, passim*.

28 The full form of the name preferred by the Bibliothèque Nationale de France (henceforth BnF) is "Chantelouve, Jean-François Gossombre de." Even though the spelling "Grossombre" is listed among rejected forms, it very much looks as if a typographical error has somehow usurped its position and now tyrannizes electronically over the catalogues (including the Catalogue Collectif de France). All the early references apparently agree on "Grossombre," which, moreover, is an actual place (in the commune of Dardenac, Gironde): its château (much rebuilt) may be seen, and (as ultimate testimony to real existence) its wine may be drunk.

29 François de Chantelouve, *Tragédie de Pharaon et autres œuvres poétiques, contenant hymnes, divers sonnets et chansons* (Paris: N. Bonfons, 1577).

30 "Elegia de Pulice," also alluded to by Marlowe in *Doctor Faustus*, where Pride declares himself to be "like to Ovid's flea; I can creep into every corner of a wench" (ed. John D. Jump, The Revels Plays [London: Methuen, 1962], vi.115–16); see n. to 116. The poem had been anthologized — e.g., in *Opuscula et moralia carmina scilicet: de Nuce, de Philomena et de Pulice* (Rouen: R. Goupil, [1500–21]).

31 *Sonnets et chansons*, in *Tragédie de Pharaon et autres oeuvres poétiques*, pp. 123 and 120. The only surviving copy of this volume is unpaginated and lacks signature markings; my page numbers refer to the electronic version published by the BnF.

32 *Sonnets et chansons*, pp. 123–24.

33 *Tragédie de Pharaon et autres œuvres poétiques*, pp. 7–8.

34 *Sonnets et chansons*, p. 82. This sonnet in praise of Chantelouve is cited by Cameron, ed., p. VII, as the work of François de Balvoine, who indeed is credited with a similar one on p. 81. The poem in question, however, is one of two attributed to a certain Martineau.

35 See *Histoire et dictionnaire des Guerres de Religion*, ed. Jouanna et al., p. 174.

36  *Déploration de la France sur la calamité des dernieres guerres ciuilles aduenues en icelle, l'an 1568* (Paris: Denis du Pré, 1568), sig. Cii[v].

37  For a succinct yet detailed account of this siege, see *Histoire et dictionnaire des Guerres de Religion*, ed. Jouanna et al., pp. 207–12. Henri arrived at La Rochelle on 11 February (p. 209), and the siege lasted until early July, when it was abandoned. The dates, then, are consistent with Chantelouve's being at home in January 1573, when he walked on the ice at Libourne, which is, after all, not far from La Rochelle. For a suggestive view of the besiegers from the other side of the ramparts (both physical and mental), cf. another tract conceivably known to Chantelouve (putatively by Nicolas Barnaud), *Le Reveille-Matin des François et de levrs voisins : Composé par Eusebe Philadelphe Cosmopolite, en forme de Dialogues* (1574; rpt. Paris: Éditions d'Histoire Sociale, 1977), Dialogue 2, p. 130:

> après que la Rochelle fut de toutes parts assiegee par les Iannissaires du tyran, ses deux freres y arriverent . . . auec bon nombre de Seigneurs Catholiques, de courtisanz, d'Atheistes, d'Epicuriés, de blasphemateurs, de Sodomites, & d'autres tels officiers, que le tyran auoit chasse d'aupres de luy & de sa cour, non qu'il fust marry de voir tels galans pres de sa personne : ce sont ses mignons fauoris, ce sont ses appuis & soutien & les délices de sa Mere : ains tout despit, tout enragé, blasphemant tousiours de cholere, de ce qu'vn chacun n'alloit pas comme il commandoit, en l'armée.

> [after La Rochelle was besieged on all sides by the Janissaries of the tyrant, his two brothers arrived . . . with a good number of Catholic nobles, courtiers, atheists, Epicureans, blasphemers, sodomites, and other such officers whom the tyrant had chased from him and from his court. Not that he was ashamed to see such gallants around him — they are his favourite minions, his supporters and sustainers, and the darlings of his mother — but all full of spite, all enraged, always blaspheming with anger because nobody did as he commanded in the army.]

This portrait of the royal "tyrant" is, of course, far closer to Chantelouve's Coligny than to his King.

There is a record, incidentally, of the performance at La Rochelle in 1572–73 of a tragedy whose loss is especially regrettable: *Holoferne* by the redoubtable Protestant militant and woman of letters, Catherine de Parthenay (1554–1631), later

Duchess of Rohan, whose first husband died defending Coligny in the Paris massacre; see Lebègue, "Tableau de la tragédie française de 1575 à 1610," *Bibliothèque d'Humanisme et Renaissance* 5 (1944): 373, 382.

38 *Sonnets et chansons*, p. 111 (text slightly regularized and corrected).

39 *Pharaon*, p. 4; see p. 5: "la rudesse du langage mal agencé, . . . les traits d'vn Gentilhomme Gasçon [*sic*] mal aiséement s'adonant a la polissure du François [the rudeness of the ill-managed expression, . . . the features of a Gascon Gentleman who does not apply himself with facility to polishing French]."

40 My account here is particularly indebted to René Taveneaux, "L'Esprit de croisade en Lorraine aux XVI^e et XVII^e siècles," in *L'Europe, l'Alsace et la France, problèmes intérieurs et réactions internationales à l'epoque modern. Études réunies en l'honneur du Doyen Georges Livet pour son 70^e anniversaire*, Publications de la Société Savante d'Alsace et des Régions de l'Est, Collection "Grandes Publications" (Colmar: Les Éditions d'Alsace, 1986), pp. 256–61.

41 For further development of this point, see Fronton Du Duc, *La Pucelle*, trans. and ed. Hillman, pp. 41 and 168–69, nn. 24–26.

42 This François is not to be confused with the eldest son, François I de Lorraine, who became Duke of Guise and passed the title to his son, Henri. (It encourages confusion that both died in the same year, 1563.)

43 A further important off-shoot of this branch of the House of Lorraine was the first son of Claude, Duke of Aumale, and elder brother of the chevalier d'Aumale — namely, Charles de Lorraine, Duke of Aumale (1556–1631), who became one of the few *Ligueurs* who never conceded to Henri IV; he was condemned to death *in absentia* and died in Spain. See *Histoire et dictionnaire des Guerres de Religion*, ed. Jouanna et al., p. 1057 ("Lorraine").

44 Michel Pernot, "Le Cardinal de Lorraine et la fondation de l'université de Pont-à-Mousson," in *L'Université de Pont-à-Mousson et les Problèmes de Son Temps. Actes du colloque organisé par l'Institut de Recherche Régionale en Sciences Sociales, Humaines et Économiques de l'Université de Nancy II (Nancy 16–19 October 1972)* (Nancy: Université de Nancy II, 1974), p. 64, n. 6, citing a

letter from the Cardinal of Lorraine dated August–September 1574.

45   Keith Cameron, ed., *La tragédie de feu Gaspard de Colligny*, by François de Chantelouve (Exeter: University of Exeter Press, 1971), p. VII.

46   Crouzet, *La nuit de la Saint-Barthélemy*, p. 405. Piles also headed the delegation of Protestants who vehemently demanded redress from the king for Coligny's wounding. See *Histoire et dictionnaire des Guerres de Religion*, ed. Jouanna et al., p. 197; Crouzet, *La nuit de la Saint-Barthélemy*, p. 388; and Cameron, ed., n. to l. 730.

47   See, notably, Forsyth, pp. 186–89.

48   Marian Meijer, ed., *Pharaon*, by François de Chantelouve, in *La tragédie à l'époque d'Henri III*, vol. 1 (1574–1579), Théâtre français de la Renaissance, ser. 2 (Florence: Leo S. Olschki; Paris: Presses Universitaires de France, 1999), pp. 153–54.

49   See Matthieu's funeral oration for the Guises, *Pompe funèbre des pénitens de Lyon, en déploration du massacre faict à Blois sur les illustres et genereuses personnes de Louys et Henry de Lorraine, avec l'oraison sur les mesme suject, prononcée par M. Pierre Matthieu, Docteur és Droicts & Aduocat à Lyon* (Lyons: J. Roussin, 1589), p. 9.

50   See *Histoire et dictionnaire des Guerres de Religion*, ed. Jouanna et al., pp. 242–45 and 1043–44 ("Ligues"); Jean-Marie Constant, *Les Guise* (Paris: Hachette, 1984), pp. 81–82; and Martine Tissier de Mallerais, "La propagande par le texte et l'image," in *La tragédie de Blois. Quatre siècles de polémique autour de l'assassinat du duc de Guise. Catalogue de l'exposition au Château de Blois 17 décembre 1988–19 février 1989*, ed. Martine Tissier de Mallerais et al. (Blois: Ville de Blois, Conservation du Château et des Musées, 1988), p. 32, who implicitly includes *Pharaon* in the wave of propaganda against the king and in favour of Guise that followed the failure of the Estates General of Blois in 1576.

51   *Histoire et dictionnaire des Guerres de Religion*, ed. Jouanna et al., pp. 244, 698 ("Batailles"), and 1237–38 ("Reîtres et Lansquenets"); Tissier de Mallerais, p. 32.

52   A telling document in this regard is *Le Vray Discovrs de la deffaicte des Reistres par Monsieur le Duc de Guyse, le lundy dixiesme d'octobre, 1575. Ensemble la poursuyte, qui a esté faicte à*

*l'encontre d'iceux* (Paris: J. De Lastre [1576]), which manages to praise the king's piety while insinuating his inaction and fearfulness — perhaps even hinting at his sinfulness, given the slippery possessive pronouns in the statement that he prayed "pour appaiser l'ire de Dieu qu'il ne s'irritast contre son peuple par ses demerites offenses [to appease the wrath of God, lest he be angry against his people, offended by their/his unworthiness]" (sig. Aiii^v). In any case, it is clear that the House of Lorraine is the answer to the royal prayers. The heroic young duke, backed by his brother Mayenne, is "celuy qui ne forlignant de la magnanimité de son pere, s'expose tousiours tresvolontiers à tous perils & hazards de guerre pour le service de son Prince [he who, nothing derogating from the magnanimity of his father, is always ready and willing to expose himself to all dangers and chances of war for the service of his prince]" (sig. Aii^v); it is his loving uncle, the Cardinal, who sends surgeons to dress his wound (sig. Bii^r).

53  It was a traditional belief that storks instinctively killed snakes.

54  François de Chantelouve, *Pharaon*, ed. Meijer, ll. 492–504.

55  Agrippa d'Aubigné, *Les tragiques*, ed. Frank Lestringant (Paris: Gallimard, 1995), 2.713ff.

56  There are two 1575 editions described as distinct in Paul Lacroix (pseud. "P.-L. Jacob, bibliophile") et al., *Bibliothèque dramatique de M. De Soleinne*, 9 parts in 6 vols. (Paris: Administration de l'Alliance des Arts, 1843–45), vol. 1, nos. 791 and 121 (the latter in the Supplement). Cameron, ed., p. XIX, cannot confirm this; neither can I. In addition to the copies at the BnF, I have located one at the Bibliothèque Municipale de Versailles (no. 120 in Trevor Peach and Jean Brunel, comps., *Le "Fonds Goujet" de la Bibliothèque Municipale de Versailles : Textes littéraires des XVI^e, XVII^e et XVIII^e siècles : Catalogue alphabétique* [Geneva: Slatkine, 1992]).

57  Cameron, ed., p. VI and nn. to ll. 1045ff., 1059–60, 1069ff., 1105–12. On Pibrac's apologia, see *Histoire et dictionnaire des Guerres de Religion*, ed. Jouanna et al., p. 260, and Crouzet, *La nuit de la Saint-Barthélemy*, pp. 100–04.

58  Camillo Capilupi, *Le Stratagème, ou la ruse de Charles IX, Roy de France, contre les Huguenots rebelles à Dieu et à luy*, in *Archives curieuses de l'histoire de France*, ed. L. Cimber and C. Danjou,

ser. 1, vol. 7 (Paris: Beauvais, Membre de l'Institut Historique, 1835), pp. 401–71. This work is the subject of an interesting exchange in *The Correspondence of Sir Philip Sidney and Hubert Languet*, ed. and trans. Steuart A. Pears (1845; rpt. Westmead, Farnborough, Hants.: Gregg, 1971), Languet 23 April 1574 and 21 May 1574. Sidney ironically mentions that the French ambassador had protested to the Pope about the praise of the king for "certain Italian virtues" (p. 60).

59  Crouzet, *La nuit de la Saint-Barthélemy*, pp. 472–73, with reference to Antoine Fleury, *Responce à un certain escrit, publié par l'Admiral et ses adherans, prentendans couvrir et excuser la rupture qu'ils on faite de l'Edict de Pacification, et leurs nouveaux remuemens et entreprinses contre l'Estat du Roi, et le bien et repos de ses subjectz* (Paris: Claude Fremy, 1568).

60  Cameron, ed., p. VIII.

61  See *Histoire et dictionnaire des Guerres de Religion*, ed. Jouanna et al., p. 238.

62  The edition is replete with technical and typographical errors. Neither the place of publication nor the publisher is identified, but Cameron (p. XIX), on the evidence of the volume's physical resemblance to *Pharaon*, reasonably considers it to be the work of the same Parisian publisher, Nicolas Bonfons.

63  François de Chantelouve, *La tragédie de feu Gaspar de Colligni, Jadis Admiral de France, contenant ce qui advint à Paris le 24 Aoust 1572. avec le nom des Personnages*, ed. N. Lenglet du Fresnoy (Paris: P. Gandouin, 1744); François de Chantelouve, *La tragédie de feu Gaspar de Colligni, Jadis Admiral de France, contenant ce qui advint à Paris le 24 Aoust 1572. avec le nom des Personnages*, in *Journal de Henri III, Roy de France et de Pologne, par Pierre de L'Estoile. Nouvelle édition. Accompagnée de remarques historiques, et des pièces manuscrites les plus curieuses de ce règne*, ed. J. Le Duchat, D. Godefroy, and N. Lenglet du Fresnoy, 5 vols. (The Hague: P. Grosse, 1744), vol. 1, pp. 549–98. My references are to the separately published edition. Apart from his numerous derogatory remarks regarding Chantelouve's language — one is to the effect that he has never seen a particular word before and trusts never to see it again — the editor (Lenglet du Fresnoy) measures the play by neo-classical standards with sublime assurance: "jamais pièce ne fut moins dans

les règles, ni pour le temps, ni pour l'ordannance [never did a play conform less to the rules, either for time or for disposition of the action]" (p. 2). It is hard to set much store by his claim that "On trouve d'ailleurs quelques autres Tragédies imprimées de cet Auteur dans la Bibliothèque de Sa Majesté [Moreover, several other printed tragedies by the same author are found in His Majesty's library]" (p. 2), but the statement remains intriguing.

64 François de Chantelouve, *La tragédie de feu Gaspard de Coligny*, ed. Lisa Wollfe, in *La tragédie à l'époque d'Henri III*, vol. 1 (1574–1579), Théâtre français de la Renaissance, ser. 2 (Florence: Leo S. Olschki, 1999).

65 Jean-Baptiste-Honoré-Raymond Capefigue, *Histoire de la Réforme, de la Ligue, et du règne de Henri IV*, 8 vols. (Paris: Duféy, 1834), vol. 3, pp. 242–43.

66 Faguet, p. 194. Faguet's sources were often dubious, and in the second edition of his study, he suppressed a number of "assertions hasardées [ventured assertions]" and "erreurs incontestables [indubitable errors]" that had appeared in the first some thirty years earlier (Paris: Hachette, 1883; see the Avant-Propos). This statement concerning *Pharaon* was allowed to stand, for better or worse, while two notes citing the *Journal du Théâtre Français* to document Parisian performances of *Coligny* (by the Besochiens in 1574) and *Pharaon* (at the Hôtel de Reims in 1575) were modified to eliminate those claims (1883 ed., p. 310, nn. 1 and 2).

67 Charles Mazouer, "Chantelouve et la Saint-Barthélemy: *La tragédie de feu Gaspard de Colligny* (1575)," in *Les écrivains et la politique dans le sud-ouest de la France autour des années 1580. Actes du Colloque de Bordeaux 6–7 novembre 1981*, ed. Claude-Gilbert Dubois et al. (Bordeaux: Presses Universitaires de Bordeaux, 1982), p. 132

68 On early modern performances of Garnier, see *Œuvres complètes de Robert Garnier: Porcie, Cornélie*, ed. Raymond Lebègue (Paris: Les Belles Lettres, 1973), pp. 22–24. As it happens, there are no records of the staging of *Porcie* or *Cornélie*, which I discuss below.

69  Cf. the discussion of Wollfe, pp. 97–102, which stresses Chantelouve's "liberties," if not ineptitude, in managing syntax, vocabulary, versification, and tone.
70  For a readily accessible summary in a useful broader context, see Margaret M. McGowan, *The Vision of Rome in Late Renaissance France* (New Haven, CT: Yale University Press, 2000), pp. 272–82.
71  On the circumstances of Garnier's undoubtedly lukewarm participation in the League in Le Mans, see Henri Chardon, *Robert Garnier. Sa vie, ses poésies inédites avec son véritable portrait et un facsimile de sa signature* (1905; rpt. Geneva: Slatkine Reprints, 1970), pp. 159–67.
72  See Cameron, ed., p. XII; he is nearly absolute on this question: "Si Chantelouve a lu les pièces de Garnier . . . il ne semble rien lui devoir [If Chantelouve has read the plays of Garnier . . . he seems to owe nothing to him]."  On Senecan influence on the French tragedy of the period, see Raymond Lebègue, "La Renaissance: les tragédies de Sénèque et le théâtre de la Renaissance," in *Études sur le théâtre français*, vol. 1, pp. 195–206.
73  See Jean-Claude Ternaux, ed., *Cornélie*, by Robert Garnier, Textes de la Renaissance, 53 (Paris: H. Champion, 2002), pp. 20–21. I cite the description (preceded by "Fin des . . .") on the final page of the 1539 edition of Grognet, published in Lyons (*Les tragédies très-éloquentes du grant Philosophe Seneque diligentement traduictes de Latin en Françoy. Avec plusieurs épitaphes, épigrammes, dictz moraulx et aultres choses mémorables nouvellement adjoustées*).  It should be emphasized that this work was in no way an edition of the plays, which are shorn of all dramatic features, beginning with direct discourse itself.
74  Cf. Forsyth, pp. 203–06, who also detects the general evolution I attempt to trace here but does not propose a "hypothetical" reading—that is, in terms of the danger of tyranny happily thwarted by timely divine vengeance. Rather, Forsyth considers that the target of the ferocious attack on tyranny in *Cornélie* is probably the abuses of provincial officials. More generally, Forsyth's discussion of the mixture of classical and biblical elements in Garnier's treatment of vengeance (pp. 211–15) is very much to the point.

75  See Jondorf, *Robert Garnier*, pp. 105–10, whose claim that Garnier here weights the case in favour of harshness seems to be swayed by the doubtful passion of Octave. The Senecan passage in question is *Octavia*, 441–84, in Lucius Annaeus Seneca, *Four Tragedies and Octavia*, trans. and ed. E.F. Watling (Harmondsworth, Middlesex: Penguin Books, 1966).

76  Robert Garnier, "Hymne de la Monarchie," in Chardon, p. 266 (sig. Ci$^v$).

77  On the date of composition, see Ternaux, ed., p. 9.

78  "Ambition des hommes la ruine, / Combien helas! tes effaicts sont malins. . . ."

79  It is not inconsistent with Garnier's eventual brief formal affiliation with the League in 1589 (after the assassination of the Guises and in view of a heretic's succession) that his introductory verse epistle to the 1585 edition of his works begins by assuring Henri III of divine protection — in terms that *Coligny* strikingly enacts ("Les Rois, enfans du Ciel, sont de Dieu les images : / Jupiter en prend cure et les garde d'outrages [Kings, the sons of Heaven, are the images of God: Jupiter takes them under his care and protects them from assaults]" ["Au Roy de France et de Pologne," in *Œuvres complètes*, ed. Lebègue, 1–2]) — then goes on to offer cautionary admonitions regarding kings who (unlike Henri, needless to say) forfeit such favour.

80  Lazard, pp. 105–06.

81  This is essentially the conclusion of Crouzet, *La nuit de la Saint-Barthélemy*, p. 104. Cf. Jondorf, *Robert Garnier*, pp. 44–45.

82  See Forsyth, pp. 206–11.

83  Guillaume de Salluste, seigneur Du Bartas, *La Judit*, ed. André Baïche, Publications de la Faculté des Lettres et Sciences Humaines de Toulouse, ser. A, vol. 12 (Toulouse: Association des Publications de la Faculté des Lettres et Sciences Humaines de Toulouse, 1971), 6.215–24. Baïche's text is based on the revised edition of 1579, but the passages I cite contain no substantial variants from that of 1574, except where indicated. Behind Du Bartas's account of Holoferne's mutilation pretty clearly lies Claudian, *In Rufinum*, 2.410ff.

84  See Baïche, ed., pp. XXI–CIXC. This reading depends very much on the established discursive patterns mediating the topical context; there is little within the poem to mandate such

specific allegory, although when Du Bartas refers to Holoferne as "duc" at telling moments (Baïche, ed., 2.22, 6.128, 6.251), it is hard not to suspect him of taking advantage of the term's common application to biblical leaders (see Huguet, *Dictionnaire de la langue française du seizième siècle*).

85         O que c'est chose bien horrible
     De tomber en ma main terrible,
     O que mes jugemens sont grands
     Sur les hommes plus apparans.

       Plustot que mon pouvoir s'efface,
     Du chaos la confuse Mace
     Les elemens rebrouillera,
     Et plustot la nuit jour sera.

       Et plustot ceste courbe voute,
     Fille de mes mains, sera toute
     Ruinée, que le meschant,
     Echappe mon glaive tranchant.

86 There were very few Elizabethan translations of French plays, none destined for the stage. Arthur Golding's version of the *Abraham sacrifiant* by the militant Calvinist Théodore de Bèze (1575, pub. 1577) seems to have stood alone in the field before Mary Sidney Herbert, Countess of Pembroke, translated Garnier's *Marc Antoine* in 1590 (*Antonius*, pub. 1592). This precedent, in turn, may have encouraged Kyd to think of Garnier, despite his Catholicism, as a respectable author, indeed one especially susceptible of appealing to an aristocratic patron: he dedicates his work to the Countess of Sussex and promises a translation of *Porcie* to follow (*Cornelia*, in *The Works of Thomas Kyd*, ed. Frederick S. Boas [Oxford: Clarendon Press 1901], p. 102). Mary Sidney Herbert, sister of Sir Philip Sidney (who had himself narrowly escaped being killed in Paris on Saint Bartholomew's day by taking refuge with the English Ambassador), would have provided impeccable authority for valuing Garnier, given the family's militant Protestant credentials. These she herself had effectively signalled, incidentally, by initially publishing her translation of Garnier as a supplement to her translation of a treatise on death by Philippe de Mornay, seigneur du Plessis-Marley. (The latter was a prominent Huguenot theologian and politician, the "Pleshé" who

figures in Marlowe's *Massacre* as an ally of Henry of Navarre.) Thematic connections between the two works may also have helped to blunt Garnier's political edge for readers of this volume — see Mary Ellen Lamb, *Gender and Authorship in the Sidney Circle* (Madison: University of Wisconsin Press, 1990), pp. 129–32 — but the politics of *Marc Antoine* are in any case less tendentious than those of *Cornélie*. On a purely speculative note, while Kyd's 1594 dedicatee is undoubtedly the young and very newly titled Bridget Radcliffe — on the question of his patron's identity, see Arthur Freeman, *Thomas Kyd: Facts and Problems* (Oxford: Clarendon Press, 1967), pp. 32–37 — the dedication reads only "the vertuously noble, and rightly honoured lady, the Countesse of Sussex" (Boas, ed., p. 102), and one wonders whether Kyd also aimed at evoking for readers a far more eminent Countess of Sussex — namely, Frances Sidney, Sir Philip's aunt (d. 1589), a notable figure of Protestant piety.

87  C'est toy, Rome, qui l'as nourri trop indulgente,
Et qui luy as armé la dextre si puissante
Qu'il leve maintenant, parricide, sur toy,
Violant de nature et des hommes la loy.
Comme un simple paisant qui de fortune trouve
Des louveaux en un bois au desceu de la Louve,
Les massacre soudain, fors un tant seulement,
Qu'il emporte et nourrist pour son esbatement.
Avecques ses aigneaux aux pastis il le meine,
Il l'estable aveque eux comme une beste humaine,
Le traitte tendrement : mais luy, grand devenu,
Au lieu d'avoir le bien du Berger recogneu,
Une nuict qu'il s'avise, estrangle insatiable
Tout le foible troupeau, puis s'enfuit de l'estable.

[It is you, Rome, who, too indulgent, have nurtured him and who have armed the right hand, so powerful, that he now, parricide, raises against you, violating the law of Nature and of men: like a simple peasant who happens to find some wolf-cubs in a wood, to the discomfiture of their mother; he kills them at once, except one only, which he takes with him and nurtures to divert himself. With his sheep he leads it to pasture; he shelters it in the barn as if it were a humane beast, treats it tenderly. But when it has grown up, instead of acknowledging the shepherd's goodness, one night it becomes

> aware and, insatiable, strangles all the feeble herd, then flees
> the barn.]                                    (Ternaux, ed., 779–92)

Garnier's passage is imitated from Aeschylus, *Agamemnon*
(Ternaux, ed., n. 168), but given the overlap with Chantelouve's favourite vocabulary ("armé la dextre si puissante,"
"humaine"), the latter seems to have had Garnier in mind (including a reference to the archetypal Roman fratricide [*Cornélie*,
599–602]) in characterizing the savage Huguenots:

> De ces deux Louveteaux Romains,
> Ainsi la fiere Nourriture,
> Monstra des effaits inhumains
> Voire mesme contre nature,
> Quand Romul en fierté supresme
> Espandit la vie de Reme.
> [Of those two wolfish cubs of Rome
> Thus did the brutal nourishment
> Drive its inhumanity home,
> In spite of nature's own intent,
> When Romulus in violent strife
> Forth on the ground poured Remus' life.]            (ll. 265–70)

88 The disgracing of the Admiral's corpse was not unusual for
condemned criminals and broadly, in fact, conformed to the
edict that had been issued against him in 1569 (although later
quashed) by the *Parlement* of Paris for involvement in the murder of François, Duke of Guise (*Arrest de la covrt de parlement
contre Gaspart de Colligny, qui fut Admiral de France, mis en huict
langues, à sçavoir, François, Latin, Italien, Espagno, Allemant, Flament, Anglois et Escoçois*, in *Archives curieuses de l'histoire de
France*, ed. Cimber and Danjou, ser. 1, vol. 6 [1835], pp. 375–
93).

89 "C'est luy, ce sont messieurs ses Freres, & c'est Guise, / Un
meschant comme moy d'un meschant fait s'advise."

90 For notes on the passages cited, see the translation.

91        O fille de Tithon du lict ensafrané
> Sortant, qui monstre aus Dieus le grand tout enjourné,
> Et qui, par tout le Ciel, les barrieres descloses,
> D'une infantive main semes d'œillets & Roses,
> Descouvris tu jamais de tes yeux vigilans,
> Tels mal-heureux que moy parmi les plus vaillans?

92    Ores la hart au col, je suis pressé si fort
      Que bavant ecumeux, je rends un venin ord.
      Ainsi le filz d'Alcmene en sa juste colere,
      Pour Pyrithoé mort estraignant de Cerbere
      Soubz son Robuste doy le gousier inhumain,
      De sa bave aperceust l'aconyte villain.

93    Si donques je me veux reposer à mon aise,
      Je me couche en un lict couvert de chaude Braise.
      Si j'ay froit j'ay le glaz tout prest pour me chaufer,
      Et si quelque appetit a mon ventre en enfer,
      De crapaux, & Serpens, ma table plus insigne
      Se couvre, pour pouvoir appaiser ma famine.

94    Et ce qui plus me fache, est que ceste Moynaille,
      Ces Prestres, Cardinaux, & toute la Prestraille,
      Que tant je mesprisois, que je tuay jadis,
      Sans mort, & sans douleur, vivent en Paradis,
      Et remplis de bon heur voyent de Dieu la face,
      Et entre les enfans de Dieu reçoivent place.

95    Ouvrés, faites moy place, à moy est le labeur
      De Sysiphe Larron, & Ixion trompeur.
      Et s'il y a nul Dieu qui ait puissance adonques,
      Car en mon cœur meschant de Dieu je ne creus onques,
      Qu'il monstre son pouvoir, & darde sur mon chef
      Et non sur un rocher, des foudres le mechef.

96 *Shakespeare, Marlowe and the Politics of France*, pp. 84, 88–89, 93.

97 Both the classical and the medieval elements are signalled by Cameron, ed., n. to l. 857.

98 Marlowe, *Faustus*, iii.78, 79.

99 Et le voyant ainsi bresphemer & desplaire, / Il sera plus enclain à ma volonté faire." Cf. Marlowe, *Faustus*:

> For when we hear one rack the name of God,
> Abjure the scriptures and his saviour Christ,
> We fly, in hope to get his glorious soul;
> Nor will we come unless he use such means
> Whereby he is in danger to be damn'd.      (iii.49–53)

100 Shakespeare is cited throughout from *The Riverside Shakespeare*, gen. eds. G. Blakemore Evans and J.J.M. Tobin, 2nd ed. (Boston: Houghton Mifflin, 1997).

101 These dramatic manifestations of Catholicism were suppressed, of course, in post-Reformation England; for a concise

summary of the situation, see Albert H. Tricomi, "Joan la Pucelle and the Inverted Saints Play in *1 Henry VI*," *Renaissance
and Reformation/Renaissance et Réforme* 25.2 (2001): 8, whose
broader discussion bears usefully on the symbolism of Jeanne
d'Arc as represented by both Shakespeare and Fronton Du
Duc.

102   Cameron, ed., pp. XIII–XV.

103   Crouzet, *La nuit de la Saint-Barthélemy*, p. 245. In " 'secrets' of
God," I echo the heading of a section of Crouzet's fascinat-
ing analysis (pp. 50ff.). On the "Paradis d'Amour," see also
Frances Yates, *The French Academies of the Sixteenth Century*,
Studies of the Warburg Institute, vol. 15 (London: Warburg
Institute, University of London, 1947), pp. 254–56.

104   See Pierre de Ronsard, *La Franciade*, in *Œuvres complètes*, ed.
Jean Céard, Daniel Ménager, et Michel Simonin, vol. 1, Bibliothèque de la Pléiade (Paris: Gallimard, 1993), 4.849ff.

105   See *Coligny*, n. 118.

106   Thus, e.g., "Vole, mon fils, . . . / Huche les vents" adapts "vade
age, nate, voca Zephyros, et labere pinnis" (*The Aeneid of Virgil*,
ed. T.E. Page, 2 vols. [London: Macmillan, 1967], 4.223).

107   See Céard et al., eds., p. 1614, n. 1.   The adventure of the
Golden Fleece was a commonplace emblem of Greek heroic
splendour; cf. Jacques Grévin, *César*, ed. Ellen S. Ginsberg,
Textes Littéraires Français (Genève: Droz, 1971):

> Ainsi le brave fils d'Æson
> Rapporta la riche toison
> Et d'une audace plus hautaine
> Rama premier l'humide plaine.

> [Thus the brave son of Aeson brought back the rich fleece and,
> with still loftier boldness, was the first to row on the watery
> plain.]                                                     (ll. 275–78)

108   It appears that, although the poem had been in Ronsard's plans
for years, he did no substantial work on it before 1568 (Céard
et al., eds., vol. 1, p. 1605). On the "Surprise de Meaux," See
*Histoire et dictionnaire des Guerres de Religion*, ed. Jouanna et al.,
pp. 163–65.

109   . . . je l'ai prins en garde
Si bien, qu'ores qu'il ne se garde,
Que sur son innocence & moy,

Je le veus garder comme Roy.

110 Cameron, ed., p. XIII.

111 *Miracle de l'Empereur Julien* (No. 13), in *Miracles de Nostre Dame par personnages*, ed. Gaston Paris and Ulysse Robert, vol. 2 (1877), pp. 171–226, ll. 61–63.

112 A further link between the tradition of the saints plays and Shakespeare's *Cymbeline* is the fact that Our Lady accompanies the comfort she offers the sleeping Saint Basil with the gift of a book "Ou moult de choses trouveras / Dont enjoir moult te pourras [Where you will find many things from which you can take much pleasure]" (ll. 696–97).

113 It may even be to the point that Iarbus is introduced as the son of Ammon (a Libyan deity, commonly identified with Jupiter): the chief god of the Egyptians in *Pharaon* is "Jupiter Hamon." Might Chantelouve have been further insinuating an association with the biblical Haman, the villain of Riveaudau's tragedy—one of the Protestant precursor dramas he was writing against?

114 François Rabelais, *Le Quart Livre*, ed. Robert Marichal, Textes Littéraires Français (Lille: Giard; Geneva: Droz, 1947), pp. 22–31.

115 See *Coligny*, n. 85.

116 "Hynne des estoiles, au sieur de Pibrac," in *Œuvres complètes*, ed. Céard et al., vol. 2 (1994), ll. 105–10; these verses are aptly cited by Cameron, ed., n. to ll. 1185ff.; cf. n. to ll. 63–70. See also Claude Postel, *Traité des invectives au temps de la Réforme* (Paris: Les Belles Lettres, 2004), pp. 184–86.

117 See François Hotman (attrib.), *La vie de Messire Gaspar de Coligny Admiral de France (c. 1577)*, ed. Émile-V. Telle (1643; fac. rpt. Geneva: Droz, 1987), p. 108. Telle's argument for Hotman's authorship of this work, which has sometimes been attributed to Jean de Serres or Jean Hotman, is quite conclusive (Introduction, pp. 99–100). It is suggestive that while German and English translations appeared in 1576—the latter by Arthur Golding, entitled, *The lyfe of the most godly, valeant and noble capteine and maintener of the trew Christian religion in Fraunce, Iasper Colignie Shatilion, sometyme greate admirall of*

*Fraunce* (London: Thomas Vautrollier, 1576)—no sixteenth-century copies have survived of the contemporary French version that must have appeared simultaneously (see Telle, ed., pp. 104–05). The extent to which the saint's life, technically a Catholic genre, was itself a contested discursive field is suggested by the famous attack on Catherine de Medici, putatively by Henri Estienne, first published in 1575 and known mockingly as the "Life of Saint Catherine"; see Henri Estienne (attrib.), *Discours merveilleux de la vie, action et deportements de Catherine de Medicis, royne-mere*, ed. Nicole Cazauran et al., Les Classiques de la Pensée Politique, 15 (Geneva: Droz, 1995), and Mireille Huchon, "Vie de Sainte Catherine ou Discours merveilleux : les avatars d'un pamphlet," *Cahiers V.-L. Saulnier* 2 (1984): 55–67. See also Kingdon, *passim*.

118  See Capilupi, p. 42; "affiché à son fondemant vn brandon [a torch attached to his arse]," records François de Belleforest, *Les Grandes Annales et histoire générale de France, dès la venue des Francs en Gaule jusques au règne du Roy très-chrestien Henry III*, 2 vols. (Paris: G. Buon, 1579), vol. 2, fol. 1687ʳ.

119  For a well-documented study of such symbolism in the historical context, see David Nicholls, "The Theatre of Martyrdom in the French Reformation," *Past and Present* 121 (1988): 49–73.

120  "O Manes noircissans es Enfers impiteus, / O mes chers compagnons. . . ."

121  A convenient chronology of Mathieu's life is provided by Gilles Ernst, ed., *Clytemnestre. De la vengeance des injures perdurable à la postérité des offencez, et des malheureuses fins de la volupté*, by Pierre Matthieu, Textes Littéraires Français (Geneva: Droz, 1984), pp. 11–20. For a full discussion of his career as a dramatist, see Louis Lobbes, "Pierre Matthieu, dramaturge phénix (1563–1621)," *Revue d'histoire du théâtre* 50 (1998): 207–36.

122  Gilles Ernst, "Des deux *Guisiade* de Pierre Matthieu," *Bibliothèque d'Humanisme et Renaissance* 47 (1985): 367.

123  Valuable bibliographies are provided by Ernst, ed., *Clytemnestre*, and Lobbes, ed., *La Guisiade*.

124  The phrase cited is the title of Chapter 17 of Crouzet's *Les guerriers de Dieu* (vol. 2, pp. 361–461); on the renewed myth

of the crusade, and its appropriation by the Guises, see esp. vol. 2, pp. 397–407.

125  *Stances svr l'hevreuse publication de la paix et saincte vnion : Avec un Hymne de même argument prins de l'Erinophile du sieur Germain d'Apchon, Chevalier de l'ordre du Roy* (Lyons: B. Rigaud, 1588). On the Union, see *The Guisiade*, n. 4.

126  These passages are indicated in the notes.

127  On Penitentialism within the League, see Crouzet, *Les guerriers de Dieu*, vol. 2, pp. 379–97. Rhetorical prowess is traditionally a lawyer's quality, of course, one valued even more highly in the Renaissance, and Matthieu's play displays a special consciousness of the orator's art — not only in the speeches he composed for the scenes of the Estates, but also in his sardonic praise of the king for his eloquence (see Argument to Act III, Scene ii[a]).

128  Lyons: [n.pub.], 1593.

129  See *Discours veritable, et sans passion*, p. 12.

130  See David Buisseret, *Henry IV, King of France* (London: Routledge, 1984), pp. 44–49.

131  *Histoire et dictionnaire des Guerres de Religion*, ed. Jouanna et al., p. 394.

132  Ernst, ed., *Clytemnestre*, p. 17.

133  Lyons: P. Michel, [1595]; BnF electronic document NUMM-49738.

134  See Lobbes, "L'exécution des Guises, prétexte à tragédie," in *Le mécénat et l'influence des Guises. Actes du colloque organisé par le Centre de Recherche sur la Littérature de la Renaissance de l'Université de Reims et tenu à Joinville du 31 mai au 4 juin 1994 (et à Reims pour la journée du 2 juin)*, ed. Yvonne Bellenger, Colloques, Congrès et Conférences sur la Renaissance, 9 (Paris: H. Champion, 1997), pp. 578–79.

135  Pierre Matthieu, *Aelius Sejanus, histoire recueillie de divers auteurs* (Paris: R. Estienne, 1617). Matthieu had included Sejanus (as well as Edward II's Gaveston) in a list of wicked counsellors doomed to destruction in the preface to his tragedy of *Aman* (1588), which was aimed at Épernon; see Lobbes, ed., *La Guisiade*, pp. 26–27 and 26, n. 1. Matthieu is almost certainly not, however, the author of a tragedy on the Concini affair that

has been attributed to him (*La magicienne étrangère* [1617])—
see Ernst, ed., *Clytemnestre*, pp. 19–20, n. 33.

136 For a more extensive discussion of Matthieu's dramatic production, with particular attention to the relation of the biblical
plays to *La Guisiade*, see Lobbes, ed., Introduction, pp. 8–55.
On the composition of *Clytemnestre*, see Ernst, ed., pp. 67–74.

137 Ernst, ed., *Clytemnestre*, p. 68.

138 See Lobbes, ed., pp. 10–12.

139 Forsyth, p. 161.

140 Lobbes has disproved this; see his edition, p. 13 and p. 13, n. 1.

141 "A Tolose: par Iaques Colomiés, 1589"; BnF RES P-YF-63. I
have verified that this copy is of the second edition. BnF also
holds a manuscript of the second edition (Lobbes, ed., p. 56).

142 Simon Belyard, *Le Guysien, ou perfidie tyrannique commise par
Henry de Valois es personnes des Princes Loys de Loraine Cardinal &
Archevesque de Rheims, & Henry de Loraine Duc de Guyse, grand
Maistre de France* (Troyes: Jean Moreau, 1592). For descrip-
tions of this work, see J. Chocheyras, "La Tragédie politique
d'actualité sous les régnes de Henri III et de Henri IV," in
*Études sur Étienne Dolet: le théâtre au XVI$^e$ siècle: le Forez, le
Lyonnais et l'histoire du livre. Publiées à la mémoire de Claude
Longeon*, ed. Gabriel-André Pérouse, Travaux d'Humanisme
et Renaissance, 270 (Geneva: Droz, 1993), pp. 167–70, and
Lobbes, "L'exécution des Guises, prétexte à tragédie," pp. 567–
79.

143 Adolf Ebert, *Entwicklungs-Geschichte der Französischen Tragödie
vornehmlich im XVI. Jahrhundert* [1856; rpt. Geneva: Slatkine
Reprints, 1970], p. 182 and n. 256; L.-V. Gofflot, *Le théâtre au
college du moyen âge à nos jours*, introd. Jules Claretie, Le cercle
français de l'Union Harvard (Paris: H. Champion, 1907), p. 61.

144 Witness Charles Mazouer, *Le théâtre français de la Renaissance*
(Paris: H. Champion, 2002), p. 240: "boursouflé, ampoulé,
maladroit et lourd [bombastic, swollen, clumsy, and heavy]."

145     Comme un second Cain, tu auras à tes pas
    L'ombre de mon enfant, en prenant ton repas,
    Le sang de ce grand Duc fera bouffir tes veines,
    Tu sera escorché, et mis entre les geines
    D'un renaissant remord, les Panniques terreurs
    Combleront ton cerveau de craintes et d'horreurs,

Et te mussant couard en un fort, la vengeance
Ira tousjours sommer ta pasle conscience.

On the characterization of Henri, cf. Lobbes, "L'exécution des Guises, p. 577: "Enfin, le monstre lui-même se présente sous des traits terriblement humains [Finally, the monster presents himself with features terribly human]."

146 See the development of this comparison in Hillman, *Shakespeare, Marlowe and the Politics of France*, pp. 178–85, and "Richard II, *La Guisiade* of Pierre Matthieu and the Invention of Tragic Heroes," in *Richard II de William Shakespeare. Une œuvre en contexte*, ed. Isabelle Schwartz-Gastine, Cahiers de la Maison de la Recherche en Sciences Humaines, numéro spécial, février 2005 (Caen: Équipe Littérature et Sociétés Anglophones, Cahiers de la Maison de la Recherche en Sciences Humaines de Caen), pp. 87–98.

147 For an intertextual discussion of Marlowe's and Matthieu's plays, see Hillman, *Shakespeare, Marlowe and the Politics of France*, pp. 84–97.

148 See above, n. 46.

149 Cameron, ed., pp. 44–47.

150 See my further comments, in that volume, on this choice of verse-form (Introduction, pp. 51–53).

# The Tragedy of the Late Gaspard de Coligny
## Formerly Admiral of France

### Containing What Occurred in Paris on 24 August 1572
### with the Names of the Persons

by

François de Chantelouve

Gaspard de Coligny, School of Clouet, Bibliothèque Ste.-Geneviève.

## *Dramatis Personae*

Gaspard de Coligny, Lord Châtillon, Admiral of France
King Charles IX
Montgomery[1]
Briquemault[2]
Cavagnes[3]
Piles[4]
The Informer[5]
Mercury
Ghost of Andelot[6]
The Furies
The King's Council
The People of France (Chorus)
Messenger

**Scene:** Act I, indefinite; Acts II–V, Paris. The action ranges from the period immediately preceding the peace of Saint-Germain-en-Laye (signed 8 August 1570), which is resolved upon by the King with his Council in Act II, Scene i, to the day of the massacre as specified in the title. The Admiral first returned to court, at the King's request, on 12 September 1571. His wounding occurred on 22 August 1572 and interrupted the festivities, which had begun on 17 August, surrounding the marriage of Henri de Navarre and Marguerite de Valois, the king's sister.

Defenestration and Decapitation of Coligny,
Dubois Panorama, Cabinet des Estampes.

# Act I

## Scene i.

ADMIRAL [*alone, with a hangman's noose*[7] ]

O ye shades of darkness in Hades pitiless —
O my dear companions — O what shame and distress
To see my fearful boldness bridled by a child![8]
What shameful act is left for one so meek and mild
But to take this hateful halter where none can spy
And use my hangman's hands to stretch my neck up high?
O death, O rage, O sword, O Pluto, O fell Furies,
Come running, beat me down beneath your bitter frenzies.
O Satan! O Calvin: open for me hell's gates,
Where my brothers[9] and you are grilled on divers grates —          10
Scorned and despised, blaspheming with horrible shrieks —
By force invincible, as He just vengeance wreaks.
Open up, make room for me, the labour is mine
Of that thieving Sisyphus, deceiving Ixion.[10]
And if there is any God upon whom to call[11]
(For in my foul heart I believe in none at all),
Let him show his power, and pour upon my pate,
Instead of some pointless rock, his thundering hate.[12]
Night, daughter of Hades, you fierce Eumenides,
Styx and Phlegethon, Cocytean vortices[13] —          20
And you, shade-herding porter, triple-headed hound,[14]
Let your ghastly gullet gape, gulp me at a bound.
All power is yours, my dear lords diabolical,
You boast a strength that is truly admirable,
And not that great God that twits children with fears
And women stooped over with the weight of their years.
For if He were capable of doing anything,
He would have caused me to triumph over the King;
And seeing I had that precious Christ in my pocket,
I should have had my will, with no Henri to block it.[15]          30
   Henceforth all religion by me shall be renounced.

Yea, I'd throw over the one that Bèze has announced,[16]
Except that I must use the shadow of piety
To mask my machinations aimed against royalty.
And since I well know it's a filthy enterprise,
I've picked up in Geneva a vile pack of lies,
Which, because on the outside it shows itself white,
Though black as black within,[17] fools the most erudite;
Thus, though we request that, since conscience should be free,
We be given in France the right to preach peacefully,                    40
For my own part I cherish nothing but the hope
Of ruining the faith of both Calvin and the Pope,
And, shunning all restraint that aims to clip my wing,
To be alone exempt from law — I would be king!
I feign to appear a reformed Christian die-hard,
The more easily to catch our King off his guard.
Thus hypocritical, I'm always apt for treason;
An old fox remains a fox[18] — while hens are in season.
But, but — alas! — how comes it that, having incited
(More thoroughly to plague that infant so benighted),                    50
The fair-haired race,[19] Thames-watered under English skies,
As well as the German pig who murdered that great Guise,[20]
My mortal enemy (once counted as my friend) —
A means of advancing my murderous royal end —
But how comes it, I say, that all this force of arms
Has served for nothing but to bring on me more harms?
   O Daughter, you who from Tithonus' saffron bed[21]
Arise to show the gods the universe outspread
By daylight, as the gate swings open and discloses
All heaven with carnations deftly strewn, and roses,                    60
Have you ever perceived, using your watchful eyes,
Brave men as unhappy as I beneath the skies?
   O most sovereign Queen and Princess of the world,[22]
Who keep uncertain footing as the globe is whirled,
What have I done to you to be thus overthrown
By a new Pyrrhus,[23] who before had scarcely known
The first thing about engaging in furious war?

Overthrown, I say — I, who men-at-arms galore
Have led in battle, and reduced to fearful trembling
Countless different nations, enemies of my King!                    70
    Must I be made to recall the Amboise disaster,[24]
When the flames of civil strife I made to burn faster,
Or when, on the shadowy druids' famous field,
In combat against our King I was forced to yield?[25]
I had fancied myself at your wheel's very height,
When by your cruelty, which of the world makes light,
To the depths was I hurtled, to the nadir thrown,
Where the blood that I bathed in included my own,[26]
Where all who had rebelled against their mother France
In the garb of innocence,[27] following my chance,                 80
With stark catastrophe could make no better deals
And again took my lead — by taking to their heels.
    Then (on various minor skirmishes not dwelling),
Being at Saint Denis and — this is much more telling —
At Bassac subjected to your disdainful frown,
We took the blow that knocked my Prince of Condé down;
And so, his life ending on the back of an ass,
Instead of destroying it, he restored the mass.[28]
Just so did Telephus, who intended to stay
The passage of the Greeks, at last show them the way,              90
When great Achilles, famous for the foes he routed,
Came to his aid with the little plant that sprouted.[29]
    And (not to amuse myself with that deadly sojourn
At the siege of Poitiers[30] ), a still more nasty turn
I feelingly received near Moncontour at Ervaux,[31]
Where the ferocious sword of that bloody Enyo
So struck me down,[32] my white-garbed reformers[33] so harmed,
That the greater part of them died, or were disarmed.
But courage: those who have no further hope yet dare
To stake a kind of hope even upon despair.                         100
Then let me either die — or, better, kill the King,
Then draw the crown to me by some sly act of cunning.
    If only, O Fortune, you deign to grant my prayer,

My invincible heart will spread death everywhere,
And, since I'm not stingy with incense in the least,
From your altars I'll send the stars a fragrant feast.
But then, does anyone fail, in the earth's whole sphere,
To thrill when my exalted name rings in his ear?[34]

### Scene ii.

*[Enter Montgomery.]*

MONTGOMERY

Truly now, I swell with gleeful elation
To think of the mass's evisceration.                           110
Those ill-fortuned losses that we deplored
By fortune have already been restored.
Have we not run the length and breadth of France
And found no one to offer real resistance?
All of Provence, the whole of Languedoc too,
Since the fight at Ervaux, confirms that true.
The Papist fools have had to recognize
That in war the Admiral bears the prize:
Take courage, then, O France's Admiral,
Repair our past reverses tragical                              120
By renewing our strength in Charity,[35]
Where either, by dying honourably,
We shall make our way to the fields Elysian,
Or we shall bring our foes into derision.
I hereby make a solemn dedication
Of my valour to France's ruination,
And just as once I served you with my arm
And did the King at Paris deadly harm,
To that good deed I hope to add another:
Killing the King and butchering his brother.                   130

ADMIRAL

I well recall, O great Montgomery,
That you not only sent to death Henri,[36]

But also by your shrewd and valiant pains
Prevented the Papists from making gains.
I remember you put your armour on
To take back the lost country of Béarn,
And, surprising by diligence and speed
The haughty arrogance of de Terride,
You drove the besieger to take a stand
And delivered Navarrenx from his hand.                    140
I don't forget your lofty qualities,
Sure harbingers of future victories.
I well know that, as far as Paris, too,
The great Prince of Papists we must pursue.
For our army, with strong reinforcements,[37]
Shall sieges lay and shock their battlements,
Where, at the least, fighting bravely in action
We shall not perish without satisfaction.
And if peace should arrive by happenstance,
We shall take it, and then await our chance               150
By underhanded means to surprise our King,
Who will believe our simple undertaking.
All it takes for a great lord to be greater —
King, yea emperor! — is to be a traitor.

### MONTGOMERY

He who attacks his prince to gain a crown,
Rightly or not,[38] for valour gains renown. *[Exeunt.]*

*[Enter the People as Chorus.]*

### CHORUS

That man who is whole within[39]
And who has kept his soul unstained
By any sense-corrupting sin,
Who has not entered unrestrained                          160
On transgressions execrable
And excesses abominable —
He who in life is whole and pure

Of Moorish dart no need has he
Or Turkish bow;[40]  to be secure
He need not practice soldiery
Nor requires any armed defence:
*A sufficient shield is innocence.*

He who in conscience undefiled
From his soul all fraud has shed                    170
Need not fear to be reviled,
Everywhere holds high his head
And never fears that some attack
Is being planned behind his back.

He is content with what he's got,
Be his riches great or small;
Thus only good shall be his lot,
To none does he do harm at all;[41]
Never does he take offence:
He gives, and receives in recompense.                180

And although, when he goes to sleep,
He does not choose to close his gate,
No one to his bed shall creep
Some violent act to perpetrate.
*In such a strong fortress does he dwell*
*Who never speaks of others but well.*

By all is such a one approved,
To give good words his certain charm.
Against him no enemy is moved;
To no one, in turn, does he wish harm.               190
*With wisdom his beloved mistress,*
*He is immune to all distress.*

But in what continual fear
Exists someone who lives by evil?
From conscience he can never clear
Tormenting knowledge of his ill.
What misery it is to know
How hatefully his actions show!

The thefts to which so many times

His crooked right hand has bent,                                    200
The upraised arm committing crimes
Of blood against the innocent —
Sight of his manifold transgressions
Shall summon him to painful sessions.
     Never shall he traverse the wood
Or through the Syrtes,[42] where wreck awaits,
Sail in assurance, like the good,
But feel the menace of the Fates;
In Proteus' turbulent motions
He shall receive the death he shuns.                                210
     And if by God's exceeding grace,
Relief from one danger is supplied,
Another shall take up the chase,
Pressing him from the other side,
And with some form of death more dire
Shall cast on him its righteous ire.[43]
     Thus the miserable pilot
Who strives to flee, at any cost,
Charybdis looming as his lot
On ravenous Scylla is tossed;[44]                                   220
Thus the bird that seeks the open air
Flees its cage but falls into the snare.
     O worse than wicked Admiral,
You would not have felt such terror
If you had shown yourself loyal,
Not thrown yourself into error.
Despite yourself, gnawing contrition
Feeds you with fear and suspicion.
     The fires set on every side
At that pirate's instigation,[45]                                   230
The massacres[46] in endless tide
He has poured across our nation,
Pillaging, treasons — low and high[47] —
Within his soul for vengeance cry.[48]
     The blood so treacherously shed

Of that excellent Duke of Guise
Frightens him nearly out of his head;
The Church's just lamenting cries
Continually his heart torment
With unrelenting punishment.                                    240
   Not that, for all this, he repents:
For he, a newfangled Judas, seeks
To shun, as he despairs, the judgements
That the righteous Father wreaks,
And, by troubling again our France,
Hopes, fool as he is, to flee vengeance.[49]
   Cease, Châtillon, wicked wretch,
Cease thus to persecute the Church,
And see before you sweetly stretch
The gentle repose for which you search.                        250
Offences earlier committed,
If you so wish, shall be remitted.
   Come from blood most thoroughly bred
And issued of most noble race,
That bosom would you turn blood-red
Of your own mother's warm embrace?
The very life would you now wrest
Of her who suckled you at her breast?
   No woman, surely, gave you suck,
But a tigress of Hyrcania,[50]                                 260
No more than that Montgomery, struck
From the sheer rock of Marpessia:[51]
To both of them a she-wolf gave
Shamelessly suck in some weird cave.
   Of those two wolfish cubs of Rome
Thus did the brutal nourishment
Drive its inhumanity home,
In spite of nature's own intent,
When Romulus in violent strife
Forth on the ground poured Remus' life.                        270
   It is not through combat and flame

That one must solicit his[52] grace,
But, leaving that disastrous[53] game,
By doing good in every place.
Then his most royal Majesty
Will grant pardon liberally.

But instead of doing as he should,
Poor fool, he has persevered in wrong,
Stirred up again, wherever he could,
A war that has lasted all too long,                    280
Trying, criminally insane,
The crown for his own head to gain.

La Charité his force renews,
Saintonge he sees to be his own —
Unless the divinity rues
The grievous trouble we bemoan,
Then we, God's Christian spouse, in sadness
Shall suffer from his double madness.[54]

Moreover, it is sure that never
Draws the Tyrant an easy breath,                       290
But always, with his nerves a-quiver,
Lives in stark terror of his death.
For the voice of his wicked conscience
Harps on others' wicked intents.

Thus this murderer, devil-driven,
Views all others in his own image,[55]
And fears his death's blow will be given
By some executioner whose rage
Will have his body ripped and rent
As token of God's punishment.                          300

Yet still, O most merciful Lord,
By whom on Oeta's[56] wilderness
Gigantic thunderbolts are poured
For nothing in your gentleness,
With bloody arm hurl them instead
Upon this Gaspard's muffled head.[57]

Listen to all the abject cries

And groans of mothers devastated
To see, alas, before their eyes,
Their helpless daughters violated,                    310
Hear, Lord, the father's suppliance,
Stricken with grief, for bitter vengeance,
   To see his child hacked in his arms—
In vain for mercy may he search;
See the peasant, who can run from harms
Only to the sorrowful church:[58]
See, Saviour, see how far from peace is
Your poor Church, in its thousand pieces.


# Act II

### Scene i.

KING [*alone*]

That serpent of Egypt which, as its tail it bites,
The year gone past with that which is to come unites,[59]        320
And you, Father Janus, who are alone assigned
Among the gods to look both before and behind,
And brilliant Titan, tracing your blazing course, who
Bear with you the searching light of day—none of you
Have seen a prince with more grievous sorrow attended,
And by his own subjects—O heartache!—so offended.
Just as one who suffers in fever's burning throes
From the pain tormenting him struggles for repose,
Finds that he sometimes turns to lie on his right side,
Then turns on his left—then another place is tried,              330
But in vain: by wakefulness he is more distressed,
The more devoured by the futile hope of rest.
Not otherwise do I, when repose I would find,
Stir up a mass of thoughts, a chaos in my mind;
Now stumbling upon hope, suddenly I despair.
I search the means, like a good father moved with care

Of his family, to preserve my subjects' peace,
But alas, I find that in passion they increase,
When I think to win them by showing myself mild —
Like a colt that kicks at the bridle, keeping wild.                340
O me, most wretched prince! O miserable king —
By no means only for myself is my lamenting,
Though when I was an infant sucking at the breast,
My subjects rose up in rebellion manifest;[60]
No, it is my French people I am wretched for,
Who suffer the many evils of cruel war.
O, I should be content if Heaven's stormy blast
Were all upon my head, and not my people, cast,
Instead of seeing thus, in a rebellious nation,
My servants forced to run to their annihilation.                  350
O my royal forefathers, what bliss you enjoyed,
Who in peace and plenty your government employed! —
When all your subjects, living under the same law,
Held faithfully the same God, the same king, in awe.
Not that I am envious at all of your peace,
But the pain that my poor life bears without surcease
Makes me long to see such repose in France appear —
Or else to have my bones soon placed upon their bier.
    I have managed (by the hands of those who proved true)
At Dreux the rebels' flanks with their blood to imbrue;[61]      360
Against them at Saint Denis, too, I gained the field:
My warlike brother's leadership forced them to yield;
At Bassac died the very stirrer-up of strife;
Henri[62] inflicted at Ervaux great loss of life
Upon the rebel Huguenots there overthrown:
O, I bear the wound, and I am cut to the bone.[63]
    For I have caused the loss of those faithful to me
In wreaking such losses among those in mutiny;
And even by such losses, though of mutineers,
Still my breast is torn, heaving with pitiful tears;             370
I have seen myself obliged to send to the grave
Those whom my benignant clemency longs to save.

Need I seek out new occasions for sorrow fresh,
When I find myself constrained to cut my own flesh?
O treasonous[64] Admiral, O you mutinous band,
Would God that you could read my heart and understand[65]
That where you might expect just harshness and cruelty,
You would encounter nothing but mildness and mercy!
But I delude myself; you have no inhibitions:
My death is at the dead centre of your ambitions —                    380
My ruin, my end, my realm, my blood: regicide
Is the only spur to action that pricks your side.
But if my death alone would satisfy your vengeance,
Your bloody hands inflict no further harm on France,
Myself to death I would most willingly expose,
So that France from that time forth might live in repose,
But your treasonous soul seeks only to wolf down,
With its gluttonous appetite, the royal crown,
And sink my blood[66] beneath my coffin in the clay.
But I wish to hear what my Council has to say.                         390

### Scene ii.

*[Enter Council.[67]]*

COUNCIL

    Sire, may He who bends His holy gaze
Upon our actions all our earthly days
And in a trice turns pomp into affliction,
Upon your Catholic hands grant benediction,
Due piety and justice to preserve.
    Now if you hope that we your good may serve
By furnishing you with counsel sound and steady,
All of us you see most humble and ready.

KING

My Lords and friends, because you are the source
Of wisdom here, to you I have recourse.                               400
*Always a king this course should closely hold[68] —*

*To treat with reverence the wise and old.*
*In times of great danger, it is the prudence*
*Of age that helps, not youth devoid of sense.*
*If their advice he will not seek, or mind it,*
*Woe to the king who in himself can't find it!*
Thus to you, my most faithful friends, I bare
My soul's complaint that this cruel warfare
I cannot check by pulling on the reins
Of peace, punishing evil with due pains,                              410
And fulfill my longing with my own hands
To have Astraea[69]  brought back to my lands.
Tell me, therefore, if I should grant a peace
Or keep the course of combat without cease.

### COUNCIL

Surely, Sire, the question that you raise
May be considered in different ways:
One who rebels against your government
Deserves, no doubt, no end of punishment;
On the other hand, to continue fighting
Is to ensure your country's further blighting.                        420
*Since mercy is the most becoming dress*
*To garb your state and kingly business,*
*And royal princes occupy God's place,*
*They should be prompt and lavish with their grace,*
*Their pity, and these as freely give*
*As God Himself is ready to forgive.*
Certainly, the Huguenot has well earned
The wrath with which our forceful arm has burned,
But when he realizes your Majesty
Has granted him a gracious amnesty,                                   430
He will confess his former insolence
By rendering you full obedience.
But, you will say, such a divided state
Will merely, with two faiths, disintegrate.
God will, by touching that bold rebel crew,

Turn the infidel Catholic for you.
Not that we argue that you should accede
To any law but the Catholic creed.
But one must choose well the hour and time
Propitious for banishing such false crime.                    440
Then, God wishes to test your constancy:
That is why He permits your enemy
To reinforce his fighting strength once more.
God wishes that all exercise of war
Give way to a peace, in order to make it
Harder on them, if they should dare to break it.
As for what his arms in Saintonge have done
In overcoming all the population,
For this God has given express permission
To test your willingness to grant remission.                  450
For those who bear their hearts as Christ intended
Are meek with those that have them most offended.
Peace will also put an end to the death,
The fire and steel, and the bellows-breath
That blows, as we watch, all France into flame.
Make peace, then, and once war's spirit is tame,
Since Hymen's are the strongest bonds there are,
Marry Madame to the prince of Navarre.[70]
And, to gain by honour their approbation,
Call the rebels to that fair celebration.                     460
Then, when they see how much humanity
Is wedded, Sire, to your Majesty,
Remorse will provoke a ready repentance;
They will put aside their former arrogance
And render themselves your humble servitors,
Leaving unheeded their lying ministers.
But if their hearts are hardened so to stone
To raise their feeble hand against your throne,
Then — kill, dash them in pieces, let them die;
Those Giants, under Aetna let them lie.[71]                   470
Thus Jupiter does not lift up at once

His flaming-red[72] right hand when man affronts;
But when he sees his grace held up to scorn,[73]
Then is the sky with smashing thunder torn,
And his bloody arms, pitiless and just,
Shatter unworthy mortals into dust.

KING

Then, my lords, since the better course is peace,
In good time let all hostilities cease.
By messenger the Admiral I'll exhort,
As well, to come and meet me here at court. [*Exeunt.*]                480

## Scene iii.

*[Enter Briquemault, Cavagnes.]*

BRIQUEMAULT

I can hardly, O Cavagnes, my great joy restrain
That the King allows such free and liberal rein
To our preaching, which is essential to our life —
That is, to our schemes and plans for stirring up strife.
But, not to amuse ourselves with matters so small,
Now that here in Paris we and the Admiral
Are honourably entertained, we need some plot
In due time to surprise this princely idiot.
But a pretext or colour, too, we must embrace
To put upon our project a plausible face.                              490
Thus are many women made attractive by make-up
Who are rather less than charming when first they wake up.

CAVAGNES

Since I have served as the chancellor to our cause,
In my diligence I have never made a pause,
But looked out always to advance Bèze's Evangile,[74]
And if I can, while I remain in this town still,
Find out some crafty colour to trick out our plotting,
I'll dip my hands in the blood of the Papist King.

Did not Judith, with a hand divinely uplifted,
To save Bethulia cut off the tyrant's head?[75]                    500
   How many rats shall we kill, these Franciscan friars?
What a mess of parish priests?[76]  How many fat priors?
How many cardinals shall we, and mitre-heads?[77]
Thus Elijah once cut the false prophets in shreds,
And Daniel was the death of those who worshipped Baal.[78]
But, to do it better, consult the Admiral,[79]
For he is the expert, and his Sinon-like[80] soul
Of treasonous practice boasts unrivalled control.
Adept as he was when horrid Mars was ascendant,
How much more than before shall he now shine resplendent? 510
Now that the King's love and preferment he has carried,
And the King of Navarre the King's sister has married,
With this, I expect to see the Admiral king,
And Guisards to die by his edict unpitying. [*Exeunt.*]

CHORUS (the People hail the peace)[81]

   Welcome to thee, O Peace;
   O Peace, I bid thee welcome;
   Never do you bring disease
   Except to the unwholesome.
   As true daughter of the Lord,
   In all lands you are adored.                               520
      You shall render us our lands
   And our desolate fields,
   Which war, with raging hands,
   Seizes and never yields;
   If, Peace, you are maintained,
   Every loss shall be regained.
      Come live with us in France
   Your olive branch in hand;
   By you shall our sufferance
   And vain anguish be banned.                                530
   Peace, lend repose at length
   To aid our failing strength.

All lands with foison teem,
O Peace, by your influence,
And in the cities gleam
Goods in all abundance.
Undoing our first Fall,
Pure bliss you can install.

Athens' divine protectress,
As is her right, produces                              540
The olive which to softness
The harm of Mars reduces,
Knowing, Peace, you are sure
To make all things endure.

Thanks to you, his little boat
The mariner can row,
Certain to remain afloat;
From his violent foe
With you he fears no harm:
You are his lucky charm.                               550

And if fierce Aeolus[82] forth
Every angry demon
Sends from the far North,
Still the stricken seaman,
Though his barque may shatter
Is rescued from the water.

So well does Peace protect
That once upon dry land,
The man who was shipwrecked
Fears no enemy's hand                                  560
Will with cursed effort strain
To give him death again.

The peasant on his plot
His tranquil bulls can herd,
By the frightening thought
Of murderers undeterred:
The soldier he need not dread
Who in war strikes him dead.

Thanks to you, pleasant Peace,
The shepherd with his tuneful                               570
Flute can pipe at his ease,
His flock to soothe and lull,
By the heat overcome,
No fear to strike him numb.
Give us, O Peace divine,
Give us long repose, free
From the rebel hand malign
Of Huguenot treachery;
And grant unto our King
The holy faith's safe-keeping.                              580


# Act III

## Scene i.

MERCURY [*alone*]

Jupiter, praised universally,
Jupiter, who from the Moorish sea[83]
As far as the haughty Ocean,
Keeps in control the whole world's motion;
Jupiter, with his red lightning
All the earth beneath him frightening,
And with all-seeing eyes like darts
Piercing the secrets of evil hearts;
Whose right hand, dread vengeance wreaking,
Cannot endure that faithless sneaking,                     590
Or a hypocrite's false outside,
A bloody heart within should hide;
And who cannot allow a crook,
Lurking behind an honest look,
To fill up a prosperous place
For long among the human race —
At last, the triple Father,[84] then,

Who regards the actions of men
(Always careful of his creation)
From his heavenly elevation, 600
   Me, his offspring and servant quick,
Me, his Mercury angelic,
Commanded my flight to prepare
Through the soft element of air.
   "Put on," he said, "your plumèd hat,
Your ivory rod, forget not that,
And down to France your way to make,
Your twin winged sandals look you take.[85]
   All Zephyrs with your speed outracing,
Your course throughout chill Juno[86] tracing, 610
Descend to Paris in a trice,
City beyond all earthly price.
   I, from my celestial seat,
Have seen the grace, the mildness sweet,
With which Charles treats the Admiral,
Though a traitor and a criminal.
   But I have taken him so well
In charge, he may in safety dwell:
His innocence and I protect him;
My chosen King I do elect him. 620
   The Admiral's depths I have sounded,
Seen the frenzy that there abounded:
I see and know he seeks one thing:
Some pretext for killing the King.
   And yet that wretched reprobate
Supposes that his work of hate,
His damnable and mad design,
He covers from these eyes of mine.
   The cruel murders of former times,
The execrable thefts — all crimes, 630
In short, that he has perpetrated
My anger have accumulated.
   I well know that his stinking soul

Hardens, sins adding to its roll;
So I have made determination
Of his final extermination.

    Therefore, Mercury, I command
That, taking this affair in hand,
Once within Paris you lie low:
Yourself to no one but me show,            640
    Until, when you have him in sight,
To Coligny is done a sleight
Of which I'll give you the description
Blow by blow, O Atlas's grand-son.[87]

    Not far removed from the riverside,
As the Seine through Paris does glide,
A great palace is seen to rise,
As rich as pleasing to the eyes,
    Whether the rich stone or, instead,
The precious metal overspread         650
Upon the beams with fine invention,
Or works of art with more attention
    You observe — whether you prefer
The tapestry fine-wrought with silver,
Gold, as well as pearls, to view
(Which does the Golden Fleece renew[88] ),
    Or, that which gives me more content,
That Prince and his mother so prudent,[89]
Who, keeping my religion pure,
Beauty everywhere assure.         660
    That palace, called the Louvre, now
Not only Catholics does allow,[90]
But followers of the Admiral
Wholly to me inimical;
    In this palace now come and go
The Admiral and his troop also,
Who feed the King with flattery,
Hearts swollen with hostility.
    In execrable fashion, then,

Worse than all villains known to men,                          670
The Louvre he is about to spurn
And secretly against it turn.

    Within a house then must you see
(This is your further charge from me)
A soldier hiding, who will shoot
An harquebus at him en route.[91]

    Then instantly apply your force,
Guiding the bullet in its course
To that criminal's hand and arm,
Thinking himself immune from harm.                             680

    I do not wish that he should die,
But be convinced that he may try
Henceforth to kill the King his lord,
For that blow will excuse afford.

    When this news his ear attains,
The King will start to rack his brains,
Intending instant punishment,
Not knowing who this shrewd stroke sent.

    But from the treason of this Gaspard
His meek innocence I will ward:                                690
All danger I will have averted
By causing him to be alerted

    Even by those within the plot;
Then his wrath, inflamed red-hot,[92]
Will cause, after due confirmation,
This traitor's just elimination.

    Mercury, it is by this course
That I desire my potent force
To be made known, and it is so
That I wish to punish him also.                                700

    O such an end may well appall,
Into my awful hand to fall,
Dread are my judgements downward sent
Upon those men most eminent.

    Sooner than my power shall cede,

Chaos's mingled mass shall breed
The elements some other way;
Night shall sooner become the day.
　　And sooner shall this vaulted sky,
Daughter of my hands, in ruins lie,　　　　　　　　710
Than the authors of crimes abhorred
Shall fly the slicing of my sword.[93]
　　Mad Châtillon-ian,[94] in vain
You think, by knowing how to feign,
My blood-red hands you can evade,
The bolts those brothers in Aetna[95] made."
　　Hardly had his discourse ended
When I in swooping flight descended
To the great city from the sky,
Faster than sudden thought can fly.　　　　　　　720
　　And, fulfilling there my charge
By shedding Gaspardine blood at large,
So that in spurts a flood he loses,
I have thus bruised the hand that bruises.[96]
　　So, as back to heaven I soar,
I shall leave Coligny once more,
Who, in his wicked blood supine,
Blasphemes the sovereign divine,
　　Even as Polyphemus Lorges,[97]
With Piles consorted, does disgorge　　　　　　　730
Against the King fierce words of hate
Offensive to God's sacred state. [*Exit.*]

## Scene ii.

[*Enter Montgomery and Piles.*]

MONTGOMERY

O Earth, gape open wide, and suddenly swallow me,
If I am to be forced an act so vile to see!
O unhappy star, O malignant force on earth,
You who presided at and reigned over my birth;

O disastrous Phoebus,[98]  who first brought light of day,
And offered me his brilliant torch to show my way;
O day ill-fortuned, with its lamp that wakes from sleep,
That first caused me to see, enabled me to peep,[99]              740
If we, with our cunning ruses, old at the game,
By a child more cunning still are now put to shame.
We—surprisers of the King, surprisers of towns,
And trying another royal surprise, mere clowns
We appear, Piles,[100]  for the King's hand is surely there,
Though he pretends to know nothing of the affair.
It's the King, it's the King who has ordered this harm,
Admiral invincible,[101]  given to your arm;
It's him, with my lords his brothers, and Guise, too—he's one:
A villain like me knows a villain when he sees one.         750

PILES

He would have to be of some log or tree-trunk born,
Not (given the rumours running wild) to be sworn
This shrewd audacious blow comes by the King's decree;[102]
He must be the son of some beast of Arcady,
And wholly blind to the rays of the mid-day sun,
Given all the evil that to the King we've done,
Not to judge this blow and treacherous injury
Ordered by the King, though he claims the contrary.[103]
No, one shouldn't go limping in front of the lame![104]
He has caught certain wind of our murderous aim,            760
Our searching for a means, and with that in his head,
Shrewdly he has chosen to get one step ahead.
Now, to pay the King back in his own cunning kind,
Let us find out what my Lord Admiral has in mind,
For the King, to conceal his subtle treachery,
Has gone to visit him, cloaked with hypocrisy.

MONTGOMERY

Then let us hasten, Piles, and may the time be short
Until, by the King's murder, we make a new court. [*Exeunt.*]

*[Enter the People as Chorus.]*

CHORUS[105]

All things are mutable
In a world of rise and fall;                               770
Only inconstancy
Constant in this world can be.
He anchors his plough upon Proteus's back,[106]
Who seeks things here below that will not go to wrack.
Laboriously in vain
He pours and would retain
In leaky pot or sieve
The waters fugitive.[107]
In vain, he would wash tile, or on the countless grains
Of sand abounding by the bridge employ his pains[108]        780
Each wave to empty
Of deep Amphitrite;[109]
Or he numbers the eyes
That shine in the night skies.
Our tidal bore[110] he would bear off to where the sun,
In distant lands, the Moorish sea[111] does look upon.
By climbing a mast-top,
Olympus he thinks to hop,
Or — a second Atlas — pack
The sky upon his back.                                    790
So, too, he dares without danger, like Him that saves,
Thanks to His divine rebuke, walk upon the waves.[112]
Unto a round ball whirled
May be likened the world:
Trying to make it stay
Only makes it roll away.
Just so it is with worldly plans: the more we make,
The more we see affairs a course contrary take.
Nothing but a good death
Can certain life bequeath —                               800
Merely an end to meet,

Good, with content replete.
O, thrice-happy — four times! — the souls of noble heroes,
Who in the Elysian fields enjoy repose.[113]
    Charles, our good prince and tender,
    His domain that he may render
    Free of the ills it bears
    And the infinite cares,
Honours the Admiral, bestows his company,
When a damaging blow gives him fresh misery;    810
    He plagues himself with doubt,
    Desperate to find out,
    Consumed with boiling fury,
    Who did this injury.
He complains that this blow, to the Admiral dire,
Is a whole new flame to set France again on fire,
    That a glad marriage hour[114]
    From joy has turned to sour,
    The love-notes of musicians
    To murmurs and suspicions;    820
That joyful Peace, who should safety to all afford,
Takes flight at such noise, threats, and felonious discord.
    The Admiral he does soothe
    With speeches kind and smooth,
    Promises him justice
    As a calming poultice.
O royal gentleness, O what a clement hand,
Still to have such pity on France's fire-brand!
    He loves his enemy,
    He is in agony,    830
    In his heart does complain
    To see the villain's pain.
And that foul traitor all the while his heart contorts,
Because he cannot harm the King who so comforts:
    The slave,[115] for damnation fit,
    Thus with cursed hand would hit
    The God in human form,

Who did his cure perform.
I do not know who determined to strike this stroke,
Although a vile Admiral, so prompt to provoke,                    840
    A fell Eriphyle,[116]
    Within such a city
    Could not for long remain
    And no such blow sustain.
It is not surprising if one who everywhere
Aims at stirring up trouble in the end must bear
    That wretch's punishment;
    But his bold heart, unbent
    By blows, however just,
    Causes me much distrust.                             850
O great son of Saturn,[117] pray keep him firmly tied
And be unto our King a favourable guide;
    And if it gives alarm
    Of any future harm—
    This blow today—may all
    Its weight upon him fall.

# Act IV

### Scene i.

ANDELOT[118] [*rising out of hell*[119]]

The earth gaping open, from Taenarus[120] I rise[121]
And from frightful Tartarus,[122] lighted by no skies,
Where, roasting amidst a fire that knows no quenching,
I suffer, torn by travails contrarily wrenching.               860
Now I roll a rock that came from a mountain's height,
Being forced at once to set it again upright;
Now to a wheel attached,[123] which sets itself in motion,
I am pursued by snakes in hideous commotion;
Or, a new Prometheus, a beak rips my flesh
And devours my lung,[124] which only grows afresh.

Now a sulphurous torch, stinking so as to choke,
Forever belching forth billows of endless smoke,
Baffles my brain; now water reeking with foul stench
With filthy mud and sand[125] my gullet's thirst will quench.    870
Now a Rhadamanthus,[126] with a rope and a whip,
Gives me a hundred thousand strokes, my skin to rip;
Then he leads me to the top of an estrapade,[127]
And, my arms backwards, to cut capers I am made;
Now my neck is squeezed so hard by a strangling noose
That I drivel scum and puke out poisonous juice.
Thus the son of Alcmene,[128] in his righteous fury,
Of Pirithous' death to venge the injury,[129]
Bent Cerberus' inhuman throat to his strong rule,
Till he perceived the putrid venom of his drool.[130]    880
    If then to repose at my ease I should desire,
I recline on a bed of coals glowing with fire.
If I am cold, to warm me I have lots of — ice;[131]
And if I feel, in hell, that a meal would be nice,
All of serpents and toads my prodigious collation
Is made ready, which serves to keep me from starvation.
Instead of lutes and songs, I hear the frenzied cries
Of those to whom, like me, damnation hope denies:
My servants are sorrow, despite, blasphemy, rage —
And devouring care still serves me as my page.    890
My train — none but Tisiphone, with snaky hair:
That makes me furious at all times, everywhere.[132]
Though, no less than I, my brother the Cardinal[133]
And apostate Calvin forever bray and yell,
Thus I suffer greater torments, and more diverse,
Than I could have thought of when in the universe.
And what angers me more is that all of those monklings,
Those cardinals and priests, the whole rabble of churchlings[134]
I went about killing, I did them so despise,
Free from death and pain are living in Paradise    900
And, filled with happiness, behold the divine face,
And among God's children have their appointed place.

Now Pluto, hell's magnifico,[135] more than prepared
To see my Admiral brother by him ensnared,
Has sent me to the world, frustrated that the King
And Guise — the two of them the Christian Church sustaining —
Should longer live.[136] So he has given me permission
To come here to see my brother upon this mission —
Which much contents me, for during this earthly visit[137]
I am exempt from that war with pain exquisite[138]                    910
I wage in hell; I'll have some measure of respite,
My wretched[139] bones a moment's truce, however slight.
One can take pleasure, though tossing in fever's throes,
When the illness affords a few minutes' repose.
But my Admiral brother I now go to see,
Who is threatening vengeance for his injury — [spying Coligny]
And, finding him thus blaspheming, with downcast mind,
I know that to my will he'll be the more inclined.

### Scene ii.

[Enter Admiral, his arm in a sling.[140] ]

ADMIRAL

Wherever can I be? And what have I perceived?[141]
I've seen my brother, if I'm not deceived!                          920
Truly, it's he — O Andelot, my brother,
Do you come when my need exceeds all other?
Where have you so long, far from us, remained,
O Andelot, whose loss has us so pained?

ANDELOT

Verily, the solid earth did vent me,
Ascending from hell, where your war sent me;
Then, mad from that, and given Condé's death,
You lost the fight; Saintes saw my dying breath.[142]
I have traversed, I say, the thick black shade,
So that you for those wrongs may be repaid                          930
Before your eyes — those countless injuries

The Papists' prince has done you in long series.
If your senses are now so wholly numb
You can't feel how far the French King has come
In ruining you—if your eye is now blind
To how Guise with him to kill you combined—
Open up the eyes of your pride, at least,
To see how much your renown is decreased
By the blow that your arm so sorely bloodied.
For brother, when the matter you have studied,                    940
O you,[143]  wise old man, among the craftiest,
You will recognize that one from the breast
Scarcely weaned your great cunning countermands,
Has crushed outright your invincible hands—
That an Admiral, the hammer of France,
Could not shun the stroke of a mere child's vengeance.
Open your eyes, coward—for you are no
Man but a women if you take things so—
And with a single hand,[144]  for vengeance hungry,
Kill the King, then with a furious army                           950
Strike down all his party, as with a fist,
Overthrow the Guisard, likewise the Papist.
Courage! No, even if your hand is hurt,
Your head is not yet trodden in the dirt.
Sure, in the din of fell Bellona's[145]  band,
The brain is five times better than the hand.
Montgomery and many others more,
Who still remain with you to fight this war,
With arms in victory well exercised
Will implement the plans you have devised.                        960
   Alas, if only my once warlike hand
Could here its former liberty command,
You would not then, my brother, need to doubt
Who brave exploits of war could carry out.
But ghostly dwellers in the caves of shades
Are not allowed to bear dangerous blades.
Ah, the spirits of that shadowy land

Are not allowed to combat, steel in hand.[146]
Take courage, therefore: kill, smash, overthrow,
And your foes strike down with blow upon blow!          970

[*Enter Furies.*]

THE FURIES

You dream still that your honour, noble lord,
To its place in the stars may be restored.
O Admiral! Where is the noble courage
That, boiling hot (when you were green in age)
Within your bowels, sent you forth resplendent
In potent virtue's rich and shining raiment?
You are deceived, O you glory of France,
If you think that he who leads the advance
As his alone the grand triumph can claim,
Not he who better realizes his aim.                    980
Where is that heart, where that sagacity,
O Admiral, to which the gallantry
Of the greatest leaders has always yielded?
Where are your cunning sleights, so shrewdly wielded,
Your stratagems, and where is your forethought,
You who to warlike France such fear have brought?
Do you not keenly feel that Henri's mocks
For beating you, nurtured on war's rough shocks?
Do you not see that through the whole of France
You will be scorned if you neglect this vengeance —    990
You, Châtillon of lofty principle,
The Admiral with hand invincible?
But what am I saying? No, I well know,
True Châtillon, that, avenging this blow,
You will make your armour's punishing steel
In Valois's hostile blood its temper seal,
And will, darting your puissant wrath with speed
Upon the King, your noble[147] brother heed,
Who, rising from hell in our company,
Here offers on his knees[148] his humble plea           1000

That you not endure this shame and reproach,
Which would upon his soul's repose encroach.

### ANDELOT

Yea, dear brother, as your arm vengeance takes,
Let it gain that honour for both our sakes.
But now, alas, the cruel Hecate
Down to eternal darkness beckons me,
And the calling of unpitying Pluto,
Draws me back to the gloomy caves below.

> [*Here Andelot returns to hell* [149] *(with the Furies).*]

### ADMIRAL

Ah, woeful me! And so, brother, you leave me.
Turn back, hard-hearted man, a while relieve me!          1010
Alas, my pursuing cry, as he flees,
Is carried off on the wings of the breeze.
But be sure of one thing, O brother mine,
A ferocious vengeance I shall design,
And the King shall feel, as his life he loses,
What this Admiral can do when he chooses.
And at once I shall spark the enterprise
Among my Huguenots to murder Guise,
And establish the means the King to send
The sooner the better where I intend. [*Exit.*]          1020

*[Enter the People as Chorus.]*

### CHORUS

O you, great deity, the master of the world,
    By whose hand bolts of thunder may be hurled,
Whose raised eyebrow [150] may deal earth and heaven a blow,
    Direct your eyes with pity here below.
See, son of Saturn, O Rhea's brave progeny,
    See your own spouse, O sacred majesty, [151]
With a sudden jolt by that same evil afflicted
    Which the Admiral has often inflicted.

The King, O Jupiter, from evil fortune ward,
   And us preserve from falling into discord.          1030
Alas, I have much fear of the clandestine humming[152]
   Of the Huguenots, their going and coming,
Their turning and returning; to me this all seems
   The Admiral's work — their menace and schemes.[153]
Lord, keep in check the Admiral's haughty disdain,
   And of our prince uphold the arm humane.[154]

# Act V

## Scene i.

*[Enter the King, his Council, the Informer.]*

KING

Who ever would have dreamed of such a heinous case
Of treason among my subjects? O Saturn's race,
Who on all living things impose your regiment,
Of the Admiral's wound you see me innocent;          1040
You know that although, with his rebellious right hand,
He would have rekindled cruel wars in this land,
And that he has attempted my death countless times,
I have notwithstanding pardoned him all those crimes.
What is more, with my mildness and merciful tact
I have met his every overweening act.
You know how much anger I did — and still do — show,
And how I have searched for the author of that blow.
Assist me then, Lord, and, my Council, now advise me
What, at this most treasonous effort to surprise me,      1050
Is best to be done — whether they should be forgiven
Or example to others by their death be given.
What do you say, my friends? Here is the man who claims
To know the wicked plot to implement their aims
Hatched by the Admiral and his henchmen in conclave:

They plan to send my bones tomorrow to their grave —
And not myself alone, or those of my blood only,
But all the loyal servants who remain to me.

### COUNCIL

Alas, can such a thing have possibly occurred?

### INFORMER

Not only did I see myself how they conferred —             1060
I swore and promised (but my countenance was feigned)
To help them in that enterprise; I was constrained:
A man will promise a great deal to save his skin.
And thereupon I instantly did determine
To seek his Majesty, nor could my heart convince
To let them by such crime take the life of my prince.
And yet, O Sire, have pity on me, I pray,
If I engaged my faith to them, you to betray.

### KING

A recompense eternal you have deserved,
Not punishment, for having so loyally served.             1070
Go, then, in safety, and be sure that for my part
I keep your faith imprinted firmly on my heart.
Now to you, my good Lords: in this urgent affair,
Tell me what should be the first object of our care.

### COUNCIL

Sire, there is no doubt that in dangers extreme
Those surgeons most expert infallibly esteem
The rule of prompt and extreme remedies applies.[155]
In such great danger, then, Sire, do you likewise.
Anticipate the enemy: upon him throw
What he plans for you today — a murderous blow.            1080
Even so does one nail another nail expel;[156]
Not otherwise does each wave the other propel.
Thus by one deceiver, another is undone.

KING

Surely, Mercy pleases God when she urges pardon.[157]

COUNCIL

But Justice pleases better and His judgement sways.

KING

Pardoning one's enemy always merits praise.

COUNCIL

Punishing the wicked was always a great virtue.

KING

Happy the king whose garments blood does not imbrue.

COUNCIL

Happy for the obstinate, always apt for war!

KING

The king, out of self-respect, vengeance should abhor.          1090

COUNCIL

Respect of the common good makes vengeance his sphere.

KING

The blood of his subjects to the king must be dear.

COUNCIL

Far dearer is his own blood, and that of his country,
Which for vengeance, vengeance cries to his majesty.[158]
Thus God pardons one who his offences would mend —
So he teaches you — and the evil without end
He damns, showing you that rebellious intent,
Persisted in, deserves a cruel punishment.
But if you give a man of hard iniquity
More grace than to our blood and God, then piety,          1100
One tender off-shoot of your sceptre, shall be blighted,
And the other, which is justice, thoroughly spited —

That is, if you do not punish the wretched scheme
Of which the Huguenots apparently now dream.
Punish, therefore, Sire, this enterprise untrue;
Deliver the people,[159] and likewise the Church rescue,
Which for rescue cries to you, and with the swift sword
Of death thrust these mutineers darkly overboard.[160]

KING

Then since clearly I can follow no other course
But to destroy with armed strength this murderous force,     1110
Let it be done, and let you yourselves make haste,
That the evil-doers their punishment may taste. *[Exeunt.]*

## Scene ii.

*[Enter the People.]*

THE PEOPLE

Either my eyes deceive me, or there does appear
A messenger running towards us in full career.
Messenger, my friend, what news do you have to tell?

*[Enter Messenger.]*

MESSENGER

I have no news to offer you but the most cruel.

THE PEOPLE

O God, what will he say to me? My leaping heart
A mortal fearfulness commences to impart.

MESSENGER

The Admiral and his crew, had formed the bold design,
Treacherously to extirpate the royal line,     1120
And were resolved tomorrow, with treasonous steel,
To kill the King, his brothers,[161] and Queen at their meal.

THE PEOPLE

O treason indeed! But tell me, I pray, one thing,

Messenger: was this plot discovered by the King?

#### MESSENGER

He found out through three lords, who had given their word
And consented on their faith to have the King murdered,
Lords worthy of belief — their noble rank gainsays
All falseness — who always followed Huguenot ways.[162]

#### THE PEOPLE

God be praised! But, messenger, will you tell me not
What the King has done in order to smash this plot?          1130

#### MESSENGER

The council done, when Aurora of golden tress
Banished the night-black horses of the Moorish goddess[163]
And, as she arose from her ancient husband's bed,[164]
Her colours throughout all the sky distributed,
Taking action first, he despatched a puissant band
(While having all parts of Paris more strongly manned):
They sank Piles, Pardaillan,[165] Pinos,[166] the Admiral,
And others deep down into Styx's gloomy channel,[167]
Although God permitted Lorges, in desperate flight,
To ride off on his swift horse with all of his might.          1140

#### THE PEOPLE

O high-minded exploit, O hand of vengeance dread,
If only you had murdered that monster instead!

#### MESSENGER

Thus, then, the King has punished their impudent face.
But I bid you adieu — God keep you in His grace. [*Exit Messenger.*]

#### CHORUS (the People)

  Ambition, to whom men's downfall is due,
Alas, how your final effects are dire.
O blessed is the one who masters you
And holds in check your mutinous desire.
      One who true measure takes

His heart never stakes,           1150
His inmost condition,
His hope and his goal,
His foresightful soul,
Upon mere ambition.
O how he basks in happiness galore
Who takes the path of golden moderation:
He does not tremble at treacherous war —
And feels he any other trepidation?[168]
    With soul serene that frowns
    With fear of no town's         1160
    Brutal magistrate,
    He never fears that might
    Could virtue and right
    To vice alienate.[169]
Alas, what use to fill the world with dread
And see oneself controlling everyone
From where Phoebus raises his gleaming head
To the Western sea of the setting sun,[170]
    If the life of man
    Has scarcely the span         1170
    Of the half of a day,
    And from hour to hour
    We must renew our
    Right of longer stay?
Now he, alas, who all France would devour,
With boundless desire to make him great,
And fixed himself the dream of royal power,
Suddenly sees himself unfortunate.
    He thought the huge sea,
    Every territory,         1180
    For him was too small;
    Now[171] his vain flesh and blood
    Is made in the mud —
    And in scorn — to sprawl.
And so, on that traitor whose spirit showed

To lord it over France such appetite,
Vengeance divine has finally bestowed
Possession of Montfaucon's greatest height.[172]
      Thus, Lords, we contemplate
      The cautionary fate                              1190
      Of base aspiration.
      Sovereign virtue
      Leads us upward, too,
      But to salvation.

[There follows the imprimatur:
    We the undersigned doctors of the Faculty of Paris certify that
we have read this tragedy and found nothing unworthy which
would prevent its publication, in witness whereof our seals
have been here affixed on the 23rd day of October in the year
of Our Lord 1574. So sealed, De Piro. F. David Berot.]

# Notes to
# The Tragedy of the
# Late Gaspard de Coligny

1 Gabriel de Lorges, comte de Montgomery, had accidentally caused the death of Henri II by wounding him in the eye during a tournament, after which, pursued by the vindictive hatred of Catherine de Medici, he fled to England, turned Reformer, and returned to fight for that cause, as he did with both valour and ruthlessness. His status as a villain from the Catholic point of view apparently earned him a starring role of his own: a lost tragedy entitled *Montgoumery* is attested before 1584 (Lebègue, "La Renaissance: théâtre et politique religieuse," p. 203). A source of personal animosity for Chantelouve might have been his involvement in a failed scheme to relieve the bloody and ultimately unsuccessful 1573 siege of La Rochelle, at which Chantelouve served; see Kingdon, pp. 126–28.

2 François de Beauvais, seigneur de Briquemault.

3 Arnaud de Cavagnes or Cavaignes (1575 ed. "Cauagne"), Counsellor to the *Parlement* of Toulouse. Briquemault and Cavagnes were close associates of Coligny tracked down after the massacre and executed for treason (29 October 1572) in order to bolster the king's claim that a conspiracy had existed. Their prominent guilt in Chantelouve's play is explicable, not only on this basis alone, but also by the fact that their rehabilitation, with that of Coligny himself, was being demanded. (They were indeed vindicated two years after the play, in 1576, by the Edict of Beaulieu.) See *Histoire et dictionnaire des Guerres de Religion*, ed. Jouanna et al., p. 708 et passim, and Cameron, ed., p. viii and n. to ll. 480–81.

4 Armand de Clermont, baron de Piles, companion in arms to the Prince of Condé, who had accompanied Jeanne d'Albret to Paris. See Introduction, pp. 28, 68, and n. 46.

5  Allowing for Chantelouve's evident distortion of the facts, this character may be based on Antoine de Bayencourt, seigneur de Bouchavannes, who is said to have reported to the court regarding Huguenot councils. See *Histoire et dictionnaire des Guerres de Religion*, ed. Jouanna et al., p. 197, n. 2; Crouzet, *La nuit de la Saint-Barthélemy*, p. 385; and Cameron, ed., n. to ll. 1059–60. By some accounts, he was one of those personally singled out for mercy by the king as the massacre began (Crouzet, *La nuit de la Saint-Barthélemy*, p. 403).

6  François de Châtillon, seigneur d'Andelot, Coligny's younger brother and fellow warrior in the Huguenot cause. He is recorded objectively as having been sincere, honourable, and personable, and was seemingly the first of the three Châtillon brothers to embrace Reform—hence, perhaps, his role in Chantelouve's scenario as a persuasive demonic agent promoting his brother's damnation. Relevant background, too, is an episode during the tumultuous political and religious events that led up to the first civil war: in 1558, Henri II imprisoned Andelot for over two months because of his supposed involvement in Protestant demonstrations and, probably, because of false accusations of treachery coming (by way of Charles, Cardinal of Lorraine) from the Spanish, who misrepresented a letter of pious exhortation he had written to the Admiral, then a prisoner of war. His subsequent rehabilitation was a slap in the face to the Guises (even if the Pope took the occasion to blame the Cardinal of Lorraine for being soft on heretics!). See Lucien Romier, *Les Origines politiques des Guerres de religion. D'après des documents originaux inédits*, 2 vols. (1913–14); rpt. Geneva Slatkine-Megariotis, 1974), vol. 2: 270–86, 327, 367–68.

7  There is no such indication in the 1575 text, but Coligny's reference to the noose in l. 5 seems to call for a prop, and I have pointed up the effect by making the definite article (*"du* vilain licol") demonstrative (*"this"*). The image adroitly combines the Admiral's shame at having had his "boldness bridled" ("bridé . . . audace" [l. 3]) with the standard emblem of suicidal (and sinful) despair, as epitomized by Judas (Matt. 27:3–5). Cf. Coligny's recovery of resolution at this conclusion of this monologue (ll. 99–100) and the Chorus's designation of him as a "newfangled Judas" ("nouveau Judas" [l. 242]) in a passage playing on the terms "hope" and "despair."

The possibility that Coligny is actually wearing the halter should not be dismissed. Condemned criminals did so when performing *amende honorable* (Nicholls, p. 49), and cf. the appearance of the knight fleeing from Despair in Edmund Spenser's *The Faerie Queene*: "In fowle reproch of knighthoodes fayre degree, / About his neck an hempen rope he weares, / That with his glistring armes does ill agree" (*The Complete Poetical Works of Spenser*, ed. R.E. Neil Dodge Cambridge ed. [Boston: Houghton Mifflin, 1908], 1.9.22.6–8). Nor would such an image have been inconceivable at least for the English stage, to judge from *Promos and Cassandra*, by George Whetstone (1578), where the hangman enters with "a greate many ropes abought his neck" (ed. Geoffrey Bullough, *Narrative and Dramatic Sources of Shakespeare*, vol. 2 [London: Routledge and Kegan Paul; New York: Columbia University Press, 1963], Pt. 1, II.vi.0.SD). More probably, however, Coligny is merely carrying the noose, like Achitophel in George Peele's *David and Bethsabe* (1594?), who appears "*solus with a halter*" (ed. Elmer Blistein, in *The Dramatic Works of George Peele*, *Life and Works of George Peele*, vol. 3 [New Haven, CT: Yale University Press, 1970], l. 1415 SD), and the comic villain Fronto in George Chapman's *The Tragedy of Caesar and Pompey* (1605–12?), described as entering "all ragged, in an overgrown red beard, black head, with a halter in his hand, looking about" (*The Plays of George Chapman: The Tragedies*, vol. 2, ed. Thomas Marc Parrott [New York: Russell and Russell, 1961], II.i.0.SD).

In fact, the latter two English *exempla* of despair deliver soliloquies roughly analogous to that of Coligny. Achitophel pleads that the earth may open "and take thy miserable sonne / Into the bowels of thy bowels of thy cursed wombe" (ll. 1432–33), then addresses the noose as the "hellish instrument of heaven" about to "execute th'arrest of Joves just doome / And stop his breast that curseth Israel" (ll. 1437–39). The self-conscious comic villainy of Fronto brings him even closer to Chantelouve's Admiral:

> Wars, wars, and presses fly in fire about;
> No more can I lurk in my lazy corners
> Nor shifting courses, and with honest means
> To rack my miserable life out more —
> The rack is not so fearful; when dishonest
> And villainous fashions fail me, can I hope
> To live with virtuous, or to raise my fortunes
> By creeping up in soldierly degrees?
> Since villainy, varied thorough all his figures,
> Will put no better case on me than this,
> Despair, come seize me! . . .                    (II.i.1–11)

Fronto is kept from suicide by the apparition of the devil, who offers him worldly prosperity in exchange for mischief-making.

8  With the despairing reference to being defeated by the "child" ("enfant") King Charles IX, in 1572 actually aged 22, cf. the initial soliloquy of the triumphant Guise in Marlowe's *Massacre*, who boasts, "Him, as a child, I daily win with words" (Oliver, ed., ii.70). The comic devil of the medieval drama, at once dangerous and ridiculous, distinctly colours Chantelouve's portrait of the Admiral, and it is tempting, in particular, to see it as shaded ironically by the *Abraham sacrifiant* of Théodore de Bèze (cf. below, l. 32), whose Satan is also routed by a heaven-assisted child: "Iamais, iamais enfant mieux ne parla. / Ie suis confus, & faut, que ie m'enfuye"; "Was neuer child that spake with better skil. / I am ashamde, and therefore take my flight" (Théodore de Bèze, *A Tragedie of Abrahams Sacrifice, Written in French by Theodore Beza and Translated into English by Arthur Golding*, ed. Malcolm W. Wallace, trans. Arthur Golding [Toronto: University of Toronto Library, 1906], ll. 858–59 [original], ll. 871–72 [translation]). With the Admiral's soliloquy more generally, cf. the invocation of demons by Épernon in *The Guisiade*, ll. 781ff.

9  Both brothers were recently deceased: François d'Andelot (d. 27 May 1569), and Odet (d. 1571), cardinal de Châtillon, who had turned Reformer and fled to England (see Introduction, p. 55).

10  Sisyphus and Ixion were subjected to the two most celebrated exemplary punishments of the underworld — the former condemned perpetually to roll a rock uphill (since it perpetually rolled back down), the latter bound upon a turning wheel. The invocation of such torments upon oneself was a neo-classical commonplace, and, as with many such, no intermediary need be posited between Chantelouve and Seneca, whose desperate Hercules, on the brink of suicide after killing his family in his madness, makes a particularly apt model for the Admiral (see *Hercules Furens*, ll. 1203ff.); similarly, the ghost of Tantalus opens *Thyestes* by longing to return from the pain of the upper world to the horrors below. Still, there were intermediaries, most prominently (and effusively) Garnier, with parallels so close that they are worth recording:

> Tonnez, cieux, foudroyez, esclairez, abysmez,
> Et ne me laissez rien de mes os consommez
> Que ceste terre ingrate enferme en sa poitrine.
> Respandez respandez vostre rage maline
> Sur mon chef blasphemeur, et tempestez si bien
> Que de moy malheureuse il ne demeure rien.
> . . . . . . . . .
> Ouvre ton sein piteux, ô terre malheureuse,

Et l'engoufre au profond de ta poitrine creuse.
Enfonce, enfonce moy dans les gouffres plus creux
Qui se puissent trouver aux Enfers tenebreux:
Englouty moi chetive, et d'une nuict espesse
Bousche mes sens esteints, que la douleur oppresse.
. . . . . . . . .
Vous antres caverneux, siege du vieil Pluton,
Vous filles de la nuict, Tisiphone, Alecton,
Vos Rages de là bas, vous Cerbere à trois testes,
Vous fleuves, qui roidis bruyez mille tempestes,
Plongez-moy dans le sein de l'ambysme souphreux,
Où logent tourmentez les esprits plus affreux.

[Thunder, ye heavens, hurl and blast with lightning, destroy, and
leave nothing of my bones, all consumed, for this ungrateful
earth to enclose in its breast. Spread, spread your furious anger
upon my blaspheming head, and storm so that nothing remains
of my wretched self. . . . Open your pitiful bosom, O miserable
earth, and engulf me in the deepest caves that may be found in
shadowy hell: swallow wretched me, and with thick darkness
stop my extinguished senses, me whom suffering oppresses. . . .
You hollow caverns, seat of old Pluto, you daughters of the night,
Tisiphone, Alecto, you Furies from below, you, three-headed
Cerberus, you raging rivers, which roar with a thousand storms,
plunge me into the bosom of the sulphurous abyss where the
most terrible ghosts dwell.]        (*Porcie*, ed. Lebègue, ll. 1603–43)

Hecate triple en noms, et triple en deïtez !
Arrachez-moi la vie, estouffez moy chetive,
Ou dans les creux Enfers poussez-moy toute vive :
Tirez-moi de ce monde, et qu'entre les esprits
Je face resonner les abysmes de cris.
. . . . . . . . .
Venez Dires, venez, venez noires Furies,
Venez, et dans mon sang soyez toujours nourries.
Le tourment d'Ixion, l'aigle de Promethé,
Le roc qui est sans fain par Sisyph remonté
Soit ma peine eternelle, et que la gesne ent[r]ee
Au dedans de mon cœur, soit de mon cœur ostée.

[Hecate triple in name and in deity! Tear out my life, suffocate
me in my wretchedness, or in the hollow underworld thrust
me still alive. Drag me from this world, and let me among the
shades make the caverns echo with my howls. . . . Come Dires,

come, come, black Furies, come, and be forever nourished with my blood. The torment of Ixion, the eagle of Prometheus, the rock endlessly rolled up again by Sisyphus—let that be my punishment eternal, and may the torture entered in my heart be taken from my heart.]    (*Cornélie*, ed. Ternaux, ll. 1828–41)

Cf. also the grieving Calpurnie's outburst in Grévin, *César*, ll. 925–28. There were parallels, too, in the biblical drama; particularly to the point, given its Protestant provenance, may be Florent Chréstien's adaptation, reissued in 1573, of George Buchanan's *Jephte*, in which the protagonist, about to sacrifice his daughter to fulfil his vow, begs the earth, "Ouure toy jusqu'au fond, & tout vif m'engloutis / Dans vn abysme creus, devore moy tandis / Que je ne suis meschant [Open wide to the bottom, and swallow me alive in a hollow abyss; devour me while I am not evil]" (Florent Chréstien, trans., *Jephté, tragédie traduicte du latin de George Buchanan, escossais* [Paris: R. Estienne, 1573], fol. 20ʳ). Such intertextual overdetermination tends to skew the Admiral's speech in a parodic direction.

11  This line points with some precision to an ironic adaptation of Marc Antoine's call for vengeance in Grévin's *César*:

> J'invoque des Fureurs la plus grande fureur,
> J'invoque le chaös de l'eternelle horreur,
> J'invoque l'Acheron, le Styx et le Cochyte,
> Et si quelque aultre dieu sous les enfers habite,
> Juste-vangeur des maux, je les invoque tous,
> Homicides cruel, pour se vanger de vous.

> [I invoke the greatest Fury of the Furies; I invoke the chaos of horror eternal; I invoke Acheron, Styx, and Cocytus; and if any other god dwells in the underworld, a just avenger of evils, I invoke them all, cruel homicides, to take vengeance on you.] (ll. 1057–62)

12  It is as if the Admiral here takes his words (and some of the tone) from the prayer that Du Rosier, in *Déploration de la France*, directed to Jupiter for vengeance against the instigator of civil war in France, clearly having Coligny in mind:

> Dresse toy contre luy, ride ton front seuere,
> Enfonce tes sourcis, enflame ta colere,
> O grand Saturnien, & n'amuse tes bras
> A batre les Rochers qui ne t'offencent pas.

> [Rise up against him with frowning forehead, furrowed brows;

inflame your anger, O great son of Saturn, and do not amuse your arms by striking the rocks that do you no harm.]     (sig. Aiiii$^v$)

13  Styx, Phlegethon, and Cocytus: the three rivers of the underworld — cf. *The Guisiade*, ll. 799–800.

14  Coligny addresses the monstrous dog Cerberus.

15  Henri, Duke of Anjou, the (slightly) younger brother of Charles IX, was the leader of the Catholic royalists who defeated Coligny at Jarnac (13 March 1569) and Moncontour (3 October 1569), so he is most immediately responsible for the Admiral's discomfiture. Having succeeded his brother in 1574, Henri III was on the throne when the play was published.

16  Bèze, based in Geneva, had been the spiritual head of the Huguenots since the death of Calvin in 1564.

17  An allusion to the image of the "whited sepulchre" used by Jesus to condemn hypocrites (Matt. 23:27–28), with a simultaneous glance at the white worn by Huguenot forces (signifying allegiance to the House of Bourbon), as in l. 80 below.

18  "Le vieus Regnard tousjours Regnard demeure": proverbial.

19  "[F]air-haired race" ("peuple blondissant"): Chantelouve may have transferred the epithet to the English from Garnier's "blons Germains, people enrageé de guerre" (*Cornélie*, ed. Ternaux, l. 57), reserving a choicer one for the latter.

20  The assassin of François, Duke of Guise, in 1563, while he was directing the siege of Orléans, was in fact a French gentleman, Jean Poltrot de Méré, but an association with the *reîtres* (see *The Guisiade*, n. 23 et passim) suits Chantelouve's purpose, as does the accusation of treacherous dealings with the English. Cf. Cameron, ed., n. to ll. 51–52. Chantelouve is, in fact, countering Protestant propaganda: the Huguenots identified François de Guise with the tyrannical Holofernes of the Book of Judith (see below, n. 75) and, on the basis of his own use of *reîtres* and Spanish troops, portrayed his army as foreign invaders. This is evident in *La Judit* of Du Bartas; see Baïche, ed., pp. XXXVII and CXXXVII, n. 16. Coligny's supposed sponsorship of this assassination, despite his official exoneration, was a key motive for Guisian involvement in the massacre of 1572. On the youthful friendship between Coligny and François, Duke of Guise, see Cameron, ed., n. to l. 53.

21  In the absence of punctuation, the inverted Latinate syntax of the original ("O fille de Tithon du lict ensafrané / Sortant") might en-

courage the supposition that Chantelouve is ignorantly calling Aurora the daughter of Tithonus (so Wollfe, ed.), whereas a comma is surely to be understood after "fille" and "de Tithon" depends on "lict." Tithonus was the lover or husband of Aurora, doomed to an immortality of increasing age — hence, presumably, the epithet "daughter" ("fille"), in the sense of "young girl," signalling her eternal youth; cf. below, l. 1133.

The evocation of dawn is a not-unpoetical rendition of a conventional motif deriving especially from Virgil (*Aeneid*, 4.584–85, 6.535, 9.459–60; see Cameron, ed., n. to ll. 57–60) but already *de rigueur* in French Neo-classical drama — witness Etienne Jodelle, *Cléopâtre captive*, ed. Françoise Charpentier, Jean-Dominique Beaudin and José Sanchez (Mugron: J. Feijóo, 1990), ll. 207ff., and Garnier, *Porcie*:

> Desja loin de Thithon, l'Aurore matineuse
> Chasse les rouges feux de la nuict sommeilleuse:
> Et ja Phebus monté sur le char radieux
> Vient de sa torche ardante illuminer les cieux.

> [Already far from Tithonus, Aurora of the morning chases away the burning lights of sleepy night, and already Phoebus, mounted on his gleaming chariot, has lit up the skies with his flaming torch.]    (Lebègue, ed., ll. 199–202)

Du Bartas, in *La Judit*, also has "l'aurore saffranée" and "l'aube saffranée" (3.97, 5.93). It is, however, the flowery dawn used in Grévin's *César* to mark the extent of the hero's domination of the world (ll. 525ff.) that seems most to the ironic point. Cf. below, nn. 164, 170.

22  Atheistic villains are typically worshippers of Fortune; the Admiral's downfall and ironic elevation on the gallows are already prefigured, as Cameron points out (n. to ll. 63–70). Cf. Introduction, pp. 55–56, and below, ll. 1185–88 and n. 172. The virtual soliloquy attributed to Coligny by Fleury in *Responce à un certain escrit, publié par l'Admiral et ses adherans* has him asking himself, on the basis of people's readiness to change in matters of government and religion, and his success so far, "pourquoy aiant un si beau subject ne pousseray-je ma fortune jusques au bout [why, having such a splendid motive, do I not push my fortune to the limit] . . . ?" (sig. Hiii[r]); he cites the success of Caesar in Gaul.

23  The son of Achilles, who avenged his father; the allusion to Henri, Duke of Anjou, seems particularly apt, given the imminent appearance of Montgomery as the Admiral's diabolical companion in arms. Chantelouve is not alone in portraying his killing of the king as in-

tentional. Cf. *The Guisiade*, ll. 137–40.

24  The 1560 Protestant-led plot to separate the young King François II from the Guises, who dominated him, was a fiasco and provoked bloody repression; see *Histoire et dictionnaire des Guerres de Religion*, ed. Jouanna et al., pp. 647–48. Cf. *The Guisiade*, ll. 617–18 and n. 82.

25  A reference to the defeat of the Protestants on 19 December 1562 at Dreux. In view of the passage from *La Vie de Messire de Coligny* cited by Cameron, ed., n. to l. 73, in which the association of the place with druids is mentioned, it is unclear why Cameron does not adopt the reading of Lenglet du Fresnoy, ed., "Druides," for "drindes" (1575 ed.); this obvious typographical error is also corrected by Wollfe, ed.

26  Here there is apparent confusion with the battle of Moncontour (see above, n. 15), where Coligny was indeed wounded.

27  Cf. above, ll. 37–38 and n. 17.

28  The battle of Saint Denis took place on 10 November 1567, that of Bassac (usually known by the name of the larger town of Jarnac) on 13 March 1569. At the latter, the Protestant Prince of Condé was indeed killed (after having surrendered, it was said) and his body treated in this insulting way; Cameron, ed., n. to ll. 86–87, cites a mocking epitaph making the same rhyme as Chantelouve ("anesse"/"messe").

29  Achilles, who had wounded Telephus, subsequently cured him by means of the plant (milfoil) that sprang up from the rust of his spear; Telephus then showed the Greeks how to reach Troy. All of this fulfilled a divine prophecy by which Telephus, who had resisted the Greeks, finally made their success possible. The rather elliptical point seems to be the mysterious ways of the Lord in using the apparent obstacle, Condé, as an instrument of promoting true religion.

30  This was abandoned after several weeks, the besiegers having suffered severe losses from dysentery.

31  Here and once below (in l. 116, but not l. 364) the 1575 text reads "Erbaux," a variant suggestive, perhaps, of contemporary pronunciation.

32  Enyo: Greek goddess of war, portrayed by Ronsard in *La Franciade* as going before the chariot of Victory in company with her Roman counterpart, Bellona (Céard et al., eds., 3.486). The reference to her sword is purely metaphorical; in fact, Coligny was wounded in the face by a pistol shot.

33  The original's "blancdres formés" is unintelligible; Wollfe convincingly corrects to "blancs réformés."

34  "Qui au bruit de mon nom superbe ne s'estonne." Cf. the tyrannical Caesar in Garnier's *Cornélie*: "Qui au cœur ne fremisse oyant parler de moy [Who does not quake in his heart when he hears me spoken of?]" (Ternaux, ed., l. 1333).

35  "[A]u pais charitable": There is an ironic play on words, since the immediate reference is to the Protestant stronghold of La Charité-sur-Loire, one of the "places of surety" accorded them by the peace of Saint Germain.

36  Montgomery was widely held responsible for the death of Henri II, and in fact there was a Protestant discourse of providential intervention surrounding the accident, for in 1559 Henri had promulgated a decree calling for the extermination of the "heretics." See Cameron, ed., *Aman. Tragédie saint*, by André Rivaudeau, pp. 33–34.

   The remainder of this passage recapitulates the dramatic and bloody campaign waged in August 1569 by Montgomery in Béarn, then independent, at the behest of the Protestant Queen of Navarre, Jeanne d'Albret (to whom Rivaudeau had dedicated his *Aman* in 1566). This followed the successful invasion of the forces of Charles IX under Antoine de Lomagne, vicomte de Terride, who was charged with pacifying the country, governing it on behalf of the French king, and restoring the Catholic religion. Montgomery relieved the siege of Navarrenx, the last place of resistance to the French royal army, and compelled Terride to take refuge in Orthez, which subsequently capitulated. A horrendous massacre followed, especially of Catholic clergy — part of what lent credibility to Montgomery's supposed desire to "eviscerate the mass" and reinforces the irony of the Admiral's praise here. This history lesson has particular typological aptness: Terride and several other Catholic leaders were executed by the Protestants for "treason" on 24 August 1569, three years to the day before the Saint Bartholomew massacre.

37  The echo of Montgomery's reference (l. 121) to recuperating the sapped strength of the Protestants ironically signals the danger of delaying action against them. In fact (and contrary to the Admiral's opening despair at his string of defeats), the peace shortly to be presented as an act of royal munificence was largely forced on the king by the dramatic reversal in Huguenot fortunes — a point effectively made by Yves Cazaux, *Jeanne d'Albret* (Paris: Éditions Albin Michel, 1973), pp. 325–26. Chantelouve, needless to say, is trying to have it both ways.

38 This translation preserves the ambiguity, in its context, of the expression "A tort ou droit" ("wrongly or rightly"), which may go with what precedes or with what follows.

39 This Chorus, as Cameron observes (n. to ll. 156–57), adapts Horace's much-echoed praise of a pure life from *Odes*, 1.22 ("Integer vitae"), although its Christian colouring, itself a commonplace, quickly develops a partisan tinge. The Lines in italics were signalled as *sententiae* by *guillemets* in the 1575 edition.

40 The Moorish dart is Horatian (*Odes*, 1.22.2), but the Turkish bow incorporates the discourse of Turkish irreligion and brutality deployed against their opponents by both sides in the Wars of Religion.

41 I follow both modern editions in restoring the rhyme scheme by inverting ll. 177–78 as printed in 1575.

42 The *Oxford Classical Dictionary* cites the exaggerated danger associated from antiquity with the navigation of the shallow Syrtic Sea. The immediate model is, again, Horace, *Odes*, 1.22.5. Cf. *The Guisiade*, l. 12.

43 The strained personification here is true to the original ("sa juste colere").

44 Scylla and Charybdis: two rocks between Italy and Sicily, the former harbouring the cave of a sea-monster and the latter, across a narrow passage, producing an irresistible whirlpool. Since Homer (*Odyssey*, Bk. 12), the legend has emblematized the idea of attempting to avoid one danger only to run into another. Cameron, n. to ll. 417–20, aptly compares the description incorporated within the tale that Aeneas recounts to Dido in Virgil, *Aeneid*, 3.420ff. (cf. also 3.558ff.); see also below, n. 50.

45 "Corsaire" (here "pirate") is a general epithet connoting ruthlessness, but, characteristically, it also plays on Coligny's official title of "Admiral" of France.

46 "Massacre" was one of the standard terms applied by both sides of the religious divide to killings by the other, as *The Guisiade* also illustrates in abundance. Here, there is an implicit refutation of its application by Protestants to what extreme Catholics like Chantelouve represented as the divine vengeance of Saint Bartholomew's day. (See Introduction, pp. 18–19, 51–52; also Hillman, *Shakespeare, Marlowe and the Politics of France*, p. 87 et passim.) The word is especially widespread and adaptable in French texts because usage permits it to be applied to the killing of (defenceless) individuals: e.g., it is the word used by Montgomery in l. 130 (translated here as "butchering")

for killing the king's brother.

47  "Low and high": my addition, signalling that the "treason" ("la trahison") of the original extends in scope beyond *lése-majesté*.

48  For "crie" ("cries"), the reading of the 1575 edition, which makes perfect sense and is followed by Cameron, Wollfe unaccountably substitutes "rie" (="rit" ["laughs"]).

49  This stanza contains an ironic (and theologically complex) play on ideas of hope ("espere" [l. 242]) and despair ("en desesperant" [l. 243]), which encapsulates the Admiral's conversion of suicidal despair into vindictive aggression. The pattern no doubt has its origin in Seneca's demented revengers (cf. Cameron, ed., pp. X–XII), but, as in the numerous off-shoots in the English revenge drama, beginning with Kyd (*The Spanish Tragedy*), the Christian context — here, in particular, the notion of God's just vengeance — considerably complicates the issue.

50  The standard association of the tigresses of Hyrcania (a region on the Caspian sea, part of the ancient Persian empire) with inhuman nurturing received its major impetus from Dido's similar accusation against Aeneas (*Aeneid*, 4.367). The Virgilian context is important here, since the following lines will extend the idea to those other legendary founders of Rome, the wolf-suckled Romulus and Remus. In this regard, it is interesting that the inhuman Admiral himself has accused Henri d'Anjou (l. 66) of conquering him like a "second Pyrrhus" ("Pyrrhe nouveau"). The nexus of Virgilian allusions (see nn. 21, 44, and 51) helps to establish the *Aeneid* as an intertext for the subsequent intervention of Mercury and Jupiter (see Introduction, pp. 48–55, passimx). A famous "Hyrcanian beast" figures in *Hamlet* (II.ii.450) in connection with the slaughter of Priam by Pyrrhus — a "slip," as noted by Harold Jenkins in the Arden Shakespeare edition (London: Methuen, 1982), n. to II.ii.446, since the passage is based on Aeneas' narration to Dido (*Aeneid*, Bk. 2), where no Hyrcanian tiger is mentioned.

51  As Cameron indicates (n. to l. 261), this image, too, is Virgilian (*Aeneid*, 6.471). The context is, this time, the coldness of Dido's spirit to Aeneas, when he meets her in the underworld. Marpessa is the name of a mountain in Paros known as a source of marble; the point is the same one conveyed by the standard English expression "marble-hearted."

52  The reference of the pronoun is intriguingly — and functionally — ambiguous. Since the Chorus's most recent theme has been divine

forgiveness, God comes first to mind, but the ground is in the process of shifting to the earthly realm, whose king seems paramount by the end of the stanza.

53 "[D]isastrous" ("disastré"): as in English usage of the period, the word carried a stronger sense than it currently does of its literal meaning — "ill-starred."

54 This stanza is grammatically obscure; in the edition of 1575, it reads:

> Renforçé à la charité,
> Et uoyant la saintonge siene,
> (Si de nous la diuinité)
> Nous, son Espouse chrestiene
> N'a compassion pour le trouble
> Il punira sa rage double.

Obviously, the closing bracket, at least, is in the wrong place, which suggests that the compositor may also have been confused. After much hesitation, I arrive at the meaning offered on the following assumptions:

1) the parenthesis was originally intended to be closed after "trouble," but a shift in the grammatical structure (see next point) rendered this impossible;

2) "Nous" in the fourth line is in apposition to "nous" in the previous line, but is then thought of also as a direct object for the verb "punira," so the syntax effectively changes in mid-course;

3) "Il" refers to Coligny;

4) a comma is to be understood after "punira," so that "sa rage double" serves as an absolute construction attributing a quality to Coligny.

The ideas, in any case, are familiar ones. The Admiral's depredations will shortly be characterized as a divine test of the faithful (below, ll. 441–50). The image of God as married to his faithful people (i.e., to the Church) derives from the standard exegetical reading of the Song of Songs, where "épouse" translates the Vulgate's "sponsa."

Despite its grammatical contortions, the stanza maintains the grim playfulness with which Chantelouve shows Coligny diabolically appropriating the trappings of Christianity. The town of La Charité has already been the subject of word-play (see above, l. 121 and n. 35), and the name "Saintonge" has similar potential, especially given the proximate pronunciations of "onge" and "ange" ("angel"). "Double" (l. 288) goes beyond general intensification to suggest both the two specific places mentioned and the double nature of the Admiral's criminality, at once political and spiritual.

55 "A soy tous les autres il mire"; for a similar use of "mirer" in the sense of "regard," cf. Montaigne: "Pour m'estre, dès mon enfance, dressé à mirer ma vie dans celle d'autruy, j'ay acquis une complexion studieuse en cela [By having trained myself, from my childhood, in regarding my own life in the lives of others, I have acquired a studious temperament in this respect]" (*Les Essais de Michel de Montaigne*, ed. Pierre Villey, rev. V.–L. Saulnier [Paris: Presses Universitaires de France, 1965], III, 13, p. 1076 B).

56 Oeta: a mountain in Thessaly, site of the death of Hercules. The allusion is evident, and the explanation of Wollfe that the adjective in "Foréts oëtées" is equivalent to "ouatée" ("cottony"), a word not even attested in this period, is far-fetched.

57 "La Gaspardine teste" is certainly an unusual application of the Admiral's name, and it is tempting to suspect some sort of word-play: in Old French, "galvardine" or "gaverdine" meant a coat or cloak, as did "gaberdine" in Shakespeare's English (see *The Tempest*, II.i.38), and the notion of a covered head, hence a concealed purpose, would be to the point here, as in l. 689 — "la trahison Gaspardine" ("the Gaspardine trechery"). On the other hand, it is more difficult to see a double-meaning in "sang Gaspardin" ("Gaspardine blood" [l. 722]) or when Chantelouve turns the Admiral's family name Châtillon into an adjective (l. 713). He may, then, simply be coining "poetic" epithets, on the model, notably, of Ronsard — cf. *La Franciade*, 1.245, 246: "la race Priamide," "la grandeur Æzonide."

With these lines, cf. above ll. 17–18 and n. 12. Du Rosier's plea is likewise to a nominally pagan God at once merciful and angry:

Et toy grand Iuppiter, qui portes en tes mains
Les traits Vulcaniens pour punir les humains,
Pourquoy vois tu si lent ceste pariure teste,
Que tu ne la gemis d'vne iuste tempeste ?
Et auec ce Tyran, sa race, à celle fin
D'eteindre tout d'vn coup vn genre si mutin.

[And you great Jupiter, who bear in your hands the bolts of Vulcan to punish human beings, why are you so slow to see that perjured head that you do not growl upon it with a merited storm and, along with that tyrant, his lineage, in order to extinguish at one stroke such a rebellious race?]     (sig. Aiiii^r–v)

Mais ô grand Dieu du ciel qui de la haut regardes,

Et qui dessus nos chefs tes gros tonneres dardes,
Qui venges les forfaicts que les hommes te font
Fais gresler dessus eus les misères qu'ilz ont.

[But O great God of heaven, who look down from on high and
hurl your great thunderbolts upon our heads, who avenge the
crimes that men commit against you, hail down on them their
own evils.]                                                    (sig. Ciii<sup>r</sup>)

58  "Nace" (usual spelling "nasse"), literally a small boat, is here used in
the sense of "church," which derives from the common expression,
"la nasse [often 'nacelle'] de Saint Pierre."

59  This is the so-called Oroboros or Ouroboros ("tail-biter") — an Egyptian symbol of eternity. In the original, too, the king begins in the
third person, then addresses Janus (the two-headed god of begin-
nings and endings). He returns to the third person, however, in
moving on to Titan (the sun) — a shift that seems too awkward to
follow in translation.

60  Charles (b. 27 June 1550), exaggerates; the political situation was relatively stable during his early childhood, the first reformed churches
on the Genevan model making their appearance in France only in
1555 (*Histoire et dictionnaire des Guerres de Religion*, ed. Jouanna et al.,
pp. 40–41). For a contemporary audience, the king's well-known
bitterness regarding the conspiracy of Meaux (1567), in particular,
might have been evoked — see Cameron, n. to l. 344, and Introduction, p. 51.

61  Cf. the listing of the same battles by Coligny, ll. 73ff., who also singles
out the death of Condé at Bassac, as Andelot will do (l. 927) in his
turn.

62  For the sake of clarity, I specify the obvious intended referent of "il"
("he") in the original.

63  The 1575 version of l. 366, "Las, ce m'est une playe assise dessus los"
is perhaps defensible as it stands, with "los" meaning "praise" or
"glory," although the usage would be strange, and the emendation
offered by Wollfe to "l'os" ("the bone") is convincing; the apostrophe
is frequently omitted in the early text.

64  The word "felon" here translated as "treasonous" implies disloyalty
to one's feudal lord.

65  For an inverted application of this notion, see *The Guisiade*, l. 1788<sup>a</sup>ff.

66  "[B]lood" ("sang"): Charles clearly envisages the end of his lineage.

67  It appears (see ll. 398, 407) that there are several councillors on stage;

the character representing the Council, therefore, is presumably to be understood as its spokesman, rather than as a purely allegorical figure, such as is common in the English late morality plays. The technique is nonetheless more symbolic than is Matthieu's use of representatives of the Estates in *The Guisiade*, where the Argument actually specifies the historical persons who delivered the equivalent speeches. Moreover, the fact that the Councillors are evidently elderly men (see ll. 401–04), according to the stereotype, further imparts a distance from historical fact, since the king's brother, Henri d'Anjou, and, most importantly, his mother, Catherine de Medici (cf. below, ll. 657–60), were key members of the council. (So, for the period omitted by the play — from his return to court in September 1571 until his wounding — was the Admiral himself.)

68  The King's precocious wisdom is reflected in his use of *sententiae*. In *The Guisiade*, the devise lends particular support to the Duke.

69  Astraea was the goddess of justice who dwelt on earth during the Golden Age but with the coming of evil withdrew to the stars (as the constellation Virgo). The philosopher Arée, in Garnier's *Porcie*, makes Faith her sister (Lebègue, ed., l. 729).

70  The reference, of course, is to the king's sister, Marguerite de Valois. The common Protestant accusation was that the wedding was a mere pretext on the part of Catholics to assemble Huguenot notables in preparation for the premeditated massacre, which followed almost immediately. In effect, Chantelouve refutes this accusation, even as, in ll. 467ff., he foresees such action as necessary, should the Huguenots fail to respond to the gesture of peace. For the later League view of Marguerite as the "pearl" or "flower" ravished by the heretic, see *The Guisiade*, l. 1152.

71  The fate of the Titans who revolted against Saturn — a myth often invoked to figure religious innovation, e.g., by Montaigne in his "Apologie de Raimond Sebond" (*Essais*, ed. Villey, II, 12, p. 533 B). Ronsard's praise of Charles in "Le tombeau du feu Roy Tres-Chrestien Charles IX" (1574) is particularly to the point:

> Puis quand la tendre barbe au menton se renforce,
> Que l'âge et la vertu s'accroissent par le temps,
> Il se vit assailli des superbes Titans,
> Qui combatoyent ce Prince en ses propres entrailles,
> Qu'à la fin il veinquit par quatre grands batailles.

> [Then, when his soft beard grew thicker on his chin, and age and virtue increased with time, he saw himself assailed by the proud

Titans, who fought against this prince within his own entrails, whom in the end he vanquished in four great battles.]      ("Le Tombeau du feu Roy tres-chrestien Charles Neufiesme," *Œuvres complètes*, ed. Céard et al., vol. 2, ll. 46–50)

Again, Du Rosier (addressing Jupiter and thinking of Coligny) affords an early example: "Arme toy tout ainsi, qu'aus sablons Phlegreans, / Tu t'armes pour briser les Titanes Geans [Arm yourself just as you did when, on the sands of Phlegra, you armed yourself to smash the Titan giants]" (sig. Aiiii^v). Cf. *The Guisiade*, l. 98.

72  Cf. below, ll. 585–92.

73  The 1575 text's "m'espriser" must be an error for "mépriser" ("disdain"); it is corrected by Wollfe.

74  Cf. above, l. 32 and n. 16.

75  Although not part of the Hebrew Bible and generally deemed apocryphal by Reformers, the Book of Judith enjoyed particular esteem among the latter for its model of an unlikely instrument employed by God to effect a liberating tyrannicide. That model was particularly applied to the assassination of François, Duke of Guise, by which the siege of Orléans was raised, and most notably by Du Bartas in *La Judit* (pub. 1574); see Introduction, pp. 41–43, and above, n. 20. Aubigné, too, so invokes it in *Les tragiques*, 5.381–86. See *Histoire et dictionnaire des Guerres de Religion*, ed. Jouanna et al., p. 120, and Cameron, ed., n. to ll. 499–500. Judith, of course, made an even more natural model for Jeanne d'Arc; see Fronton Du Duc, *La Pucelle*, trans. and ed. Hillman, ll. 712–13, 1598–1601, and 2393–400.

76  Cavagnes's word for priests, "capelans," suggests his (or Chantelouve's) origins in the south of France. The word might also have evoked the fish of the same name—hence my translation.

77  "[M]itre-heads": prelates, especially bishops. The original, "Mytreuses testes," coins an adjective to pejorative effect.

78  For Elijah, see 1 Kings 18:40; the story of Daniel's less direct destruction of the followers of Baal—he exposes their trickery and they are put to death by the king—is appended to the canonical book of that prophet in the Catholic Bible but otherwise appears in the Apocryphal book usually known as Bel [i.e., Baal] and the Dragon. The rhetoric here is perhaps less an exaggeration of Protestant polemic (Cameron, ed., n. to ll. 501–03) than a discrediting of it through its ironic interweaving with crude Machiavelism, if not sadism.

79  The rhyme "Baal"/"Admiral" is in the original, and is suggestive.

80  Sinon: the traitor responsible for the fall of Troy, who became emblematic of treachery; see Virgil, *Aeneid*, 2.57ff.

81  "Le peuple salue la paix." The dramatic irony produced by the interposition of the previous scene has an equivalent in *The Guisiade*, where the Chorus at the end of Act III pathetically celebrates the Union, which the audience knows to be doomed. The invocation of peace has a particularly rich history as a commonplace in the French literature of the late medieval and early modern periods; see, e.g., James Hutton, *Themes of Peace in Renaissance Poetry*, ed. Rita Guerlac (Ithaca, NY: Cornell University Press, 1984), and my *Shakespeare, Marlowe and the Politics of France*, pp. 123–30. Chantelouve's Chorus here may be particularly paralleled with that of Garnier in *Porcie*, ed. Lebègue, ll. 283–402.

82  Aeolus: the god who controlled the winds.

83  "Moorish sea" ["onde more"]: conceivably, the Mediterranean sea bordering North Africa (from the ancient Roman region of Mauretania), but the point is to indicate the whole extent of the (classically imagined) world from East to West, so the 1744 editor is probably right to understand an allusion to the Black Sea (Lenglet du Fresnoy, ed., p. 70, n. 69).

84  Jupiter is clearly now assimilated to the Christian Trinity. Cf. below, ll. 657–64.

85  These are the three traditional iconographic emblems of Mercury or Hermes. The broad-brimmed traveller's hat ("capeline") is usually winged, like his sandals, so I supply feathers in the translation. Chantelouve recalls Ronsard, "À Mercure, Ode XXVII" (1550), also in octosyllabics: "Je garniray tes talons d'ailes, / Ta capeline de deux belles, / Ton baston je n'oubliray pas [I shall adorn your heels with wings, with two fine ones for your hat; I shall not forget your rod]" (*Œuvres complètes*, ed. Céard et al., vol. 1: 952, ll. 13–15). One of Chantelouve's love sonnets is worth citing here for its radically different use of the same motifs:

> Nepueu d'Atlas: plein d'eloquence digne
> Ange diuin, courrier du haut-tonnant,
> Aelé Dæmon! ou vas-tu maintenant,
> Ou vas-tu las! auec ta Capeline?
>     Ou pousse-tu [*sic*] ta volee diuine,
> Dieu inuentif ou va ton cours fuyant!
> Tu ne dis mot? ha? Mon cueur deuinant,
> Presage bien quelque chose en ta mine

Tu viens cruel, de ta verge sorciere,
(Ayant au pieds ta double talonniere)
Charmer les yeux, de mon aimé soucy
De ton parler tu veux gaigner ma dame,
Pour appaiser de toy maistre flame:
Qui du haut ciel t'a faict caler icy.

[Grandson of Atlas, full of worthy eloquence, divine angel, messenger of the high thunderer, winged daemon, where are you going now? Alas, where are you going with your traveller's hat? Where are you pressing your divine flight, ingenious god; where is your fugitive course directed? Not a word do you say, eh? My divining heart foresees something in your countenance. You come, cruel one, with your double-winged sandals on your feet, with your magic staff to charm the eyes of the beloved object of my trouble. With your speaking you seek to win my lady to appease the flame of your master, who has caused you to descend here from the lofty sky.]        (*Sonnets et Chansons*, pp. 118–19)

Lines 601–12 in Cameron, ed., read as follows:

A moy sa serve geniture,
A moy son angelic Mercure,
A commandé prendre le vol,
Fendant de l'ær l'element mol.

Pren (macil dit) la capeline,
Empogne ta verge yvoirine,
Et pour caller en France bas,
Le talonnier jumeau prendras.

D'un vol qui les Zephirs surpasse
Toute la froide Junon trace:
Et descend dedans ce Paris
Laquelle n'eut iamais de pris.

Cf. Rabelais, *Le Quart Livre*, ed. Marichal, Prologue:

"Cza, ça, dist Juppiter à Mercure, descendez præsentement là bas, et jectez es pieds de Couillatris troys coingnées. . . . S'il en prend aultre que la sienne, couppez luy la teste avecques la sienne propre. Et desormais ainsi faictes à ces perdeurs de coingnées." . . .

Mercure avecques son chappeau poinctu, sa capeline, talonnieres et caducée, se jecte par la trappe des Cieulx, fend le vuyde de l'air, descend legierement en terre. . . .

["Go on, then," said Jupiter to Mercury, "descend at once below and throw three axes at the feet of [the woodsman] Couillatris. . . . If he takes any but his, cut off his head with his own. And henceforth do the same to these losers of axes." . . .

Mercury, with his pointed cap, his broad-brimmed hat, winged sandals and caduceus hurled himself through the trap-door of the heavens, split the emptiness of the air, alighted delicately upon the earth. . . .]                                                        (p. 26)

For discussion of this parallel, see Introduction, pp. 54–55. The two hats of Mercury mentioned by Rabelais go strangely together, as pointed out by Marichal, p. 26, 354n., and two traditional images seem to be combined.

86   Juno: a poeticism, of medical origin, for air — see Cameron, ed., n. to l. 610.

87   Mercury was the son of Maia, the daughter of Atlas. The original's "neveu" was not an error, as claimed in Lenglet du Fresnoy, ed., p. 29–30, n. 72: the older meaning of the word was grand-son; cf. the opening line of Ronsard, "À Mercure": "Facond neveu d'Atlas, Mercure [Eloquent grand-son of Atlas, Mercury]."

88   The allusion is not merely decorative. Seneca's Atreus, taking (to put it mildly) the side of "harshness" in discussion with his Minister (*Thyestes*, Act II, ll. 243ff.), makes the Golden Fleece symbolic of the sacred sovereignty that his brother has impiously violated, thereby sowing discord in the land and earning a terrible retribution. The parallel with the intentions of the Admiral would hardly have escaped Chantelouve. See also Introduction, p. 51.

89   That is, of course, Catherine de Medici, whose role as power behind the throne is notably kept at a distance by Chantelouve.

90   In the original, there is a pointed rhyme (regrettably untranslatable) on "Louvre" and "s'ouvre" ("opens itself").

91   It is fairly certain that the gunman in question was Charles de Louviers, seigneur de Maurevert; who was behind the act is more difficult to say, although from that day to this speculation has centred on the Duke of Guise and the royal family (especially Catherine de Medici); the house used was that of a follower of the Guises. See *Histoire et dictionnaire des Guerres de Religion*, ed. Jouanna et al., pp. 196–97 and 1088.

92   "[S]a fureur esprise": the pronoun is technically ambiguous, and "fureur" might seems a more appropriate term for Coligny, but it could be applied to the justified wrath of God, and it seems clear from

the context that such wrath is here being purposefully transferred to the otherwise mild and forgiving king; it is, indeed, the word applied to the king's reaction to the wounding of Coligny (l. 813), which is mistaken but noble — one of the mysterious ways in which God moves. The theology implied by Jupiter's intervention is particularly interesting; it might be supposed, for instance — and is, in fact, by Donald Stone, Jr. (*French Humanist Tragedy: A Reassessment* [Manchester: Manchester University Press, 1974], p. 108) — that God would inflict the wound on Coligny in order to warn him, rather than to tempt him to further crime, but then God knows that Coligny has incorrigibly chosen the path of evil.

93 On this self-sworn oath and a parallel passage in Garnier's *Porcie*, see Introduction, p. 43; cf. *The Guisiade*, ll. 1157–60.

94 "Mad Châtillon-ian": I attempt to convey something of the verbal exuberance with which Chantelouve converts Coligny's family name into an adjective, addressing his "chatillone rage." Similarly, in the next line, the noun and adjective "hypocrite" is made into a verb ("Ypocrisant," translated "feign") — an unusual coinage (though one warranted by the existence of a cognate Greek verb).

95 That is, as pointed out in Cameron, ed., n. to l. 716, the Cyclops, Virgil's "Aetnaeos fratres" (*Aeneid*, 3.678), who worked in Vulcan's smithy within Aetna and produced the thunderbolts hurled by Jupiter; see especially *Aeneid*, 8.418ff. Cf. Du Rosier, sig. Aiiii$^r$ ("traits Vulcaniens"), and Rabelais, *Le Quart Livre*, p. 22. There is an obvious analogy with the devils who were cast out from heaven yet serve God in punishing mankind (cf. below, l. 729.) Presumably in support of this sense, the 1744 edition, followed by Cameron, emends to "les" the original's "mes" in "mes mains / Sanglantes des frères Etnains" (Lenglet du Fresnoy, ed., ll. 715–16). This seems unnecessary, even confusing: the bloody hands are not those of the "frères Etnains"; they are Jupiter's hands, which are "bloody" (fiery red) with the thunderbolts provided to him, "des" indicating cause or origin. Wollfe keeps the original reading and must therefore share my understanding of the syntax, although she appears (from her note) not to grasp the allusion.

96 "J'ai meurtri la meurtriere main." Cf. the relish of the Admiral's ironic fate expressed by Gabriel de Saconay, Archbishop of Lyons, in *Généalogie et la fin des Huguenaux et découverte du calvinisme* (1573): "L'exterminateur à été exterminé" (cited Postel, p. 185). As reflected in the translation, the verb used in l. 636 is also "exterminer."

97 Polyphemus: a Cyclops of barbarous cruelty derived from Bk. 9 of

the *Odyssey*. Apart from the common imputation of such cruelty to Montgomery (see above, nn. 1, 36), the horrible retribution inflicted on Polyphemus by Odysseus — gouging and burning his eye with a sharpened stake — would surely have come to mind in connection with Montgomery's fatal wounding of Henri II in the eye with his lance. A mediating text may be Ronsard's *La Franciade*, 2.973ff., where Polyphemus is evoked to characterize the tyrannical giant Phovère. The latter is eventually slain by the young hero Francus, the mythical founder of France's royal line, thereby succouring Dicée, the just king, in a sequence that includes an encounter with spears and wounding in the eye. Ironically, Chantelouve's Montgomery, in the following speech, will shortly be wishing he were blind.

98    "Phoebus": a common epithet for Apollo; here, of course, the sun.

99    "Eclouant ma paupiere": the verb is an archaic form and transitive usage of "éclore" (lit. "hatch"), employed figuratively to mean "open"; see Huguet, *Dictionnaire de la langue française du seizième siècle*.

100   The name "Piles" contributes at least to the alliterative energy of ll. 743–45 — "Nous surpreneurs du Roy, nous surpreneurs de villes, / Et retaschans encore surprendre le Roy, Pilles, / Sommes les premiers pris" — and it is tempting to look for word-play, too, based on "pile" as the "tails" side of a coin, although expressions such as "tomber pile" ("fall on one's back") and "s'arréter pile" ("stop abruptly") are apparently more recent.

101   More irony: the Admiral is conspicuously far from invincible.

102   This line, as printed in the original (followed in Cameron, ed., except for the obviously erroneous accent in "Rougé") seems to me impossible: "Que fait faire a le Roy cete Rougé bravade." Lenglet du Fresnoy's edition renders it intelligible as "Qu'a fait faire le Roy cette estrange bravade," but the simplest solution is to restore the normal word order ("Que le Roy a fait faire . . . " — see Wollfe, ed., n. to l. 753), and "rouge" poses no problem: as is indicated by Cameron, ed., n. to l. 753, the word at the time could bear the sense of "cunning," "shrewd." See Huguet, *Dictionnaire de la langue française du seizième siècle*.

103   Again, Chantelouve's arrangement of his material, with this dialogue following the revelations of Mercury and fulfilling the project of Jupiter, produces effective irony, which here further damns the conspirators. The more they insist on their interpretation of events as obvious, the more they expose themselves as measuring others by

their own perverse perspective.

104 "Non, devant le boiteux il ne faut point clocher": proverbial.

105 Lines 769–804, in their expression of the commonplace of worldly instability, strongly resemble choruses in Garnier's *Cornélie* (ll. 551–622, 985–1064); with the latter speech, in turn, Ternaux, ed., n. 192, aptly compares Seneca, *Thyestes*, ll. 612–21. Especially close in rhetorical structure and imagery is also Du Bartas, *La Judit*, where the innumerable tears shed by the widow grieving for her husband point the familiar moral regarding the vanity of worldly wealth:

> Celuy qui peut [conter] combien le vent arctois
> En novembre fait choir de feuilles par les bois,
> Celuy qui peut [conter] les gouttes que l'Hyade,
> L'Orion pluvieux et la moite Pleiade
> Versent dessus les champs, celuy seul peut compter
> Les larmes qu'elle fit alors desgouster. . . .
> [Quand elle eust possedé tous les tresors d'Assur,]
> Quand elle eut possedé tout cet or qu'à la rive
> Du fleuve lydien parmy le sable arrive,
> Elle n'eust esté riche, ayant perdu celuy
> Sans qui tous les thresors ne luy portoyent qu'ennuy.

[He who can (number) how many leaves in the forest the arctic wind causes to fall in November, he who can (number) how many drops the Hyades, rainy Orion, and moist Pleiades pour upon the fields—he alone can number the tears she shed then.... (Had she possessed all the treasures of Assyria;) had she possessed all that gold which arrives on the bank on the Lydian river among the sand, she would not have been rich, having lost him without whom those treasures brought her nothing but care.]    (Baïche, ed., 4.277–90, with, in brackets, the variants of 1574 from p. 121)

106 Proteus: the water-monster of infinite shapes, metonymic of the sea, as noted in Lenglet du Fresnoy, ed., p. 34, n. 80.

107 This was the punishment of the Danaides in Hades.

108 Lines 779–82, as printed in 1575, present multiple difficulties: "Il laue en vain le thuyle, ou bien contre du sable, / A la Riue du pont le grain instant nobrable / Il veut espuyser londe, / D'amphytrite proffonde." Editors have made the obvious corrections to "nombrable" and "l'onde," but this leaves "instant nombrable" stubbornly obscure. I propose that it represents the printer's quite plausible error for the archaic (but biblical) "nïent nombrable," which translates

Latin "innumerabilis" (Tobler-Lommatzsch, *Altfranzösischer Wörterbuch*) and gives good sense. The combination of ideas remains strange and the syntax elliptical, but these are not uncharacteristic qualities of Chantelouve's verse. It is tempting to follow Wollfe by introducing a period at the end of l. 780, but this would seem to require emending "contre" ("against") to "conte" ("count" in archaic spelling) to produce a grammatical statement. Since the grammar is otherwise intelligible, if tortuous, I have resisted these further emendations.

109   Amphitrite: again, a metonymy for the sea, of which she was the queen.

110   "[N]otre Mascaret": a touch of local colour; the word "mascaret" is now generalized, but it is indeed of Gascon origin and for Randall Cotgrave (*A Dictionarie of the French and English Tongues*, Anglistica and Americana, 77 [1611; fac. rpt. Hildesheim: Georg Holms, 1970]) specifically designated the particularly (and mysteriously) powerful estuarial tidal bore of the Dordogne near Libourne, to which Chantelouve also paid tribute in his collection of verses; see Cameron, ed., n. to l. 785.

111   Cf. above, l. 582 and n. 83.

112   I have restructured ll. 791–92 to preserve the ambiguous referentiality of "his" ("sa"), which in the original, too, can apply grammatically either to the Saviour or to the deluded mortal: "Et comme le Sauveur souz sa plainte divine / Il ose sans danger ejamber la Marine"; the logical referent is clear, but the technical ambiguity reinforces the point ironically by teasing the reader. The allusion combines the biblical miracle of walking upon water with that of calming the stormy elements by rebuking them. See Matt. 8:23–28, 14:22–36; Mark 4:33–35–41, 6:45–52; Luke 8:22–25; John 6:45–51.

113   Chantelouve's mingling of late-medieval Catholicism ("good death" ["la bonne mort"]) and neo-classicism is particularly striking in ll. 799–804. Lines 801–02 are similarly awkward and cryptic in the original: "La fin tant seulement, / Bonne, à contentement."

114   In the original, ll. 817–22 read as follows (making in l. 817 the obvious correction of the 1575 edition's "isyeux" to "joyeus"):

> Qu'un joyeus Hymænée
> A sa feste tournée,
> Et son amoureux son
> En murmure, & soupçon:
> Que la joyeuse paix, guarde de toutes places,
> S'enfuit souz un tel bruit, & felones menaces.

Cf. the anticipation by Guise, in Marlowe's *Massacre*, of the transformation to be effected by the two murders he proceeds to set in
motion—of Jeanne d'Albret and Coligny:

> If ever Hymen lour'd at marriage-rites
> And had his altars deck'd with dusky lights;
> If ever sun stain'd heaven with bloody clouds
> And made it look with terror on the world;
> If ever day were turn'd to ugly night,
> And night made semblance of the hue of hell;
> This day, this hour, this fatal night,
> Shall fully show the fury of them all. (ii.1–8)

As in Marlowe's version generally, the diabolical Guise here takes
the place of divine providence in Chantelouve's, where it is the
uncomprehending king who is stricken with "fureur" (l. 813).

115 Cameron's correction of the original "sert" to "serf" is clearly correct.

116 Orig. "Eriphille": Chantelouve might have been thinking of Eriphile,
the daughter of Helen (cause of the Trojan war); she took her name
from Eris, goddess of spite and discord. (This figure is the original
for a later famous dramatic development by Racine in *Iphégenie*.)
The referent making far richer sense, however—in a provocatively
ambivalent way—is Eriphyle, wife of Amphiaraus; this is the identification made by Lenglet du Fresnoy, although he admits to not
seeing the point (p. 37, n. 84). Eriphyle was famous for betraying
her husband, who was endowed with prophetic powers, by per-
suading him to take part in the fratricidal war of "Seven against
Thebes" despite his foreknowledge of his death. (He was in fact
swallowed by the earth, split by Zeus's thunderbolt, just before being killed.) Amphiaraus had sworn to accept Eriphyle's decision,
and she was bribed by her son Polynices with the gift of a golden
necklace, which had originally been a wedding gift to Harmonia
(wife of Cadmus). The motif of harmonious wedding treacherously
perverted thus lurks in the background, as does even the Admiral's
murder of God's champion, François, Duke of Guise. Moreover,
Amphiaraus' son Alcmaeon, on divine authority, avenged his death
by murdering his mother. Still, it seems impossible to exclude from
the intertextual field—especially considering the allusions by Virgil
and Ovid—an element less clearly compatible with Chantelouve's
presumed application of the story: the further vengeance subsequently visited upon Alcmaeon for his matricide. The numerous
classical references to aspects of this myth include Homer, *Odyssey*,

11.326, 15.2; Pausanias, *Description of Greece*, 3.7, 5.17, 8.24, 10.41; Plato, *Republic*, 589e; Apollodorus, *Library*ain , 3.4–7; Virgil, *Aeneid*, 6.426; and Ovid, *Metamorphoses*, 9.324.

117 "O grand Saturnien": i.e., Jupiter, as in Du Rosier (see above, n. 12).

118 The effect of the ghost's grimly comic recital of underworld horrors depends, as in the Admiral's opening speech, on the ultra-serious background of Seneca — no doubt directly, but also as filtred through such precedents as that of Garnier's *Cornélie* (see above, n. 10) and Ronsard's *La Franciade* (Céard et al., eds., 4.831ff., but see esp. the original 1572 version, p. 1648, n. *a* to p. 1129). Cf. Claudian, *In Rufinum*, 2.498, whose preceding account of his villain's earthly punishment (decapitation and mutilation) may well have contributed to Du Bartas's *La Judit*. The bathetic element, however, appears to have its closest analogue in Du Rosier, who, having begged Jupiter to send France's enemy of peace to the underworld, proceeds to request his eternal torment:

> Puis vos Demons affreus, satelites fidelles
> Du Roy Tartarean, punisseur des rebelles,
> Ne vous lassés iamais, iamais ne vous soulés,
> De batre incessamment ses membres martelés
> A coups de grosse barre, & d'infester ses leures
> De Crapaus, de Lesars, de sifflantes Couleures,
> Qui luy beuront le sang: & dedans & dehors
> Enfleront de poison son miserable corps,
> Son corps de celuy la, qui dans nos poures terres
> Rapporta le premier la semence des guerres
> Et qui pour pasturer l'insatiable faim
> De son cœur convoiteux, nous met la dague au sein.

> [Then, you fearful demons, faithful servants of the King of Tartarus, the punisher of rebels, may you never tire, never get enough of incessantly beating his hammered limbs with blows of a heavy bar, and infesting his lips with toads, lizards, hissing serpents, which will drink his blood and, from within and without, bloat with poison his wretched body — the body of him who to our poor land was first to bring the seed of war, and who, to feed the insatiable hunger of his covetous heart, puts the dagger to our breast.]                                          (sig. Aiiii^v–B^r)

Chantelouve's conception of the vengeful ghost backed by the Fury is obviously indebted to the opening of *Thyestes*, but there is a fascinating Christian skewing; see Introduction, pp. 47–48.

119 Original stage direction ("sortant des Enfers").

120 Taenarus: a headland in Laconia (the nearby town is Taenarum), where a cavern traditionally gives entrance to the underworld, and where Hercules was supposed to have dragged up Cerberus. Cf. *The Guisiade*, l. 1025.

121 Lenglet du Fresnoy, followed by Cameron, emends the original's "sers" to "sors," which must be the word intended.

122 Tartarus: the underworld in general, often identified with hell in Christian writing.

123 The case is doubtful, but here I prefer the emendation of Lenglet du Fresnoy, who supplied the accent to "attache" in the original ("roüe, attache qui s'enfuit") to change it from the rather incongruous noun meaning "attachment" to the past participle of the verb "attacher."

124 More classically, it was Prometheus' liver that was perpetually devoured, but the organ was variable, as well as renewable; in Garnier, *Porcie*, l. 52, it is his heart. Du Bartas, *La Judit*, ed. Baïche, 5.49, specifies heart, lung, and liver in a passage that also includes Ixion's wheel.

125 "[S]and": Cameron, n. to l. 870, cites Cotgrave to show that the original's "falaise," normally meaning "bank" or "cliff," could also carry this sense.

126 "Rhadamanthus": underworld enforcer of punishments; cf. *The Guisiade*, l. 871. The article before the name (present in the original) may simply reinforce the sense of sequential enumeration, or it may indicate that the name is being used generically; it is not capitalized in the original text, but that means very little, given the erratic typography. There is an acknowledgement, however, in the form of an apostrophe, that the name is being shortened (to "rhadamanth"), obviously for metrical purposes. Cf. *The Guisiade*, l. 871.

127 An estrapade, or strappado, was the instrument of torture or punishment, widespread in the Renaissance, to which victims were tied with their arms behind them, then let go and stopped with a jolt.

128 Hercules was Alcmene's son by Zeus. Seneca's *Hercules Furens*, where the hero's underworld journey figures prominently, again makes its intertextual presence felt (cf. nn. 10, 140).

129 Pirithous, with his friend Theseus, had been treacherously confined in Hades, and Hercules tried unsuccessfully to free him when on his mission to bring back Cerberus to the upper world.

130 Poisonous plants were supposed to have sprung up where Cerberus'

drool touched the ground. It is worth keeping Chantelouve's epithet for Cerberus' throat, "inhumain" ("inhuman"/"inhumane"), which stands out for conspicuous redundancy, the more so because it seems to have been dictated by the need for a rhyme.

131   The word for "ice" here is "le glaz," which is quite common in the period, especially in the context of Petrarchan poetry, where lovers regularly both burn and freeze; see Huguet, *Dictionnaire de la langue française du seizième siècle*. The sense is bizarre but clear, and the line thus confirms the self-conscious humour riddling this speech: Andelot, like the Admiral himself, is ridiculously evil in the medieval tradition of stage devils and gargoyles. Wollfe prints "glas" and unaccountably glosses it as "glaise" ("clay"); apart from the objection that "glaise" seems always to have been a feminine noun, this explanation hardly makes for clarity.

132   Tisiphone: one of the Eumenides, or Furies. (Cf. *The Guisiade*, l. 870.) Chantelouve must be giving Andelot a play on the word "furious" ("furieus"). He is also subtly preparing for the striking effect of the Furies' appearance (l. 971ff).

133   See above, l. 10 and n. 9.

134   "[M]onklings" translates "Moynaille," "rabble of churchlings" "Prestraille" — pejorative coinages common in Reform rhetoric.

135   "Magnifico": I attempt to give the flavour of the original, which elliptically refers only to "le riche d'enfer" ("the rich one of hell"), playing on the etymology on Pluto ("ploutos" is Greek for "wealth").

136   That the devil awaits the Admiral's soul could hardly be hidden from Andelot, but that he, and presumably the devil, suppose that the Admiral's plot has a chance of succeeding again throws into relief, ironically, the ultimate control mysteriously exercised by God.

137   I follow Cameron in adopting Lenglet du Fresnoy's reading, "tant que" ["while," here "during"], in place of the original's "tant qu'as," which does not give good sense in the context.

138   The 1575 text's "penille" is an obvious error for "penible" ["painful"], corrected by Lenglet du Fresnoy and Cameron.

139   "[W]retched" ("miserables"): both Lenglet du Fresnoy and Cameron make the necessary correction of the original text's singular ("miserable").

140   Stage direction added; such a staging is a natural inference in the circumstances, especially given the numerous references to Coligny's wound, and fittingly counterpoints his probable initial appearance

with a noose. In historical fact, the Admiral's wound was seriously disabling, and he was killed in his bedchamber, if not quite in his bed, as is pathetically depicted in Marlowe's *Massacre*. It would hardly suit Chantelouve's purpose to show him as completely helpless.

141  Doubting one's senses in such terms was a commonplace, but the close reminiscence here of Seneca, *Hercules Furens*, ll. 1138–39 (noted by Cameron, ed., n. to l. 919), recalls the Admiral's initial appearance as a figure of heroism turned perversely destructive (see above, n. 10). The shift within ll. 919–20 from the more formal Alexandrine, regularly used for monologue, to the decasyllabics adapted to livelier dialogue shows Chantelouve's care in matching modes of speech to stage business.

142  The sequence of events is not wholly clear in the original: "Quand enragé dequoy deffait tu feus / Et Condé mort, à Xaintes je moureus." (The rhyme with "feus" in l. 927 confirms the emendation of l. 928's grammatically anomalous "mourons" to "moureus" by Cameron, again following Lenglet du Fresnoy.) The Prince of Condé was already dead, having been killed in the battle of Jarnac (or Bassac) on 13 March 1569, when François d'Andelot succumbed in May of that year to what the Protestants suspected to be poison. (Chantelouve has him blame the Admiral's war, not necessarily for his death, but for his presence in hell.) The defeat Andelot refers to must therefore be that of Moncontour (13 October 1569). See *Histoire et dictionnaire des Guerres de Religion*, ed. Jouanna et al., pp. 182–84.

143  Cameron, following Lenglet du Fresnoy, drops the vocative "O" beginning the line, presumably to correct Chantelouve's metre.

144  "D'une main" might simply mean "with a hand," but given all the plays on "hand" in the passage, it may also signal that he has only one good hand remaining.

145  Bellona: goddess of war; see above, n. 32.

146  Lines 965–66 and 967–68 are redundant to the point of suggesting two versions of what was originally intended as a single couplet. The reiteration effectively insists, however, on Andelot's distinctly mild representation of life in the underworld, in contrast to his previous monologue (and indeed the one by the Admiral that opens the play) — confirmation that he actively abets the diabolical project of luring his brother into regicidal vengeance.

147  François was born in 1521, Gaspard in 1519, so "grand" must mean "noble" instead of "elder," as might be supposed.

148  If Andelot were to kneel at this point, as if on cue or even prompted

by a significant look or gesture, the action would effectively reflect the Furies' stage-managing. A touch of exaggeration seems in order. Certainly, given Andelot's recent recital of infernal horrors, the reference to the repose of his soul (l. 1002) rings absurdly hollow.

149    Original stage direction ("Icy d'Andelot retourne aux Enfers.").

150    The original's "cil" ("eyelash") is used, as is not uncommon, in the sense of "sourcil" ("eyebrow").

151    The blend of classical and Christian ideas in ll. 1025–26 is especially flagrant but not indiscriminate. In the figure of Rhea (the mother of Jupiter), the Virgin Mary is adumbrated — the tradition represented by the *Miracles de Notre Dame* would probably have sharpened her presence — while the reiteration of the idea of God as married to his people (cf. l. 287) hints particularly at God the Son. It is the latter, of course, who will figure as judge on Doomsday.

152    The original prints the noun "pourparler" (lit. "negotiation," "discussion," here "humming") as two words; Wollfe makes the correction.

153    Lines 131–33 in the 1575 edition read: "Las que je crains beaucoup le secret pour parler / Des huguenots, leur venir, & aller, / Leurs tours, & leurs retours, à l'Admiral le porte." This may be a case where the original punctuation clarifies the syntax: the comma after "retours" seems to place the verb "porte" in parallel with "crains," the pronoun being omitted, as is common. Wollfe, who suppresses this comma, apparently has difficulty with the sentence. Note that the People's well-founded suspicion and fear highlight the need for the Informer, who, like the would-be assassin, is effectively doing God's work and answering their prayers.

154    Another occurrence of the "arm" motif; the king's strong arm, human but sustained by God's own ("A nostre prince, & tens le bras humain"), contrasts with the Admiral's, which God has shattered, and it is never more "humane" (this sense of the word "humain" is also clearly functional here) than when it punishes the enemies of God and the people.

155    A commonplace as counsel not necessarily welcome but sometimes necessary for kings — cf. *The Guisiade*, l. 631 and n. 85.

156    Proverbial; cf. *The Guisiade*, l. 593, where the context is similar.

157    As in ll. 415ff., evoked here, across the conventional weighing of mildness and harshness in political terms (see Introduction, pp. 14, 36–37, and n. 15), is the Christian paradigm of the debate in heaven, often represented in the medieval drama. The positions of the King

and Council are reversed from those in the Senecan *Octavia*, so that Charles's human/humane predilection for mercy is given full scope before he yields to the claims of retributive justice — the outcome we know to have been divinely predetermined. Stichomythia is skilfully used here to sustain a sense of veritable debate, the couplets actually resisting the closure promised by the structure of argument and refutation: the losing argument (the King's, for mercy) in each case completes the rhyme. The technique is used more conventionally in *The Guisiade* — e.g., in ll. 579ff.

158    The evocation of the blood of Abel calling to God (Gen. 4:10) prepares for the king's assimilation to the role of instrument of divine vengeance.

159    Emending the "vous" of the 1575 text ("Deliures, vous le Peuple") to "nous" (Cameron, ed.) seems to me unnecessary and blurs the otherwise clear distinction between the People and the Council.

160    The commonplace image of the ship of state blends with that of the Church as "la nace [nacelle] de Saint Pierre" — see above, l. 316 and n. 58.

161    I.e., Henri, Duke of Anjou, and François-Hercule, Duke of Alençon.

162    In the account of Pibrac, too, which Chantelouve elsewhere follows closely, first a single informer, then three, are mentioned. See Cameron, ed., nn. to ll. 1059–60 and 1069ff.

163    "The Moorish goddess": Hecate, the goddess who drove the chariot of the night. Making her Moorish suggests the east (cf. ll. 582–83) — and helps Chantelouve with a rhyme ("Aurore"/"More"). Modern editors interpolate the article "la," absent from the 1575 text, before "blonde Aurore" (l. 1131) on grammatical and metrical grounds.

164    Cf. above, ll. 57–60 and n. 21. An analogue especially to the point here is Du Bartas, *La Judit*:

> L'Aurore ja quittoit le froid embrassement
> De son vieillard espoux et d'un bigarrement
> Peignoit l'indique ciel, quand les plus fiers gend'armes
> Qui defendoyent le fort sortent auec leurs armes. . . .

> [Aurora had already left the cold embraces of her ancient spouse and was painting the Indian sky with variegated colours when the fiercest warriors defending the fort came out with their weapons. . . .]                                                    (6.225–28)

This is the prelude, in the poem, to the pagans' discovery of the divine punishment of Holoferne, which then extends to include them all.

165 "Pardaillan" is presumably the "baron de Pardaillon," a page of Henri de Navarre (Wollfe, ed., n. to l. 1137), to be distinguished from the better-known François de Ségur-Pardaillan. The latter was one of a small group of Protestant nobles in the faubourg Saint-Germain, including Montgomery, who had enough time to escape; he was later to serve Henri de Navarre as a diplomat. (See Crouzet, *La nuit de la Saint-Barthélemy*, pp. 405 and 408, and *Histoire et dictionnaire des Guerres de Religion*, ed. Jouanna et al., pp. 319 and 586). "Pardaillan" also figures in the account by Agrippa d'Aubigné (in his *Histoire universelle*, cited by Cameron, ed., n. to 1137) of those killed in or at the gate of the Louvre. So does Piles, but so, wrongly, does Beauvais (i.e., Briquemault), who was arrested and executed later.

166 I have not been able to identify "Pinos" here, under this or other possible spellings; neither has Denis Crouzet, whose knowledge of the facts is unrivalled and who graciously looked into the question at my request (personal communication). Wollfe, the only editor to venture a note, produces a masterstroke of circularity, identifying him only as a victim of the massacre. The text is seemingly correct, since there is a rhyme with "flos" (mod. "flots," i.e., "floods," here "channel"), but of course Chantelouve himself may have transcribed the name erroneously or even invented it. Given the other evidence of regionally grounded animosity on his part, it may be to the point that "Pineau" (in various forms) is a common name in the Southwest, turning up, for instance, in the records of Protestant families in La Rochelle. It would not be out of keeping with Chantelouve's grim playfulness for him to have included some personal enemy in his list of the dead.

167 In context, this allusion can hardly help evoking one of the central images of the massacre, the casting of corpses into the Seine (see Crouzet, *La nuit de la Saint-Barthélemy*, passim), although this was not actually, of course, the fate of the Admiral. Also involved, again, is a sort of discursive retribution for the fate of the Admiral's erst-while supposed victim, François, Duke of Guise, as celebrated by way of Du Bartas's Holoferne: "Mais un somme eternal a bouché les conduis / De l'oreille du duc, qui deja, miserable, / A passé du noir Styx la rive irrepassable [But an eternal slumber had stopped the conduits of the ears of the general (lit. "duke"), who already, wretched, had passed the bank of the dark Styx, from which there is no return]" (*La Judit*, 6.250–52). Thus, too, the prayer of Du Rosier has been answered: "Fay les precipiter dans les tristes manoirs / Que

l'ardant Phlegeton enclost d'abismes noirs [Have them cast into
the gloomy dwellings that burning Phlegethon encloses with dark
chasms]" (sig. Aiiiiᵛ). Cf. also Claudian, *In Rufinum*, 2.454ff.

168 "Elle ne craint aucun danger encor?" The word-order does not
suggest a question, but there is no strong imperative for discounting
the original interrogative punctuation.

169 In this period, local governors wielded great power. Cf. Garnier's
point, in "Hymne de la Monarchie," ed. Chardon, that magistrates
ruling towns in republics are as prone to display abusive behaviour
as outright tyrants (p. 261 [sig. Biiiʳ]).

170 Unaccountably, Wollfe glosses "Dès où" (l. 1167) as indicating time
("from the moment when") rather than place ("from where"), although the latter meaning is within the bounds of normality and the
former makes inferior sense. The language here is very close to that
of Cicero's opening jeremiad in Garnier's *Cornélie* on the destructive
effects of Rome's — in effect, Caesar's — ambitious pride:

> Romme, helas! que te sert d'assugettir le monde?
> Que te sert d'ordonner de la terre et de l'onde?
> Que te sert d'enfermer sous le pouvoir Latin,
> L'Aquilon, le Midy, le Couchant, le Matin,
> Et que le blond Soleil, quelque part qu'il pourmeine
> Son char estincelant, trouve l'Aigle romaine:
> Puis que ce grand Empire à tes enfans ne sert
> Que d'allechante amorce à l'orgueil qui les pert,
> Qui les pert et embarque en piteuse ruine,
> Que ja desja je voy de leur teste voisine?

[Rome, alas, what does it serve you to subjugate the world?
What does it serve you to command the land and the sea? What
does it serve you to enclose under Roman power the north, the
south, the west, the east, and to have the blond sun, wherever
he drives his sparkling chariot, find the Roman eagle, since this
great empire will serve your children as nothing but a tempting
bait to the pride that ruins them, that ruins them and draws
them to pitiful destruction, which now already I see close to
their heads.]                                               (ll. 65–74)

The original of Chantelouve's l. 1165 is "Las [Cameron, ed., gives
"Là"] que sert-il de maistriser le monde," while his adjective for
Phoebus in l. 1167 (translated here as "gleaming"), like Garnier's,
is "blond." Cf. also Garnier's Chorus on Caesar's delusion of
immunity to fortune, in a speech that Chantelouve seems to have

drawn on previously (see above, n. 105):

> Ore, Cesar, qui gros d'honneur
> Se voit de la terre seigneur,
> Presomptueux n'y pense,
> Ne prevoyant de son bon-heur
> La constante inconstance.

[Now Caesar, who, great with honour, sees himself master of the world, presumptuous, does not think of this, not foreseeing the constant inconstancy of his good fortune.]     (ll. 1055–59)

Garnier, in turn, may well have been responding to the evocation of César's grandeur by one of his soldiers in Grévin's tragedy (ll. 525ff.). Finally, cf. Claudian, *In Rufinum*, 2.440–53.

Again, the moral and the imagery of Chantelouve's religious adversary Du Bartas are also very much to the point:

> O grand Dieu, qui croira que cil qui possedoit
> Et l'Aube et l'Occident, qui ses bras estendoit
> Des Syrtes jusqu'au Nort, mort ne trouve à cette heure
> Un pouce de gazon pour toute sepulture?
> . . . . . . . . .
> Non, il ne gist pas sur terre, ains l'affamé corbeau
> Est de son corps haché le merité tombeau . . .

[O great God, who would believe that he who possessed the dawn-sky and the West, who stretched his arms from the Syrtes to the North, now in death finds not an inch of earth to be his tomb. . . . No, he lies not on the earth, but the hungry crow is the merited tomb of his hacked body . . . ]     (*La Judit*, 6.345–54)

171   Cameron emends "ores" ("now") in the 1575 text to the more modern "or," presumably to correct the metre; there is no difference in meaning.

172   Montfaucon, outside Paris, was the site of the public gallows, where Coligny's mutilated body was displayed in grotesque mockery. The irony was recorded approvingly by many Catholic partisans — see Introduction, pp. 41–43, 55–56, as well as Cameron, ed., n. to ll. 63–70 and n. to ll. 1185ff.

Compare, once more, Du Bartas, *La Judit*, at the point when the heroine discloses the wondrous vengeance wrought upon Holoferne. This moves the Hebrews to thanksgiving, effects the conversion of a former pagan enemy (Achior), and is moralized by the poet — all in terms that *Coligny* seems ironically to appropriate and redeploy:

Adonc les citadins, voyans en sa main pendre
Le chef du chef d'Assur, humbles commencent rendre
Graces au Tout-Puissant, qui par la foible main
D'une femme a puny ce tyran inhumain.
. . . . . . . . .
O Dieu, que dextrement ta saincte providence
Renverse les desseigns de l'humaine prudence!
Car pour guider l'esleu au salut destiné,
Quand mesme il en est plus, comme il semble, esloigné,
Tu tires bien du mal et fais que sa malice,
Forcée, l'achemine au sainct mont de justice.

[Then the townspeople, seeing hanging in her hand the head of the head of the Assyrians, humble, began to render thanks to the Almighty, who by the weak hand of a women punished that inhuman tyrant. . . . O God, how ably your sacred providence overthrows the designs of human wisdom. For to guide the elected one to his destined salvation, even when he seems farthest from it, you draw good out of evil and bring it about that his evil, compelled, leads him to the sacred mount of justice.] (6.175–88)

On the contemporary application of the mutilations and slaughters in *La Judit*, see Introduction, pp. 41–43. In effect, the degradation/elevation of Coligny's body by the Paris mob is evoked by Chantelouve as a "live" refutation of Du Bartas' celebration of the destruction of François, Duke of Guise. Intertextually, too, the Guises thus got their revenge—in the name of God's.

*The Guisiade*


by


*Pierre Matthieu*

Henri, Duke of Guise. Bibliothèque Nationale.

## Discourse on the Subject of This Tragedy

The envious jealousy that Henri III, King of France and Poland, bore towards the noble enterprises and happy feats of prowess of Henri de Lorraine, Duke of Guise, developed into such rage and spite as are illustrated by the events of this Tragedy, so recent that it has scarcely allowed those sensible to the miseries of such unheard-of vengeance the time to dry their eyes. On this foundation the poet, in the manner of the Greeks and Romans, in verse grave and flowing, sets up the theatre of this history, no less prodigious than tragic, which takes up the subject from its beginning, with the proposal to hold the Estates, when my lord of Guise, after the Paris barricades,[1] came, on the assurance of faith publicly pledged, to the place where all the Estates of the orders of France were appointed to meet.[2]

And so the first act of this *Guisiade* consists entirely of a declaration of the most Christian[3] and Catholic soul of the Duke of Guise, burning with a sincere zeal to extirpate heresy, to relieve the people, and to secure the public welfare — contrary to the opinion of those who slandered his holy affection as an ambitious desire to possess the state and succeed to the crown, or rather to take it away from the King, so as to reap the benefit of being chosen in the course of usurping it.

For he desires nothing more dearly than to make his innocence manifest to His Majesty, and what motives compelled his soul to his sacred resolutions to preserve in exclusivity the religion of Catholics by banishing heresy and to relieve the people by procuring the reduction of taxes and irregular surcharges — the pernicious invention of the harpies of the court. He presents himself to the King, persuaded by the Queen Mother, who seems to have sweetened the bitter anger that the King unceasingly ruminated as he recalled the trouble stirred up in Paris, and between them several articles of peace were agreed on. The most notable of these was that the King appointed himself head of the Union; all leagues and associations were to cease.[4]

The upshot was that the Duke of Guise, having apparent reason to hope for the fulfilment of his expectations, laid down his arms and followed the King. All regions received with great happiness the salutary Edict, which, in order to lend it greater authority, the King wished to be established among the three fundamental laws of the realm: for this reason, the Estates were summoned, at which were chosen to be present, from all regions, such notable persons as might be found most highly esteemed for diligence, for faith, for piety, in order to support the purpose of one who, in appearance, seemed to aspire to nothing but the good of the state and the reform of the government of his realm. Yet those who took part most closely in the secrets of his affairs were well aware of the prodigious effects to follow from that long and all-too-cunning dissimulation. Who might express by how many and various demonstrations of friendship he charmed the will of the Duke of Guise, in order to lull him, freely attributing the cause of the troubles to those who had abused his grace, and against whom he feigned to have conceived a just indignation?

And from this came about the absence of Épernon, who, impatient at this disgrace, at the beginning of the third Act despairs, invokes the Furies of hell, relates the abuses by which he has thrown into disorder the finances of France, and as a reward for this beseeches them to incite the King to the massacre of the House of Lorraine.

Nevertheless, the Estates get underway as auspiciously as they ended unhappily. The King began his speech in such a finely crafted style, and with such delivery, that he seemed to desire the prize for eloquence exclusively for himself.

The Church, the Nobility, and the people unfolded freely the proper remedies for France's illness and asked for nothing more than to maintain the Edict of Union, which ought to have realized every hope for the public welfare. They caused the King to accept it and to ratify it by oaths so solemn and serious that, without extreme impiety, one could not have doubted his faith.

Yet the King could not so thoroughly smother the flames of his vengeance beneath the ashes of his diverse favours but that my lord of Guise was pressed to withdraw. To clarify doubt on this matter, he raised it with the King, but, at the latter's words full of grace and love, he was reassured to such a degree that he would not thereafter hear urgings to the contrary. Upon which, the King took occasion to hasten the execrable and wicked plan that he had conceived under the cover of his faith so solemnly sworn.

And as it is not plausible that such an act could ever have met with a human soul—and, moreover, a French one, issued from the monarchs of France—so inclined to evil as even to entertain the thought of such a wrong, unless he had yielded to some sort of treacherous and devious counsel, the poet in the fourth Act presents the King discussing the murder of my lord of Guise with an anonymous person, or several, signified by the two letters "N.N.," on the presumption that devils incarnate, Machiavellians, heretics, sworn enemies of the Catholic religion incited him to attack the defenders of that religion on the vain and slanderous pretexts of ambition and the League. These exercised such sway over the King's heart that, forgetting all his promises, his oaths— forgetting himself—he resolved to execute that bloody tragedy on the 23rd of December 1588. He caused to be announced in the chambers of the three Estates his intention on that day, early in the morning, to press forward with some special resolution concerning the matters set forth in their memoranda. And for the same purpose he commanded his council to meet, assuring the presence of the main element of that tragedy, my lord of Guise, who alone, securely wrapped in the promises of the king, disdaining concern for his own person, thought only of the public good and harboured in his mind no apprehension of these difficulties.

And nevertheless a single rumour ran throughout the town of Blois—that Saint Thomas's day was appointed for that murder. He saw the King's guards wearing more armour than was customary, the unusual conspiratorial activity. He was not ignorant of the warnings from abroad—from Rome, from Spain, from Germany. A notable person from Lyons of weighty and distinguished authority had warned his council, speaking of this deed with such assurance as should have dissuaded the heart of this prince so close to the brink. He had forgotten the long-standing hostilities associated with the galleries of the Louvre, Saint-Maur-des-Fossés,[5] Meaux,[6] the Tuileries, and the barricades of Paris. His confidence in the King's oath and his zealous care for his reputation, lest he be judged to have deserted the Estates, which he had used all his power to bring about, caused him not to believe those who, in the interest of saving his life, begged him to withdraw. And so, once he had arrived at the council, having been in great haste to get there, he was sent for to the study, in the ante-chamber of which the forty-five cut-throats threw themselves upon him and killed him, which is the end of the fourth Act. For the fifth, there remains only the grieving, sighs, and laments of Madame de Nemours, which deserved an ample volume, in order to console not her alone, but all France, which feels along with her this deplorable disaster.

For those who have found the wherewithal to satisfy their ancient grudge against the blood of the magnanimous and noble House of Lorraine, there are maxims befitting their passion and encouraging such behaviour in kings, such as "perjure yourself boldly," "dissemble cleverly," "ride roughshod over others," "break faith and promise," all of which keep company beneath a wretched and cowardly disloyalty. Now, as Marc Antony said,[7] the most pitiful thing there is in this world is when faith is broken by one's friends, without which no virtue may be sustained; nor indeed are monarchies beneficial to their rulers when faith is banished from them. The Romans held it in such reference that they established a temple where solemn vows were sworn on the occasion of oaths, alliances, truces, even contracts, and such scrupulous and exact observers of their faith were they that they considered it to be violated, not only when one performed something contrary, but also when one permitted something to be done by others which appeared to be to its detriment. Examples of such firm and incredible fidelity are to be found throughout Livy, Salust, and Dion with reference to Scipio, Jugurtha, and Nerva. But to leave aside profane authors and convince a French king by his own ancestors, who does not know how great was the faith of Louis XII at the point when the Pope and the Emperor had defaulted on their alliance made at Cambrai against the Venetians in the year 1508? He kept the treaty in such a way that, although he would have been justified in paying them back with this adage, *Frangenti fidem, fides frangatur eidem,*[8] he fulfilled everything belonging to his promise towards those who had broken it. Thus that good prince had this in common with Caesar, that he would in no way imitate the perfidy of his enemies, nor break faith, although they had broken it on their side. And in that regard (as the wise commander Quintius Cincinnatus said), natural reason shows us that one should by no means do wrong on the example of others, break a law, although others have already broken it, or commit the same fault that we reprove and condemn in others. Neither imprisonment nor the inveterate hatred attested by so many battles, and by so many writings published against the faith of one or the other, could persuade King François I not to keep his own with the Emperor, crossing all of France and putting himself at the mercy of the promise of his ancient enemy; and he kept it so sincerely that posterity is astonished at, as much as it abhors and decries, the act of the King of France his grandson, who could have learnt the lesson of that perfidy only from Machiavelli, or from some offspring of Edward II of England, who, in a general assembly of the Estates, with no legal justification, caused to be beheaded twenty-two of the gravest princes and lords of the realm.[9] And by the same Estates he was stripped of his royalty and confined in a strait prison. From such perfidy have come the most striking downfalls of monarchies, and there is nothing within them more dangerous or pernicious. That is what ruined Carthage, the ornament of Africa, Corinth, Thebes, Colchis (three rich cities of Greece), and already it has begun to turn France upside-down, causing the murder — treacherously, disloyally, and in cowardly fashion — of one of its pillars, the magnanimous Duke of Guise, in the assembly of the Estates. In this the King greatly misjudged, reasoning that as soon as that prince was struck down, he would reign alone and securely, and that a dead man would no longer make war — a most offensive and highly doubtful affirmation to serve as a basis for the murders and impieties produced by his cruelty, and one that comes from Theodotos in Plutarch, not from Saint Paul.[10]

When Louis, Duke of Orléans, the brother of King Charles VI, was killed by Jean, Duke of Burgundy, he did not revenge his death by his own arms, but he was rather the cause of a war that ravaged France for more than sixty years.[11] Did not the abduction and rape of the wife of the Levite cause a war which was the death of sixty thousand men?[12] Pompey, once he was killed, made war no more; but his death provoked a long and cruel one through the whole Roman empire. Julius Caesar, stabbed in the Senate, left it stained with his blood, and the noble Duke of Guise, murdered in the King's study, not only leaves the place reddened with his own but renders France all bloody with it. And perfidy, amongst all crimes, approaches most closely to the punishment and vengeance of God, for God is directly involved in it, seeing His name treated with contempt and His majesty thereby made complicit in the treason committed in the shadow of faith.

# Dramatis Personae

Henri de Lorraine, Duke of Guise
Henri III, King of France
Queen Mother (Catherine de Medici)
Duke of Épernon[13]
Duchess of Nemours (mother of the Duke of Guise)
"N.N."[14]
Representatives of the assembled Estates of France:
  The Clergy
  The Nobility
  The Commons
Messenger
Chorus (voice of the "Union")

**Scene:** The time and settings of the first two acts and the first scene of Act III are indefinite, but the action is obviously conceived as occurring between the Paris revolt (the "barricades") of mid-May 1588 and the meeting of the national "Estates" in Blois during the fall and winter of that year. The Estates provide a more precise setting for the subsequent scenes. Historically, the king signed the Edict of Union in Rouen on 15 July; the swearing of the oath of Union at the Estates took place on 18 October; the Duke of Guise was murdered on 23 December.

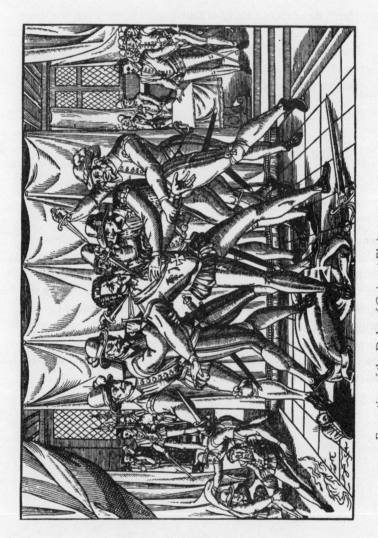

Execution of the Duke of Guise at Blois,
Dec. 24, 1588. Bibliothèque nationale.

# Act I

*Argument*[15]

*The Duke of Guise, who plays the principal part in the tragedy,
is the first to enter the theatre and manifests the ardent zeal with
which he burns to maintain State and Religion inseparable. He
responds with singular modesty to the calumnies of his detractors,
placing his frank enterprise in opposition to their ambition and
conspiracy, and represents to the eyes of those ingrates his own
accomplishments and those of his ancestors, undertaken for the
good of France; then, banishing from himself all vain fear of the
enmity of the King, with the assurance of his own conscience,
which serves as an impregnable wall of defence, he considers
whether to go and seek out the King, who out of fearful panic had
left Paris on the day after the Barricades.*[16]

DUKE OF GUISE [*alone*]

A lofty and a Christian heart never gives way
To worldly vanities that would lead it astray.
It never listens to the siren-song advice
Of those who, seeking for honours at any price,
Ambition-driven, with doses of lethal brew,
By crooked ways their fortunes purchase and pursue,
Open the door to vice, and without fear or shame,
Cloak what they do beneath religion's holy name,
Proclaim that one whose royal greatness would desire
To manage without restraint the reins of empire                    10
May violate justice and without a bridge traverse
The Syrtic Sea of Libya, with its rocky dangers,[17]
Must arm himself with strength and play the soldier, even
By turning against his own men with his weapon.
If those who have at heart what they outwardly show
Follow me where justice and chance would have us go;
If, with arms so valiant and souls so well directed,

The generous French respond as I had expected;
If the Pilot of Faith's barque,[18] in its fragility,
Cries up to heaven, and calls to heaven for me;                    20
If the most holy order of the faithful Church,
To shield itself from error, of me comes in search;
If the dear devotees of those ever-green bays
Make the universe resound with the Guise's praise;
If the people troop after me, love me, prize me;
If they count on me as the hope of all liberty —
It is not against my King, nor that royal flower,[19]
The lily of France, to challenge — or to devour;
It is not to reassert the right of Charlemagne
Or to impose upon France a marriage with Spain;                    30
It is not to gain triumphs of cypress and laurel[20]
(Of valorous warriors the wages immortal),
But for the faith, for my King, to defend my land,
That steel and lead, war's thunderbolts, I bear in hand.
But the honour is Yours, O Monarch Eternal:
A humble soldier am I — You are my colonel.
Beneath the bright rays that stream from Your holy face,
I show forth radiant, brimming with love and grace.
    If always I have armed myself with such a shield,
Often victorious, and rarely forced to yield;                      40
If always I have harkened to the trumpet's call,
Foremost in the assault, retreating last of all;
If, amid the furor of a heretic compound,
With my scar[21] I have been seen, bloodying the ground;
If I have vowed the flower of my age to alarms;
If my delights have been in combats and in arms;
If always on my back this harness I've kept wearing —
That, too, is for You, for the faith, for my King.
If always my hand has wielded sword or lance,
Lord, it is for Your sake, and that of poor France:                50
Impelled by that desire, which burns in every part,
To the wounds of a million spears I bare my heart.
    As if the Dirae,[22] those dark Furies infernal,

Had wished to have dominion here, instead of hell,
We have seen German fury, in flood after flood,
Spewing horror, impiety, shedding of blood[23] —
Against You, against us — and bloated with arrogance,
Thinking to spurn underfoot the flower of France,
With the aim in the self-same grave of entombing
Law, justice, right — France itself with its King —      60
Their souls in the grip of a vain and futile craving
For this ample realm's dismemberment and enslaving.
This barbarous army, or rather this wild herd,
Has found itself in France not enriched but interred.
For this, Lord, to You alone we render glory,
As to the primal author of such a victory.[24]
The foreigner is defeated, in shame he flees;
Sharp regret and mourning compound his miseries.
He curses his misfortune; but a foe remains,
Presumes on intimacy to plague France with pains —    70
France, alas, like a body by diseases tried,
Which suffers inwardly much more than from outside.
For Schism and Heresy, her organs inflaming,
Her mournful funeral already are proclaiming.
Her sons — O heart-break! — her bastards, not her sons,
Ensure that daily into countless harms she runs.

Father, who with a single word the pole can jolt,
Hurl Your decree upon them like a thunderbolt —
That utterance whose power once gave defiance
To the arrogant will of the frenzied Giants.      80
Infuse with strength our arms, and arm our hearts with courage,
To preserve from these wolves Your sacred heritage:
Kindle with holy zeal the coward hearts of those
Who, in our greatest need, quit us to seek repose;
Chase far from the court that envy, worthy of hate,
Which measures our life's achievements by its own weight,
Which renders us loathsome to him whose very being
Depends on You — who, but for us, would be no king.

Who held out more strongly against the haughty army[25]
Of Caesar,[26] as he trampled underfoot the glory          90
Of the magnanimous French? Who hazarded more
To maintain our lily against the rage of war?
Who retook Calais, secure for two hundred years,
Gave the English forces the taste of our own fears?
At Metz who chased the Eagle, caused the Rhine to cease
Its flow, but the Guisian arm, bulwark of peace?[27]
Who in civil combat could more ably resist
The earth-born giants of the fifth Evangelist?[28]
Who has more ably parried the dangerous blows
Of conspiring traitors, rebel Huguenots,                   100
Than I? With shield of faith and helm of esperance,
For my God, for my King — but for what recompense?
The King nurtures in his heart the wish inhumane
To slake his minions' thirst with the blood of Lorraine.
With venomous tongue, his councillors' defamation
Falsely poisons the honour of our reputation,
Enchants his mind,[29] and into his very bones deep
Instilling bitter arsenic, keeps him from sleep.
    They are constantly renewing their fine tirades[30]
Concerning our Holy League and our barricades;            110
Incessantly returning like dogs to their vomit,
No chance to cry out against me do they omit:
That I'm itching, they yap, without catching their breath,
To snatch his honour and sceptre, and cause his death;
That the people love me and loathe his partisans,
That against them I stir up all the Parisians.

Before this evil disturbs us more seriously,
And this sad fear acquires new intensity,
I am resolved to make a stand against their game
And will suffer ten thousand deaths to save my name.      120
I will go and speak with the King; my sound conscience
Is at my constant service as shield and defence.
*He whose heart is valiant, and from all vice is clear,*

*Will never be seen to blench — with shame or with fear.*
*The King's majesty, which from heaven takes its essence,*
*Does not excuse the crime of blaming innocence.*[31]
I shall not quit his Court, despite my deep vexation,
Until of hate or love I have a declaration.

CHORUS

What foreign nation
Has known more sufferance,                                    130
Greater tribulation,
Than miserable France?

Sacked cities, the sword, all horrors,
The fiercest cruelties,
War's dire furors,
For us are banalities.

Since the sad jousting,
Since that tournament so fell
That murdered our king,
The second Henri, at Tournelles,[32]                         140

Our kings, young orphans, more quick
To take to tears than arms,
Of the cunning heretic
Have heard the alarms.

Since then heaven, displeased,
Our miseries to crown,
Avenger of ill, has not ceased
Its anger to pour down.

We have seen our cities
Reduced from rich to poor,                                    150
Teeming with calamities
From incessant civil war.

Murdered before our faces
Our fathers, sons, relations;
Defiled are God's holy places
By shameful profanations.

Yet heaven has not conceded
To the enemy the triumph;
By its arm in combat speeded,
We cause the Church to triumph.[33]      016

The bee-like German who comes zooming
At the jingle of money bags,
When he hears bronze pieces booming,
Leaves in France his battle-flags.

He carries this tormenting
Sorrow with him as he flies:
That he came here for the King
Against the House of Guise.[34]

# Act II

### Scene i.

## Argument

*In imitation of the ancient writers of tragedy, in the place of the counsellor appears the Queen Mother, who, being Italian and, moreover, Florentine, is shrewd in the management of her affairs, but who also, as the mother of three kings, and consequently more intimately acquainted with their intentions, speaks with a freedom appropriate to her authority and, as occasion serves, tempers the corrupt humours of him whose only thought is of bloody vengeance against the holy league of the Princes.[35] But the needful remonstrances she employs, foreseeing the precipice towards which the King is hurtling to his own danger, restrain him and in-*

*duce him to agree and forget the hatred he has conceived against the House of Lorraine, to the point where he requests her to cause the Duke of Guise to come, on the assurance of his faith, to the Estates appointed at Blois.*

*[Enter the King and the Queen Mother.]*

KING

What does it serve to be a kind and humane king?
To have the sovereign sceptre of France in my keeping?          170
With a speech to have led the fiercest hearts along,
As if by links of chain they were bound to my tongue?
To have prevailed over a hundred thousand dangers?
What good is my subjects' love or the fear of strangers,
Madame, if always I feel such anxiety?
If under my native sky, I can find no safety?
If always the Guisards,[36] enjoying their free lives,
Keep brandishing their murderously slicing knives?
If the bold Leaguer who shelters under your wing
Would turn me into a submissive underling?          180
I wish to be king alone — after the Most High,
To have to see no other higher up than I.

QUEEN MOTHER

What, from being a royal recluse — *not* humane,[37]
Fitter for distaff than for sceptre — do you gain?
Thinking to nourish hearts with the breath of your speeches,
When your mouth with double tongue inconstantly preaches,
Blindly unable to foresee your daily dangers,
Yielding our lilies to be devoured by strangers?
Sire, what good do you get from setting your France
In resentment against you, in livid defiance?          190
What serves it to have let your mind become depraved —
To wayward minions, to Cyprian joys enslaved?
What novel fit of madness, I pray you recount,
Of anger and spite, torments you on that account?

KING

To form leagues against me? To aim their schemes at me?
At me, great master of a double monarchy?[38]
And shall I not put my right of revenge to use?

QUEEN MOTHER

If some offence there is, speak rather of excuse.

KING

An act deserving death, offence beyond reclaim.

QUEEN MOTHER

*Accusing someone else means not accepting blame.*      200

KING

*Great crime always asks to be punished with great torment.*

QUEEN MOTHER

*Great evil asks of us to show ourselves more clement.*

KING

Barricades in Paris! By my subjects subjected!

QUEEN MOTHER

Why should you be angry, if you were kept protected?

KING[39]

Paris, whom I honoured with my ennobling presence,
Where I caused to run freely the horn of abundance,
Where I caused to flourish the high arts of Athena,
The Court and the Senate, twin delights of Astraea,[40]
My battering tempest on your head hurling down,
I will see you reduced to the smallest small town.      210
Your overthrown ramparts I will sow full of salt;
The children shall curse their fathers, lured into fault.
Detesting your unbridled boldness, your descendants
Shall see you strewn in a hundred bush-covered fragments:
The survivors shall say to their children, this space

Was Paris once, and was our monarchs' dwelling-place.
The bitter cold of your winter has now arrived;
Of flowers, fruit, all green things, you shall be deprived.
Paris thrice feeble, which once was the ornament
Of all that appears in this lower element,                     220
The pearl of all cities, of the world the Princess,
By me raised to honour, by me brought to distress.
Your towers that in the heavens their foreheads hide,
Your palaces for kings, my ancestors, edified,
Your sumptuous homes, your houses of sanctity,
My Court your Ilium, my Louvre your ecstasy,
My Seine, which for your service raises its deep flows,
Your rich bridges, which in themselves are more like boroughs,
Your flourishing commerce, your shops so prosperously
Abounding in rich produce from the land and sea,              230
Thus all you have that's holy, beautiful, distinguished,
Is lost, because the torchlight of your king's extinguished.

QUEEN MOTHER

I believe you wish yourself to let the door gape
Open and all the happiness of France escape,
And to become a bloody prince, hardly a mild,
When you give rein in this way to anger so wild.

KING

Madame, you are never lacking in excuses,
Cunning as you are, to disguise the plots and ruses
Of rebellious subjects; but I am amply strong
To maintain the right, as well as to punish wrong.          240

QUEEN MOTHER

And do you wish never to display anything
Of justice or faith, the two bulwarks of a king?

KING

Madame, is it your wish the law should be violated
To allow that revolt the Leaguers instigated?

QUEEN MOTHER

Around your heart you have set up some solid wall
Of stone: it's you who violate right, faith, nature — all.

KING

Tossed by every wind, I can steer no other course
Than to conjure the death of these conspirators.[41]

QUEEN MOTHER

With a wound that will not heal, ulcerate your mind,
Have a soul as haughty-proud as it is unkind,                    250
Have a Scythian or a Sarmat's heart,[42] cast down
To earth everyone you look on with your mere frown,
Let your breast with the blackest poison be infused,
With horror and madness let your will be suffused,
Live on human blood, eschew all other delights
Apart from cowardly killings, murders, and fights,
Show yourself a bastard to your ancestral race,
Have nothing of their uprightness, their heart, their grace,
From a king, become a tyrant — all this unless
You shake off the shadow of your unhappiness,                    260
Unless, foreseeing wisely the ills of discord,
With the Princes you can reach an honest accord.

KING

Accord against myself? League with my enemies?
Defend rebels who would bring their king to his knees?

QUEEN MOTHER

Despoil those who themselves have put France to spoil; ravage
Those who have subjected your France to sack and pillage;
Beat into submission those hideous mad snakes
Whose fury our minds with panic and terror shakes.

KING

That's not the prey, Madame, of which this League's in search.

QUEEN MOTHER

The reason for their war is the Faith and the Church.          270
All against your enemies have taken up arms,
While you take no action to defend them from harms.
Do they not have good reason, those generous souls,
To haul us from the floods, filled with perilous shoals,
To prevent schism, allied with impiety,
From subverting the honour of your Majesty,
And so that your hypocrisy shall not inter
Your ancestors' religion in your sepulchre,
Nor France, which for twelve hundred years the flourishing
Sprays[43] of the cross to heaven has been brandishing,          280
Regret that in the end the faith is withered, dried
Up in its bosom, which Saint Denis sowed so wide.
Open your eyes and observe the heretic furor,
The reason why we suffer from this civil horror.
Why, with its serpentine hair, the colour of blood,
Does despair, does fear, become a terrible flood?[44]
Inconstant and uncertain, you forever sway
To the words of the first one to bid you good-day.
Nothing but pure duty, desire within bound,
Inspires them your lily, your life, to keep sound.          290
O what rare love they feel!

KING

What exquisite ambition!

QUEEN MOTHER

Nothing but abounding zeal.

KING

Nothing but a fiction.[45]

QUEEN MOTHER

God knows their inner state.

KING

Their souls are plain to me.

QUEEN MOTHER

They are strong and great.

KING

In burning and thievery.

QUEEN MOTHER

Alas, I am all seized with trembling, and my heart,
Astonished at these fearful words, resigns its part,
When the bitter memory of fortunes endured
Batters the chamber where my sad thoughts are immured;
When I think of all the hardships they have been through —
Their sorrows, sighs, and blows — for me, for France, for you,   300
I say that some demon has control of your mind[46]
You so forget your cousin Guise, and turn unkind.

KING

To my thorough regret, I made the Guisards great,
Since I've bought their services at such a high rate.

QUEEN MOTHER

Neither name, nor sceptre, nor Church were yours to prize,
Nor religion itself, without the House of Guise —
Those noble heroes, who preserved you by their aid,
Who came to your defence, and whose exertions stayed
Your tottering state, whose fortitude ever shows
Itself most constant amid the bloodiest blows.               310
Schism has a hundred throats, and the strange delusion
Seizing on French hearts, and sowing in them confusion,
That came from Germany (stronghold of those bold liars
Who would plunder our souls, filch the faith of our sires),
Was already sapping the foundations of France,
If those good Guisians had not offered resistance.
Two noble-minded brothers:[47] a Pollux, a Castor;
A good prelate and a duke; a Nestor, a Hector:
François with the law, the valour, the soldier's might;
Charles by his prayer, his tears, and his prudent foresight.   320

With love of religion teeming in both their hearts
Those two served our country as formidable ramparts.

KING

That breed was never valued but in evil days.

QUEEN MOTHER

*Blessed be the evils that add lustre to praise.*[48]

KING

The Guisards gain praise by heaping dispraise on me.

QUEEN MOTHER

When they were victorious, you have seized the trophy.

KING

I kept the Germans from sacking many a town.

QUEEN MOTHER

Saul a mere thousand, David ten thousand cut down.

KING

I vanquished the *reîtres* in returning to Paris.

QUEEN MOTHER

And your weapons? — delight, the simper, the caress!　　330
That's how you led the fight against that mighty host —
And you would steal the credit from Guise with your boast?
When that courageous Duke takes the field in your place,
When the people tremble as the drum beats apace,
When fear and terror strike the whole of France with wonder,
When heaven seems to rain down cannon-shot as thunder,
When all — sword, fire, and blood — with rage seethes and boils,
You wallow in your pleasure's voluptuous toils
With those minions, greedy harpies insatiable,
Their talons teeming with choice morsels from the table,　　340
Whose gluttonous stomachs wolf down the people's bread,
And who famish for more, the fuller they are fed —

Court sponges, whose society you so entices,
Inconstant octopuses, perfect in all vices.
Like those bears that let themselves be led by their noses,
You're abused by a devil human form encloses:
Treacherous Épernon, who at no plot will stick
Aimed against God, or you, to please the heretic.[49]

KING

Épernon, above all others, my love has won,
Without him at court my life drags wearily on.[50]                   350
Return my minion, return, and comfort afford
To the half-dead person of the King, your good lord!
But then, you wouldn't dare: envious of your worth,
These Guisards make you hated in heaven and earth.
Desperate and jealous, with passion so extreme,
For their accusations they have no other theme
Than your devotion to me, my love to you, snarling
Because you follow me, because you are my darling.

QUEEN MOTHER

Prince pitifully abused! Do you not see how
All you possess, the very state, is wasting now?                      360
Tyrant and Atheist — those names you've come to own
By insisting on pleasing Épernon alone.

KING

How am I a Tyrant?

QUEEN MOTHER
                              You plague tyrannically
Your people with taxes, the Church with impiety.
You dissipate its goods, breaking the sacred canons;
Its holy patrimony you give to the minions.
You steal the wealth of the Crucifix to prepare
The bloody fight against it that one day you will dare.
Kings live for subjects, tyrants for themselves alone.
A king loves right and law, a tyrant makes his own.                  370

You live for no one — not even yourself: it's true;
You do not love yourself, and nobody loves you.[51]

KING

And how then an Atheist?

QUEEN MOTHER
                                        In you not a thing
May be seen that's worthy of a Most Christian King.[52]
If holy knowledge of God in you had its part
Or nurturing faith were imprinted on your heart,
Neither Turk nor Alcoran[53] nor Epicurean,
Neither yet the Calvinist nor the Lutheran,
Nor the Machiavel, that worshipper of fortune,[54]
Would meet with a welcome in you so opportune.                380
Geneva would not have your hand to be its shield
But rather by its Prince[55] would have been forced to yield —
Geneva that great whore,[56] whose impudence pretends,
Thanks to Bourbon,[57] that royalty from her descends,
Who makes flow around her a constant bloody tide,
Who, without your seeing her, stabs you in the side.
If your soul were wholly God's, pure and without blemish,
Never would you have had the garter from the English.[58]
You would not be caressing, sister-like, their queen;
The Huguenot in France would not be so serene.                390
Then Justice and Faith your spirit would truly know,
And you would boldly sally forth against the foe.

KING

Do I not amply show my virtues as a Christian
Towards the reformed cloisters, Flagellant and Cistercian?

QUEEN MOTHER

In that way do falsehood, vice, and hypocrisy
Assume the arms of justice, truth, and piety.

KING

It is pure zeal for our faith that burns in my heart.

QUEEN MOTHER

To become a lion you play the fox's part.[59]

KING

Heaven will stay with me, if every subject flies;
If heaven denies me, I've got Hell against Guise.[60]          400

QUEEN MOTHER

You cause to perish the hope that in you did thrive
When François[61] was on the throne and Charles was alive —
That Charles who, when from this ungrateful world he fled,
In an age replete with fire, warfare, and dread,
Pronounced his great regret at having to abandon
France to a heretic, a trifler with religion.

KING

I think that with my sacrifice God should be thrilled,
When as due punishment I have that Leaguer killed.

QUEEN MOTHER

What bloodthirsty spirit, what demon loving pain,
What torturer's fantasy rages in your brain?          410
What thunderbolt consumes you, or what lightning-flashes
Make the fire in your heart again burst from ashes?
Against innocent men you apply the decrees
Of your precious minion.

KING

                              In my nets I shall seize
Them; they shall not escape; it will please me to teach
Them a king is out of their League, beyond their reach.[62]

QUEEN MOTHER

Do you doubt the faith of the Princes from Lorraine?

KING

I doubt the faith of those men who are inhumane.

QUEEN MOTHER

They cause their just consciences to appear to you.

KING

I'll cause all to see what to them is justly due. 420

QUEEN MOTHER

*One purges the head to keep the body in measure.*

KING

They purge me everyday of my strength and my treasure.

QUEEN MOTHER

They always served your father's interests and your own.

KING

They've always sought to occupy the royal throne.

QUEEN MOTHER

No such impudence is in their hearts.

KING

Yes, it's true!

QUEEN MOTHER

They don't think of that, trust me.

KING

Yes, they do, they do!

QUEEN MOTHER

I'm sure of their loyal feeling.

KING

I'm not — not very.

QUEEN MOTHER

They hold you to be King —

KING

King of some monastery![63]

QUEEN MOTHER

May heaven ever render such presages vain!
*Fortune holds human sceptres in amused disdain.*          430

KING

I have Fortune with me, and hope is in my breast.

QUEEN MOTHER

*Unhappy is the king whose mind can never rest.*

KING

But still I am the King, and I cannot agree
That any but the Lord should lord it over me.
By punishing the authors of this tribulation
I shall force from God His fiery indignation.

QUEEN MOTHER

True, but I fear that you will scarcely thus assuage
So many hearts inflamed against you with just rage—
That you will reign alone, with no man's good opinion
And no one left to serve the crown, except some minion.          440

KING

Madam, you know that never did I go to bed
Angry, harbouring thoughts of vengeance in my head:
I vow to be reconciled, assure him from me,
To my cousin of Guise—in all sincerity.

QUEEN MOTHER

Having your royal oath the faith you will maintain,
He is coming to the Estates.

KING

                                        And not in vain.

CHORUS

The king who masters not his heart,
Who cannot give himself a law,
Will seem unworthy of his part,
However many he keeps in awe.                    450

In vain one unable to command
Or rule his own emotions
Will try to countermand
Foreign-bred commotions.

Will he who as his only arms
Has laughter, games, and distaff,
Be first to answer to alarms
When factions threaten mischief?

Will he who merely dons the clothes
Of zeal but lacks true piety,                    460
Tame the barbarous strength of those
Who practice heretic liberty?

He who for one he loves alone
Forfeits all popular support,
Prefers to lose what is his own
Than to chase him from his court.

He who dissimulates his rancour
Beneath benevolence and smiles,
Far from Paris him to lure
Now the Duke of Guise beguiles.                   470

## Scene ii.

### Argument

*The King considers the ultimate proof of his natural inclination to
the welfare of his people to be his departure from Poland, amid
so many dangers, to take in hand the troubles that surrounded*

*them after the death of King Charles* IX *on 3 May 1574. Address-*
*ing himself to Paris, which he believes he has honoured with his*
*presence more than did any of his predecessors, he accuses it of*
*ingratitude and treason, calling to mind the barricades, and he*
*threatens it with everything cruel and furious that an angered*
*Prince can vomit forth against those he does not love. He says*
*that the Duke of Guise controlled the mainsprings of that rebel-*
*lion and engages in the bitterest language against him, unwilling*
*to be persuaded to undertake the destruction of the Huguenots,*
*even though this is the certain remedy for pacifying his realm.*
*His speech sets forth various antitheses, with the idea of keep-*
*ing the two religions together and reintegrating the Huguenots*
*by persuasion rather than by the pistol—upon which, the Duke*
*of Guise presses the point and argues for force as a solution, so*
*as not to maintain in the same family a legitimate spouse and a*
*concubine, pointing out that, since warnings have had no greater*
*effect than patience, mildness should no longer be permitted to*
*harm the nation. Finally the king, convinced by right and truth,*
*agrees with his urgings and authorizes the League, of which he*
*has himself proclaimed leader, and gives order for the holding of*
*the Estates at Blois, desiring the Duke's presence there to give his*
*advice on the articles presented at Chartres.*

KING [*alone*]

For you the sceptre of Sarmatia[64] I rejected,
Your lily's gleam to Arctic peoples I reflected;
With pity for your cries, in your love firm belief,
I thought not of myself but rushed to your relief.
For you, ungrateful France, from Cracow I took flight,
Endangering my life, under cover of night.
I broke the oath on which I'd staked my royalty
And to succour you revealed my disloyalty.[65]
My departure stunned the people there, who lament
Still the majesty of Henri of France absent.                    480
That shows how foolish I was: I should have remained,

Not kept you from harm while letting myself be pained;
I should have abandoned you as my enemy
To those who were making you an anatomy.[66]
When I saw you again you were in wretched state,
Lying stretched out like a body inanimate,
Thinking of nothing but your ruin, with your soul
Tortured in flames, eyes in tears, grief out of control.
I saw your dear children at your feet massacred,
Desecration that temples and altars incurred;[67]                490
I saw your foes flee when I loomed on the horizon,
As night skulks off to hide from the rays of the sun.
I came and dried the flood of tears where you were drowning,
By entry into Paris my victory crowning[68] —
Paris, the only worthy seat of royal greatness;
Paris, so honoured by my liberal largess;
That Paris, that Proteus, changing out of hand,
Which refuses to stoop and bend to my command,
Abused by the Leaguer, who subtly disguises[69]
In piety's name his treacherous enterprises.                500
O Paris, your perfidy my welcome repeals,
Puts me out at your gate and sets wings to my heels.
My dead body alone will re-enter your walls—
Unless I breech them with my crashing cannon-balls.[70]
I am a great and potent king, the Lord's anointed,
As judge of last resort over the French appointed;
My breast and my back, as if clad in armour plates,
My true right protects; from my face love radiates;
I have courage in my heart, and in my hand power,
Sure means to bring about my victorious hour.                510
The impervious shield that my arm boldly wears
Is blind equity itself, which no person spares.
And as my cruel lance, aimed at your mutiny,
I wield what will amaze you: stark authority.
Here stands the king of France, all ready to do battle
With any French traitor who makes of Guise an idol;
Forces are mobilizing from the earth's four corners

To rally with my host against those raving scorners.[71]

But for my friends I have a soft and warming light,
Just like that of the sun, in splendour gleaming bright,      520
Which illuminates their souls, so that they can see,
On one side, mildness, my heart filled with piety,
While, on the other, it discloses their own crime
And will cause them to acknowledge my grace in time.
But for those disloyal hold-outs a flaming torch
I brandish: vengeful lightning, which threatens to scorch
And blast, deformed offspring of the thunder's uproar,
A signal, not to be doubted, of unleashed war.
Unbending, I will make my fierce enemies feed
On their own flesh, on their blood;[72] for having agreed      530
To obey a foreign prince,[73] they'll find themselves thrilling
In madness from drinking the blood of their own spilling;
They shall murder themselves, themselves they thus shall
                                                    vanquish,
A thousand times tortured by the sharpest of anguish.
Like Jupiter the Great, for tears I shall have fire;
My tongue shall shoot forth, as weapons deadly and dire,
An infinite squadron of tempestuous shocks,
Such as my invincible arm already stocks.[74]
Then, mingling the spirit, the breath, the raging storm
To which my lips, mouth, and tongue give violent form,      540
Down upon those fools all that evil shall I fling,
They who form a faction divided from their King —
Divided from their King, from their head, from their father,[75]
Driven by hatred and anger, without a tether[76]
Running in wild fury, boasting of breaking free
Of the natural duty that they owe to me.

*[Enter Duke of Guise.]*

Ah! Here I see the mover of those rebels' actions,
Coming, I don't doubt, to assail me with new factions.

So, then, Cousin, what have you got to say? The fires
You've kindled may spread beyond even your desires.                    550
Everyone says that the blaze is fed by a flame,
Burning in your soul, that deserves ambition's name;
They tell me that, breaking your oath of loyalty,
You form leagues, day by day, of subjects against me.

DUKE OF GUISE

That I arm against you? That I spend thus cruelly
Our Holy League's high blood to do you injury?
That I am a rebel? That my heart would invent
Against the fleur-de-lys some treacherous intent?
That under a holy quarrel's deceptive mask
Lurks a faithless traitor to be taken to task?                        560
That I aspire to royalty's happy state,
That punishment for high treason should be my fate?
That tainted with such crime I should blanch in your presence?
Rather, let just heaven give me death as my sentence!
It is by no means you, my Prince, that I oppose.
For God, for you, for myself, I combat two foes:[77]
One takes your right; the other wrongs you with a spell.
One is your minion, the other an open rebel:
One with open boldness declares his hostile end;
The other, more dangerous, plagues you as a friend.                   570
Yet even they are not my final adversary:
It is that execrable tigress, Heresy.
Atheism, Schism, Presumption I've defied,
Which, with their passport from those two, range far and wide.
For my God, for my faith, for you, and for your France,
We are all in league, but under your dominance.
If you are not content, I have offended you,
Not by rebelling, but only by being true.

KING

Ambition in France was never a useful thing.

DUKE OF GUISE

Ambitious the French do not accuse me of being.                    580

KING

Your devotion, they say, aims at another prize.

DUKE OF GUISE

Never can such talk my honest intents disguise.[78]

KING

Heaven alone knows you, and your designs can weigh.

DUKE OF GUISE

For all France I have put my designs on display.

KING

But for your meddling, France could stop and catch its breath.

DUKE OF GUISE

Yes, if skin and bones can breathe — the image of death.

KING

It's I alone who bear the weight of France's ills.

DUKE OF GUISE

All the state feels that pain, and my own soul it fills.

KING

Keep yourself out of it; to me belongs redress.

DUKE OF GUISE

You will not free yourself alone from such distress.                    590

KING

Patience can teach me how to find the remedy.

DUKE OF GUISE

*Patience turns weak when overwhelmed by misery.*[79]

KING

You seek by one evil another to expel.[80]

DUKE OF GUISE

*Curing by contraries is seen to work quite well.*

KING

Bloodshed should not be the price to bring about concord.[81]

DUKE OF GUISE

*Unhappy is the accord that nourishes discord.*

KING

Peace can never be born out of such bloody throes.

DUKE OF GUISE

*In order to command in peace, there must be blows.*

KING

That means to peace I find difficult to pursue.

DUKE OF GUISE

*All things are easy to a heart open and true.*[82]                    600

KING

Let us devise, Cousin, some strategy more sure.

DUKE OF GUISE

*Infinitely more than mildness force will procure.*

KING

To force the body is not to compel the soul.

DUKE OF GUISE

*The soul lacks force with the body under control.*

KING

Let's content ourselves with bodies; let the hearts go.

DUKE OF GUISE

*Without having both, we will not have crushed the foe.*

KING

We will have outward Catholics, atheists within.

DUKE OF GUISE

*The trappings of our faith cannot conceal such sin.*

KING

They will make a show with hypocritical zeal.

DUKE OF GUISE

*The face cannot show a faith the heart does not feel.*                              610

KING

Not in the body but the soul the sore does lie.

DUKE OF GUISE

*After milder treatment, hot iron we apply.*

KING

I am prompt to pardon, slow to punish offenses.

DUKE OF GUISE

*Chastisements must go hand in hand with recompenses.*

KING

Often harms are avenged when gentleness is used.

DUKE OF GUISE

Your gentleness is universally abused.

KING

A gentle king hangs back[83] when his subjects rebel.

DUKE OF GUISE

So at Amboise and Meaux your brothers knew quite well.

KING

Sooner will fierce lions at our compulsion yield
To plough the ground for us, when we would plant a field,     620
Than this resistant people, raised in liberty,
Born into rebellion against our Majesty.

DUKE OF GUISE

You'll be a second Hercules in victory,
When of that seven-headed beast you've made a trophy.[84]

KING

How many have we seen in massacres mowed down
On the field like ears of wheat, but now, town by town,
Off-shoots from that monstrous stem are coming to light,
Like foul summer caterpillars plaguing our sight.

DUKE OF GUISE

Now or never, as you well know, the crucial thing
Is to perform indeed like a Most Christian King:[85]                    630
*When torments are extreme, extreme must be the cure.*[86]
For you to be able to keep this crown secure,
You cannot simply on the Cross alone rely;
The rod, instead, you must courageously apply.
Provide for dangers of the shipwreck close at hand;
Give evil-doers a lesson they'll understand.
What other counsel do you need but present harms,
Which of themselves cry out to drive you into arms?
Sire, be mindful of that Bohemian king[87]
Who lost his crown for his cowardly wavering —                         640
Who saw his reign fall prey, his country set on fire,
When he failed to do what religion did require.
His cunning enemies, who never gave him cause
To believe that they wished to rise against his laws —
Great in arms, not right, not in faith, but soldiers, strong —
Forced that good king to suffer their ambitious wrong.
Brazenly they increased, against his fertile lands
Launched biting sickles, wielded by their neighbours' hands.
Wenceslas, hard-pressed, their hatred clearly discerned;
He armed, but all too late: the tide could not be turned,                650
And angry heaven, his soul's indolence to punish,
Struck him down with illness, in his sick-bed to languish
And repent, because he had not in good time killed

That dragon of Heresy, as strong as strong-willed;
By fits of madness he was day and night tormented
For having left alone that sect newly invented.
   While the Huguenot step by step concocts his schemes,
According to his appetite pursues his dreams,
Claims to seek only peace, that souls by words are won,[88]
Since Christ did not plant faith at the point of a gun,      660
While he conceals his pillage and impiety,
Pretends to hate warfare and all hostility,
And that one fed on error, if brought to perceive
And know it to be false, is bound then to believe—
Is this not a sign he continues to aspire,
That he seeks to draw back only to leap up higher?
Meanwhile, Sire, it is patent that your restraint
Feeds all this evil, to the whole Church brings a taint.
Rather, for a Christian prince like you, it is meet
To stand up for his God, and to die on his feet.      670

### KING

Believe me, Cousin, my desire is intense
Thoroughly to purge my realm of this pestilence.

### DUKE OF GUISE

If such a benefit to France you can afford,
You will be her darling, her father, and her lord,
The haven of her desires; indeed, ovations
To your heart's content will resound from foreign nations.

### KING

But tell me, how shall we bring about their downfall?

### DUKE OF GUISE

These rebels we shall never overcome at all,
If we do not root out the discord in our hearts,
If your Majesty and we do not accord our parts—      680
If, with visage frank and open, courage entire,
You do not manifest with us a zealous fire.

If you wish this war to see its final hour,
You must unite with our own your royal power.
Banish from your sight those provocative advisers,
Those mere leeches of the people, those tax-devisers;
Let your arm no longer be a shield that protects
Huguenots when, beneath your wing, they brave your subjects.[89]
Give heed to your treasury, wasted by expense,
Your finances the prey of those with influence.                    690
Cut off corrupt amusements, banish idle pleasure;
Run full tilt at vices, impose becoming measure;
Punish that young upstart[90] who lulls you with his charms
To maintain untruth and give licence to all harms.
Abrogate with the Turks that faithless alliance,
And with the English — a stinking sewer for France.
To your people, fearful of ill, you must make known
Who it is that will be successor to your throne.

KING

I accept the Union; I wish to bear the name
Of your chief in pursuing such a sacred aim.                       700
The recent articles[91] I am far from refusing;
They shall be granted after a proper perusing
By the Estates we shall hold at Blois, publicly
Maintaining faith with all, as is my sacred duty.
Meanwhile, so as not by negligence to allow
The least fuel to feed the fire burning now,
I shall have one army dispatched into Guyenne,
Another to Dauphiné with the Duke of Mayenne;
Do not doubt, Cousin, that I'll keep my royal word:
I am a Prince of faith; a king is never perjured.                  710

DUKE OF GUISE

I wish that propitious heaven may long enrol
These longed-for sentiments within your Christian soul.

KING

If, breaking this sacred Union, from faith I swerve,

If all of you in safety I do not preserve,
If for your sake into battle I fail to ride,
If with strength and courage I am not at your side,
If the zeal of my faith shows the least sign of slack,
May heaven, just heaven, crash down upon my back,
May the Eternal, who has made me doubly crowned,
To fell Avernus[92] hurl me, its pit most profound,        720
And, bearing the infamous shame of such a spurn,
May I abandon France, and to Poland return.

### DUKE OF GUISE

I call to witness Him who holds the hearts of kings,
Who by his laws to your Majesty honour brings,
Who led my ancestors to Eastern victory,[93]
Whose faith and love imprint my mind indelibly,
That all-good, great, and holy triple Sovereign,
Who for champions elects the stock of Lorraine:
I avow by heaven, by the earth, and by fire,
And by my motive for war, that sacred desire,        730
That I will be true to you, and shall never cease
Till France, under you, is brought to a state of peace.

### CHORUS

The hideous monster Discord
Rolls her burning eyes,
Her gnashing teeth applies
To devour Concord.

Now she crouches concealed
Beneath the ashes of her Mars;
Here and there her fire smoulders,
But her flame is repealed.        740

The efforts of ruinous war
By Concord shall be banned,
From this rich and fertile land
Expelled forevermore.

The Union, of nurturing faith
And Heaven sole daughter born,
Together with the King is sworn
The heretic to scathe.

The Union's proclamation,
Ordained by edict holy,                              750
Takes hope and credit wholly
From the rebel to his nation.

The Church obtains the prize
Of service and liberty;
The Union joins by decree
The King and the Duke of Guise.

O stars, whose ample dance,
With due order, compass, weight,
Holds the world in governance,
Do not our hopes frustrate.                          760

Do not deceive our esperance
With a false opinion:
Do not deceive poor France,
Trusting to the Union.

If the God of Battles grants
Rewards that match our merit,
We would have no chance
A single pardon to inherit.

But His grace, which surpasses,
In its just perfection,                              770
The weight of our trespasses,
Saves His people from destruction.[94]

# Act III

## Scene i.

### Argument

*Against his will was the poet constrained to interpose amidst the majesty and grandeur of those who play this Tragedy a man of such slight value as Épernon. Yet the certain opinion which the entire people of France have regarding his behaviour, and the fact that he above all others enkindled the King's bloody deliberations against the House of Lorraine, have caused him to enter in this third Act, in the form of a desperate man, a sorcerer, with all his demonism, having no other present instrument at his disposition but the opportunity afforded by the Estates and the public pledge of faith for deceiving all religion in France in the person of our Princes.*

ÉPERNON [*alone*]

Heaven endowed my father with a noble state,[95]
But I am worth no more for that, degenerate[96]
As I am from the Nogarets' nobility:
Neither their honour nor faith in myself I see,
No trace of ancestral virtue. A putrid bane
Of fury, itch of frenzy, tortures my foul brain
By day and night; dragons, demons of every kind
In their thousands, ride on my breath, ravage my mind.[97]        780

Come, you fell Eumenides, issue out of Hell;[98]
Now let loose the imprisoned souls you force to dwell
In the obscure dungeons of that dim habitation
Which never from the daylight receives visitation.
All of you I invoke, O shadows pale and gaunt,
Who the gloomiest caverns of the Styx do haunt:
Rage, run forth, burst out, come carrying in your hands,
To harry humanity, terror, steel, fire-brands;
Guide, execute, the enterprise of my nightmare,

And then I shall set you at liberty — I swear.                              790
Abortions of the night, the offspring of confusion,[99]
Raging-mad ministers of discord's wild diffusion,
Who arm against the father the son's stubborn heart,
Who inspire children to tear their mothers apart,
Who witness the frustration that subverts my pleasure
When the party of the heretics fails to prosper —
Come, cursed spirits, to the rescue of your race,
Which that Barricader[100] seeks to doom to disgrace;
Surge from sulphurous Styx, from boiling Phlegethon,
From bloody Cocytus, and from black Acheron.[101]              800

Come, companion monsters, with your horrid images,
Turn upon Blois the terror of frightful visages,
Let your hands become hooks, your eyes with fire glare;
Let your voices be cannon, writhing snakes your hair.
Change Blois into hell; there transport your instruments
Of pain: your wheels and gibbets, flames, and whips —
                                                        all torments.

O daughters of the night, whirled in pain as you are,
Revolted spirits of the faction of Navarre,
I offer you my soul, my life, all I possess,
If only you will grant my longed-for happiness;              810
If, with the full fire of your fierce agonies,
On the life of the chief of the Leaguers you seize:
Snatch that wretched Guise away from his stubborn band,
He who dandles the will of the King in his hand,
And has so thoroughly wrought him to his opinion
As to make him his partner in his splendid Union.[102]
Of the faithful church's innocent blood[103] a torrent
He sheds to slake his heart's thirst, cruel and abhorrent;
As tall as he is strong, as brave as he is cruel,
Pluto himself he would encounter in a duel;                  820
Twice already he has wielded his valiant blade
To defeat the German forces bringing us aid.[104]

A great prince and soldier, a great Duke and great knight,
The pillar of his faith unfailingly upright —
The people swarm after, Nobles and Church, with cries
Far and wide, "Long live Guise!" —and again, "Long live Guise!"
Lording thus over us, he will trample athwart
The King's body one day, not to mention the court[105] —
The court, by me adorned with all ills that abound,
Deformities anywhere on earth to be found.                             830
(For I, already damned, slavish captive of sin,
Carry all faults, all wretchedness, hidden within.)
There my example the most sordid acts inspires,
To swell your booty and add fuel to your fires.
The glittering jewel of my career of vices
The scum of the earth to my base service entices;
Pleasure, incest, and Eros I put though their paces
To prodigious effect in the Louvre's dark places.
My manifold evil the court so bows and pinions,
It is nothing but the foul haunt of perverse minions.                  840
I grant, by false counsel, my King the privilege
Of giving free rein to rape, theft, and sacrilege;
I teach him that pleasure alone should be obeyed,
That enemies are to be flattered, then betrayed,
That the recipe for peace is simple and clear:
Crush rebels, for their crimes, with massacres and fear;
That a king is not subject to keeping his word,
If his hunger for vengeance is thereby deterred;
That a means of avoiding princes' insolence,
Is to give much to do and little recompense;                           850
That it's enough for a king to put falsely on
An outward show of faith or of zeal for religion.
This sacred lore he would have put in practice soon,
If Guise had not induced him to alter his tune,
If the splendid Union urged by that Cataline[106]
Had not persuaded him to take a different line:
That Union, which promises to put Mars in chains,
To have Heresy sent back to suffer hell-pains;

That Union which unites, brings together, accords
All France against us and will pacify discords;                    860
That Union which means that Bourbon's grand champion ,
That great and goodly Prince, my master and companion,
Shall never see the crown of France upon his head —
That crown by which his heart to warfare is incited.
Miserable Union, bulwark to all the state,
That banishes the Bourbon, calls him apostate.[107]

Megaera,[108] of total ruin the fell harbinger,
By my soul, which acts as your faithful messenger,
By Cocytus, Tantalus,[109] burning Phlegeton,
By your two sisters Alecto and Tisiphone,                          870
By Minos the cruel, Rhadamanthus the potent,[110]
By the poison that from your gaping[111] throat you vent,
By the numberless demons that with me consort,
By Lechery and Pride, which provide me with sport,
By mad, outrageous Error, by infidel Schism,
By stinking Heresy and filthy Atheism,
By the infinite evils that breed in my bones,
By extortions and taxes my power condones —
With cruelty and horror, by means inhumane,
Annihilate, kill them, shed the blood of Lorraine;                 880
Make these Guisards' massacre live in memories:
Strong they are as Caesars, dauntless as Maccabees.[112]
To assist your betrayal of that valiant race,
Make use of the Estates to hide your cruel face —
Of faith and mercy vowed in solemn testament,
Sworn in the eyes of God upon the sacrament,
That thereby our King, who dissembles with such ease,
May be esteemed by all a second Hercules.[113]

CHORUS

Dull, sad, and pale, Envy
Now eats out her heart,                                            890
Because royal Majesty
With our League takes part.

Like an octopus voracious,
Her own flesh she does tear,
To see the King no longer gracious
To one who had been so dear.

Like a thunderbolt that smashes
An edifice great and noble,
She explodes and flashes
To effect a minion's will.                    900

She rallies all Avernus
To the banner of Épernon,
Against a great Duke who honours
All his designs with renown.

With her fury she defies
Those who follow merit,
Who have a heart lofty and wise,
And equity of spirit.

She gave the sword of war
To Marius, to Sulla,                          910
To Pompey and to Caesar,
When Rome she oversaw.

A plague she is far worse
Than Busiris the brutal,
Than Stygian Cerberus
Or Agrigentum's brazen bull.[114]

### Scene ii(a) [The Estates of Blois].

### Argument

*The city of Blois was chosen for the assembly of the Estates, which began as happily as they were unhappily interrupted. They were initiated by the surest means possible of invoking divine assistance: processions, fastings, holy communion, the regular stations*

of the cross in all the churches — all these were observed by com-
mandment of the King himself. The sessions of all the groups were
placed in order, so as to avoid altercations, according to the rank of
the provinces and the towns, which had their deputies representing the Clergy, the Nobility, and the Third Estate. The venue of
this royal, venerable, and illustrious assembly was a hall measuring twenty-two toises[115] in length, of considerable width, in which
were set up the seats of all the participants, enclosed with barriers,
and in the middle a scaffold supporting a great stage with the King
on his royal throne, the Queen Mother, and the Queen Consort.
At the base of this, beside their chairs, were certain officers of the
crown. And still lower were two benches whose backs and seats
were covered with purple velvet adorned with fleurs-de-lys, on
one of which were four Princes of the Blood, namely the Cardinals
of Bourbon and of Vendôme, and the Counts of Soissons and of
Montpensier. On the other were my lords the Dukes of Nemours,
of Nevers, and of Retz. Facing these benches to the left of the
King were, on another, three cardinals — of Guise, of Lenoncourt,
and of Gondi — and on the other, further back towards the barrier,
the Archbishop of Langres and the Bishop of Châlons. My lord
of Guise was on a chair covered with purple velvet as the Grand
Master of France, with his baton in his hand, his back turned towards the King, and his face towards the people.[116] His brother,
my lord the Duke of Mayenne, whose assigned place was at the
King's foot, as representing the position of Grand Chamberlain
of France, by the grace of God was not present,[117] and there was
nobody in his place or in those of the four Marshals. The other
officers had eminent positions according to their degrees, such as
the Commanders of the Order of the Holy Spirit, the Councillors
of State, and the Comptrollers of Finance. The bishops, abbots,
and chiefs of the Orders had their places assigned according to
the responsibilities they bore. The first order of business was the
election of the Presidents of all the Orders. The Cardinals of Guise
and of Bourbon presided for the Clergy, the Count of Brissac and
the Baron of Matignac for the Nobility, and, for the third Estate,
the Provost of the Merchants of the city of Paris. The King entered

*the hall wearing his great Order around his neck, the whole as-*
*sembly standing with heads uncovered until, he and the queens*
*having been seated, he pronounced his speech, of which the poet*
*has given a reduced version, which, however, has neither the elo-*
*quence nor the grace with which it was delivered.*

*[The Estates assemble. The King enters with the Queen and Queen Mother.*
*They take their seats.]*

KING

Eternal God, who in the air, by land and sea
Make manifest the torches of Your Majesty,
Who have raised me up as Prince of so many Princes,
Entrusted to my hand two mighty provinces,[118]                    920
Honoured me by granting of each the laurel crown;
You who of all the universe bear the renown,
And of my ancestors, direct Your calming gaze
And spirit on this congress in these troubled days.
In Your sight and mine this people is here united,
That our hopes for heaven's blessing may be requited.

I rejoice to see here all the Orders of France,
Reflecting with me to reduce her sufferance—
Sufferance tenacious, but for just cause imposed
On our wild hearts by Him who has all things disposed,     930
Headlong to propel us, as with our crimes we surfeit,
From the evil-spawning monster[119] into the pit.
So does my reign, alas, seem nothing but a ship
Delivering to the world a cargo of hardship.
After following a thousand different courses
Through so many storms raised up by contrary forces,
To banish once and for all discord and division,
From this moment forth I embrace your sacred Union;
And, willing to hazard death, freely for its sake
My power, my kingdom, my life I put at stake.                    940
As in my cradle faith furnished my nursery,

I would wish my tomb to be that of Heresy,[120]
And that by such a death I may strangle the anguish
In which our conflicts cause us painfully to languish.
The many worthy trophies I have brought to France,
The love of my allies, the fear of my opponents,
Are certain testimonies of my right hand's zeal
In preserving both the faith and the commonweal.
Did Heaven not make me its chosen instrument
For repulsing the Germans' arrogant intent?[121]          950
I saw myself sole conqueror of their wild bands,
Which were certain of destroying France in my hands.
When on the banks of the Loire my resolute bearing
They saw fearlessly opposed to their shameful daring,
Like a thief on his way to the gallows, they showed
On their faces what desperate terror I sowed.
My well-ordered battalions inspired such fright,
That they vanished with lightning speed at the mere sight,
And the remnants of that great army, come to seize
Its booty greedily from a France on its knees,          960
Found no other refuge than my frank charity:
I pardon those wretches who have offended me;
I show that far greater love and grace I possess
Than they can manifest audacity or madness.

It has never been seen that my courage has failed;
I've resisted more strongly, more strongly assailed.
Youthful in years, but with courage beyond my age,
All saw me boldly oppose the renegade rage
Of those disturbers of the peace; my resolute
Deeds were credited with bearing the longed-for fruit.          970
There never has been seen, nor shall there ever be,
A king who manifests his faith more openly,
Whose friendship to the good matches his enmity
To those who ravage towns and fields with cruelty;
The French Alcides[122] on the lips of everyone
Flies from Paris to Fez, land of the setting sun.

If the heavens appear to thwart us constantly,
Cruel and resistant, deaf to our every plea,
If our France a thousand grim adversities knows,
And seems all but beaten down by such grievous blows;          980
If beneath the burden of war we feel her groan
Without truce or rest, the fault is not mine alone.
Though for this evil I do not myself excuse,
To your faces your factions also I accuse,
Regretting that so many foremost in the realm
Direct their course against me, I who man the helm:
Your divisions, my subjects and good Catholics,
Have played into the hands of scheming heretics.
What king has ever found himself in such upheaval?
What monarch has been subjected to greater evil?          990
This division has sadly impeded our progress;
In Poitou it frustrated my personal prowess,
Where Heaven, I think, would as much success have lent me
As victory and honour elsewhere it has sent me.[123]
What was I to do, poor man, caught in those contraries,
Doubtful both of my friends and of my adversaries?
At the same time, I witnessed my sceptre ringed round
By rebels, the very same whom heaven had bound
To me as vassals, as subjects. They did not shame
To put their souls in service to another's aim.          1000
To arm and form leagues without our authority —
Is that not a crime against royal majesty?
The authors of that evil, despite my long patience,
One day shall come to own their cowardly offence.

Courage, then, gentlemen; from now on may you cease
To be, by your divisions, enemies to peace.
Combat along with me the heretic's wild hate,
And everything that harms the welfare of the state.
With eyes, hearts, and hands, good subjects, take arms with me
Against those embodiments of obstinacy          1010
Who, spreading amongst us Heresy's sordid bane,

Maintain bodies in bloodshed and the soul in pain.
Your fear that, at my death, you may be left behind
As subjects of an apostate[124]  is in my mind;
Yet my God, if He pleases, on my faithful marriage
Will bestow the ornament of male lineage —
One who, like me, shall bear piety in his heart,
Prudence in his mind, in his eye a gentle part,
Who shall deliver you from this cruel slavery,
And crush your raging enemies with his bravery.                    1020
*The strong are born of the strong; high-minded desires*
*Descend necessarily from valiant sires.*[125]
Meanwhile, to hurl back the evil in preparation
Upon our enemies, who swarm, by conjuration,
From deep Taenarus,[126] swearing as their common cause
To steal our faith, soil our lily, impose their laws,
I set myself against them, declare my life's aim
The rescue of Religion, so reduced to shame,
And give my flesh to be pierced by spear, steel, or fire
For my God, for my faith,[127] as honest thoughts require.[128]    1030
I shall not be seen my royal power to spare —
If I do not lack funds:[129] my treasury is bare;
I need little myself; I would not ask for more,
*Yet money remains the true fire-brand of war,*
*War's instrument, its nerve and sinew; no expense*
*Can be deemed excessive in one's country's defence;*
*Armaments and soldiers to warfare are essential,*
*Yet without money they become inconsequential.*
*A combattant may easily enter the lists;*
*With difficulty then he suddenly desists.*                        1040
*A king takes upon himself all matters of state,*
*Yet his people must help him to carry the weight.*
But given that the will and money are not lacking,
It is imperative to have the Union's backing.
*The enterprise of warfare never worse succeeds*
*Than when upon dissension constantly it feeds.*
Never hope to see peace's concord and relief,

Unless you see France get behind a single chief.

I join with you: now follow — all of you — your King,
And never lend your faith to Fortune as a play-thing.          1050
This will cause happiness to open wide its gate
And from shipwreck so imminent preserve the state.
I subject myself to the canons of my law:
If I lapse, the duty and faith you may withdraw
That bind you to me; then let no one ever after
Live in fear of my hand or to my crown defer.
The whole extent I claim for my authority
Is a desire to observe what I decree.
*And I seek to prove that a good Prince must obey*
*The self-same law that he applies where he holds sway.*          1060

By the body of my Christ, holy sacrament
That I take tomorrow — immortal nourishment,
Antidote to death — my friends, I pledge you my troth
To uphold the Union, and if I break that oath,
May the Eternal shrink my lofty royalty
To pettiness, sans power, pomp, or loyalty;
From the Prince I am, holding slavery in scorn,
Make me a mere serf to those on my manor born;
Let the emboldened vassal, in his indignation,
Trample my potency into humiliation;          1070
In all my battles, I hope that my valour fails —
And may I be made to vomit blood through my entrails.[130]

I command you all — yea, I conjure all of you
By Him who gave me this high station in your view:[131]

By the ancient zeal of true Frenchmen, who, above
Themselves or their families, give the crown their love;
By my fathers, your kings, by their innocent bones,
Which rest at Saint Denis[132] beneath the graven stones;
By the passionate devotion with which you cherish

Your country, so battered it seems about to perish; 1080
By what your fathers' toil has made your legacy,
And by your very selves, my vassals dear to me,
I beseech you to embrace this most sacred quarrel,
Doubting no more than I do that the cause is moral.
No longer be divided; give over your factions,
Which against the state foment these seditious actions.
Otherwise the Eternal, our fathers' great God,
Will afflict you again with his punishing rod;
His justice will hurl its hail of thunder and fire
Upon you, your children, and those that they shall sire. 1090
And on that day when He shall doom perpetually
Your leagues, your factions, and your rank duplicity,
From His holy will I shall have my vindication,
Which endures no false painting or dissimulation.[133]
Now, never have I hoped from you the furtherance
Of any other aim than the good of our France—
France, which I see, even in seeing you, alas,
Craving for its miseries safe harbour and solace.

### Scene ii(b) [The Estates of Blois, continued].

## Argument

*This is a summary of the remonstrances delivered by the Arch-bishop of Bourges, Patriarch and Primate of Aquitaine, in the name of the clergy, in which he deplores the contempt of the Catholic religion, now in the possession of France for more than fourteen hundred years. In order to maintain and preserve it in its integrity, restoring it to its former lustre, he urges, as the remedy, the need to leave discord and authorize the holy Union of the Princes, for one sole and fundamental purpose, namely, to prevent the crown of France from falling, after the King's death, into the hands of a prince opposed to that Catholic faith which he has followed from his childhood. And he exhorts the Union not to suffer a heresy to be set up against the religion of himself and his fathers, a new altar against the true altar, a king against the source of his royal*

*authority, a people separate from him who possesses its towns*
*and levies taxes upon it.*


### THE CLERGY

Hear us, O Heavens, you souls of the holy saints;
Give ear to our laments, our sighs, and our complaints,          1100
Dwellers in immortality, who share the bliss
Of sacred angels in that starry edifice.
Of the ills that plague us, and bitter sufferance,
I complain in the presence of a King of France.
I make my complaint of the demise of religion,[134]
Which heaven has seen fit to banish from this region;
I tell the story of the Church's injury,
Which ravishes its freedom, right, and property.

Alas, the only beloved of God, Christ's own bride,[135]
Abandons this place, in America must hide.[136]          1110
The very ones whom she first nurtured at her breast
Are the first, O sorrow, revolt to manifest,
Abused by a charlatan, deceiver, and liar,
The premier imposter, of all discord the sire.[137]
These curious spirits have followed Heresy
And forged a God to fit their merest fantasy;
Conspiring against us in disloyal accord,
They have thought to league Belial with Christ our Lord,
Likewise the Ark with Dagon.[138]  But He who commands
Above the elements requires no helping hands:          1120
Sole, without peer or tutor, this world He maintains;
Ourselves with mercy and favour His grace sustains.
But why does He tolerate factions so diverse?
Why does He give us such obstacles to traverse?
Why do we see everywhere the priests leave their altars,
The great lacking piety, and a faith that falters?
Why do we see mad Heresy so boldly striding
Through Gaul, which in a hundred parts she is dividing?[139]

Where do these swarming evils have their origins?
Why do we tremble? Alas, it is for our sins.                    1130
The evil that plagues us is not worth flattering;
The world wastes time in seeking peace by chattering.
The cause of Christ requires no other accord
But to ban Heresy and to expel discord;
The end of all our troubles consists in alliance,
The perfect Union of the three estates of France,
Whereby, our faith renewed, these rebels we may tame,
Who, to deform all things, take "reformed" as their name;
Nor is there any hope of our just war's conclusion,
Till far from this land they are driven in confusion.          1140
*He deceives himself sorely who counts them as friends*
*Who have taken their oath to pursue hostile ends.*
*We must not exercise such an excess of patience,*
*Which offends against right by sanctioning offence.*
We have called unto them, and they seemed not to hear;[140]
When we have pursued them, they have fled to the rear.
They boast of continual guardedness of spirit,
Fearful as they are of incurring some demerit.
What more shall we endure? It is high time to die,
And by a holy death due remedy apply,                          1150
Lest the sheer madness of an arrogant apostate
Ravish the fleur-de-lys and the pearl of the state.[141]
*The sceptre of true Frenchmen never yet could stand*
*The grip of a Huguenot's — or a Tyrant's — hand.*
*That sacred flower holds heretics as alien —*
*Like a Nero, a Turk, pagan or barbarian.*
Sooner shall sailing ships be carried in the air,
Sooner shall the heavens of their stars be stripped bare,
Sooner in the dust our Salic law shall we fling
Than endure to be ruled by a heretic king.[142]                1160

Therefore, great Prince and wise, who show forth the puissance
Of the Merovingians from Poland to France,[143]
O valorous Martel,[144] Prince with a true French heart,

Having of Christian courage and Valois blood your part,
Do you march at the head, and, radiant with glory,
Seek out for the Union immortal victory.
Be the first to swear; we will follow what you teach:
By the strength of the Almighty's arm and yours, each
Shall make himself a Christian Hercules,[145] whose power
Shall procure of lasting peace both the fruit and flower;          1170
Keep our Union safe beneath your sheltering wing.
*Showing mercy to subjects but bold rebels taming;*
*Never separating reward and punishment:*
*That is a king's true duty, who bears, heaven-sent,*
*The evergreen laurels both of Love and of Justice,*
*And must not nourish vice to virtue's prejudice.*
Recover all those trophies forfeited of late;
Reunite your lost subjects, divided through hate;[146]
Ensure that your bright crown resplendently appears
Beyond the far-flung girdle of Latona's spheres;[147]          1180
Conjoin with your honour both law and obligation;
Uphold the faith, and relieve your wretched nation.
Emulate the virtues of that great Charlemagne
Whose fortune enabled France Germany to gain.[148]
For this purpose feel free to make use of our treasure —
But not to indulge your minions' dissolute pleasure.
(Please excuse us, sire, if the outrageous wrong
The Church receives from this lends freedom to our tongue.)
Those resources must be employed against Opinion,[149]
Heresy and Schism, and to preserve the Union.          1190

Why do you bear the name of the Church's first son,
Why of Most Christian King, if not with the intention
That you are to guard the honour and privilege
Of the faith in safe-keeping against sacrilege?
And because the Eternal, as a sure solution,
This day, by His gracious will, accords us the Union,
Thus in His sight we seal it, Sire, with our breath,
And for its sake at any time will suffer death.

**Scene ii(c) [The Estates of Blois, continued].**

## Argument

*Of all those who delivered speeches for the Nobility on the occasion of the Estates, in my opinion Lord Charles de Cossé, the Count of Brissac, Seigneur of Estelant, etc., Grand Panetier[150] and Falconer of France, took the prize for eloquence. The poet has therefore chosen his discourse to be reported here in summary form. It is a sort of panegyric of the King, whom he praises, not for retaining the marks of valour universal among the French, but for the piety, the faith, the mercy, and the magnanimity with which he is adorned. Also for being born in an age afflicted on all sides, so that he may administer the appropriate remedies and that France may be, by the hands of such an august Prince, not rescued but avenged, not saved but enhanced, not made to flourish but raised above all nations. And this by the continuation of his victories, like that over the fearful army of the reîtres, and by his faithful discharge of the duty of a Most Christian King, who, he says, must be as charitable towards his Catholic subjects as he is a strict instrument of divine justice with regard to the heretics — justice that must be exercised by means of a just war, not feigned, not simulated, not subject to truces, agreements, peaces, and treaties; a war truly just, the kind that has always adorned with laurels the crowns of kings of France, such as Clovis, Charles Martel,[151] Charlemagne, Saint Louis. He exhorts him to such a war by appealing to public tranquillity and urgent necessity, and, in conclusion, cites the hereditary generosity of the entire nobility of France, its values and its resources, which it has never spared in the cause of religion. Finally, he promises the King, God willing, the multiplication of his grandeur and the advancement of his empire.*

### THE NOBILITY

Monarchs whose happiness exceeds what they deserve,
Who mere fortune or chance as deity observe,                    1200
Whose sudden importance often swells their renown

Above the sceptres and laurels linked to their crown —
When they suppose they reign in most security,
They perceive such a goddess's inconstancy.
By contrast, the prince who sacredly wears the garment
Of holy virtue — of kings the true ornament —
Fearlessly the assaults of adverse fortune bears,
For merit alone maintains and guides his affairs.
Such are you, O mighty King, to whose governance
The Ruler of All has lent the sceptre of France —                          1210
Not to be a flower of that notable race
Which has put so many palms and trophies in place,
Not, phoenix-like, the Valois heroes to recall,
Not to be esteemed the Alexander of Gaul,
Not that your forehead may shine with so many marks
Of the masculine virtue of previous monarchs[152] —
But for qualities of justice, faith, piety,
Prudence combined with law, strength matched with equity,
Which dwell within your soul, and which have in their care
This France of yours, now deemed as poor as she is fair.                   1220
Your France, alas, in terror, on all sides surrounded,
By Nemean lions[153] and savage leopards hounded,
Who presents herself before you with unbound hair,
All covered over with blood, but otherwise bare,
And, showing you her breast, wounded by deadly shot,
Begs you to hurl down your thunderbolt flaming hot
Upon her enemies — or rather upon ours,
Those who seek to ravish from you your rightful powers,
Yours by true inheritance and heaven's bestowing
(Grace into your heart like nectar and honey flowing).                     1230
If the fortunate aspect of your blessed star
Grants you may break her cruel chains, her cell unbar,
From the break of dawn, where the day adorns its head
With the sun's bright tresses, to the watery bed
Of renowned Gibralter, from Ganges unto Nile,
Trumpets in soaring notes your praises shall compile.

Hear her dolorous lamenting, laden with sighs;
Regard her pallid cheeks, washed by her teeming eyes,
As her wail bursts into words and she makes her plea
For the hearing of her cause by this whole assembly.          1240
We, who have had our part in her tormented grief,
Implore your helping hand to offer her relief.
By the ardent torches of those great lights divine,
Which to the souls in the empyrean must shine;
By the tortures and irons, the stakes and the prisons
Of the Princes of the Faith, those great champions
So prodigal of their blood,[154] and whose very relics
Have not been spared by the claws of the heretics;
By all the elements against France furious
Because of our struggles hard and injurious —               1250
France, your France, beseeches humbly your royal favour
In the form of your power raised upright to save her,
And, lest she be orphaned, bereft of religion,
That you uphold the virtue of the holy Union.
We who claim, by our virtue, strength, and chivalry,
The sacred name of the ancient nobility;
We who have ardently enkindled hearts, on fire
To preserve what is ours and raise our trophies higher,
For such a war will burst the bonds of life in sunder
And challenge Jove himself to a duel of thunder,            1260
Making war without compromise, without surcease;
Never without such war will we see fertile peace.
We are sons of those who to Italy and Greece[155]
By their warlike prowess carried the fleur-de-lys,
Of those whom purest holy virtue did incite
Against Scythians and Goths valiantly to fight;
Who, to exalt more highly the royal renown,
Albigenses, Arians, and Vandals[156] cast down;
Who, armed with courage on the loftiest ramparts,
Have checked the pride of pagans and haughty Lombards;      1270
Who, under Charles Martel and doughty Charlemagne,
Have spread fear and terror across the open plain;

Who have traversed the sea and marched through
                              burning sands,[157]
And climes far distant from the sun in northern lands;
Who had nothing but the faith kindled in their soul
To make a valiant army in God's cause enrol;
Whose deeds and deaths remembered now in us begets,
At each and every moment, a thousand regrets,
Makes the alarm bell sound to awaken our conscience,
And accuses our ingrate laxness in defence                    1280
Of religion, since in our sight we tolerate
The outrages these brazen truants perpetrate.
They look down upon us, their eyes with anger fraught,
To see if our souls will remain forever caught
Up in this cowardly fear, or whether ambition,
A hungering for power in disguise, division,
Or a taste for luxury, pleasure's soft sojourning,
Will smother entirely the courageous yearning
The same route to follow, the paths already worn
By the great triumphs of their shining virtue born.          1290

Therefore, lest the praise and the lustre we obscure
Of our bold forefathers, whose memory in pure
Splendour has the wild eagle's power to traverse
The spheres and match the greatest of the universe,
Sire, to maintain the crown of France against plotters
Now swarming to beset it with traitorous horrors;
To see again the Saviour adored at the altar,
So that the gift of immortal faith shall not falter;
To preserve ourselves in our full privileges —
We shall all arm ourselves against these sacrileges.         1300
Who could achieve more glory, happier reward,
Than by dying for the faith, for God, for one's lord?
Thus, potent Prince, Prince as virtuously inclined
As Tarquin was wicked, Nero of bloody mind,[158]
The heavens will bless you; they will bestow upon you
A thousand trophies — besides, moreover, a son, who

Shall bear the august name of France, and his bright light
Shall restore the Golden Age to our famished sight.
Thus we shall see those lilies, their glory now waned,
Be reborn more freshly, and those places profaned —               1310
The temples, the altars, the churches in decay —
Regain their beauty, their service, their rightful sway.
Thus even in your time shall nurturing religion
Stand alone to exercise command in our region;
Thus shall we see again, after the nights of sorrow,
The sun of your eyes dispensing a brilliant morrow.
Happiness shall return, and so we shall rejoice,
Drawing life from peace, till peace hears our dying voice.

### Scene ii(d) [The Estates of Blois, continued].

## Argument

*For the Third Estate the speech was delivered by Monsieur Étienne Bernard, advocate to the Parlement of Dijon, who complained to the King of the wrong the Church endured in witnessing so many schisms, whereas formerly it was known as the house of God, where one sole and unique religion held sway. To return it to its original estate, he finds no way more certain than the observation of the Edict of Union, the cutting-off of vices, which seem to have taken right of possession by long usage[159] in this realm, and the utter abolition of the abuses which are committed by those of all social conditions. For it is seen that men are rather esteemed for the value of the rank they have purchased than for the splendour of the virtue and learning which should make them shine forth, and this puts vice in authority and causes it to march in triumph everywhere in France. And after this he complains in the name of the people of the insolence and the hostility, more than barbaric, of the soldiery; of the tyranny and extortion of the taxes devised by those who, wallowing up to their ears in luxury and dissolution, laugh at the despoiling of the poor; of contempt for the laws, which are printed and published without being observed. In his estimation, once these things have been restored to their integrity,*

*faith and the Catholic religion will enjoy full and complete power,*
*as was formerly the case in the King's realm.*

### THE PEOPLE

*They are truly unhappy who, addressing kings,*
*Offend against the laws by concealing true things;*                    1320
*Who are afraid their stinging ulcers to palpate*
*And show the disease that causes their wretched state.*
Before a King of France, who holds nothing more dear
Than Peace and Virtue, the people through me appear
In search of soothing solace for the injuries
They unceasingly endure from base Heresy's
Cruel abuses, and to show their skeleton,
Reduced to its bare bones by excessive taxation.
Sire, you who of great God are the living image,
Who have so much honour, and to whom we do homage;    1330
Who in this age of wickedness have been ordained
To see the widow succoured, the orphan maintained;
Who have in your hand alone such capacity
To keep all in order, justice, and equity —
Hear the throbbing sighs of the people, who complain
Of the constant ills they suffer in your domain,
And reflect that these injuries are chiefly born
Of the fact that religion is held up to scorn.
Your France in former times was her true sanctuary;
Now the fifth Evangile[160] makes her his tributary.          1340
France was the house, the very family of God,
The place where the ancient faith first and foremost trod,
Without yet having suffered the assault of Schism,
Of raving Heresy and of false Atheism,
Yet unheard that word which to our ears is foe,
Frightens the people, and is pronounced "Huguenot."
Not yet had that foul air blown in from Saxony;
This Gallic earth remained still from its poison free.
We had not yet received so many thieving shocks

From wolves decked in the fleeces of innocent flocks.          1350
Thus, O France, of your pride and joy are you beguiled!
O Faith, daughter of heaven, thus are you exiled
From our dear harbourage! Into your bowels, O France,
Do your own bloody hands your piercing knives advance?
You hurtle in madness down the slippery slope
Toward pain perpetual, unless God grants you hope.
Yet His goodness He makes gleam again, full of pity,
On the fearful danger of your calamity.
*There shall never be a lack of strength or of grace*
*For someone who loves right, who concord will embrace.*          1360
As sure and certain remedy for your religion,
He offers the principles of a holy Union.
But even if heretic madness is extinguished
By the Union, even killed, from France wholly banished,
Still so many vices in us proliferate
That heaven's righteous blows will justly lay us prostrate.

Blasphemy to the common man remains a fable —
For the nobility it is their talk at table.
Everywhere one hears without fear of penalty
God's majesty profaned and put to perjury.          1370
These bears of Muscovy, these Hyrcanian tigers,[161]
Like Jews again become the Messiah's torturers.
The court, which sees a multitude of spirits stray
From the starry mansions, the Olympian way,
To slip along the path of vicious decadence,
Makes plenty of decrees but gives few punishments.

Medea[162] is in credit, and do you not see
The great abuse of divining and prophecy?
All the arts of Circe are currently the rage,
A prognosticating fool, a star-gazing sage          1380
Will dare to tell you the Eternal Power's size
And the course of the heavens, using his mere eyes.

The other monster which follows Heresy's tracks,
Renounces God's power and God himself attacks,
Which impudently hurls up to the height of His heaven
Its arsenic, its bile, its malodorous poison,
Is called Simony, a madness abominable,
Which has now reduced the clergy under its spell,
Which corrupts the Estates, assigning dignities
Out of respect for gold, and not for qualities,                    1390
Which causes Justice, outraged by our shameful fault,
To withdraw herself from us to the starry vault.[163]

A stronger monster still, with violent aggression
Visits on your subjects his murderous oppression;
This thief with crooked hands is able to disguise
Exorbitant interest rates as free enterprise,
With a bold lying face, and gestures quarrelsome,
Producing pride and greatness from cowardly scum—
Italian Usury,[164] the honoured guest of France,
Devouring in a day the people's whole substance,                   1400
Minion of the minions, whose flaunting knows no measure,
As they heap gold upon gold, treasure upon treasure,
Who have tyrannized the people into privation,
Who, charming your spirits,[165] abusing your high station,
Although hatched overnight, now hold authority
Sufficient to impose any brutal decree,
Well knowing how new impositions to invent
And for their murderous actions obtain consent:
Thus bailiffs fill your prisons with the innocent,
And on our very household ashes we pay rent.[166]                  1410

What has more greatly excited the indignation
Of God against us than disgraceful fornication,
Incest and rape, refined perversions by the score,
All those infectious members of one filthy whore?
Nowadays one witnesses the young people crazed,
By the thrill of sordid pleasures thoroughly dazed;

The honour of their essential divinity
They soil, slaking their hot lust in obscenity,
Staking, fools as they are, on that unworthy glory —
Pleasure ill-omened — their laurels of victory.                    1420
Their elders still drink in, tasting no bitterness,
As if it were sweet brew, the error and the madness.
This pleasure and, with it, sumptuous pride conspire
The loss and the demise of your mighty empire;
Such pleasure once, beneath the stream of oblivion,
Wholly submerged the reign of the Assyrian.[167]
To kings she does great damage: for a king to drown
Himself in dissolution is to risk his crown;
He falls into idleness;[168] he puts the law down,
Drives Virtue into hiding, and exiles Renown.[169]               1430
Then to various vices Hell opens the door,
And Discord arises, from which all evils pour —
Discord full of dangers, which is the counterweight
Holding up the ills that hang over the French state;
Frenchmen divided — in ruining themselves united,
Since their land without the Union will remain blighted.
In this very way we see that, when the crew jostle
Each other, thinking nothing of the ocean's peril,
The vessel through a hole takes on sufficient water
To sink, in sinking itself, those who sail in her.                 1440

That is why, Sire, you must muster all your strength
To uphold the Union. You have been taught at length
About the evils with which Discord plagues your reign,
Preventing us from seeing France its triumph gain
Over that clawed monster, which no one can appease,
In former times struck down by Charles, our Hercules.[170]
On that day when we are pleasing in Heaven's sight,
God will make us giddy with a flood of delight,
And in the sweet sugar of those pleasures that nourish,
His hand shall candy us, with rich savours to flourish,            1450
Our hearts with nectar fill brim-full, by His grace given;

He shall open wide our eyes, our breasts shall be riven:
Then this proud heart of stone from our sides shall He tear
And give us instead one of tender flesh to wear;[171]
Then shall He mitigate those destructive emotions
That inspire against you such criminal notions,
And His liberal arm shall bountifully strew
Upon us a holy and purifying dew —
All chosen vessels of His grace — and ever hence
Shall your glory shine forth in highest eminence.                1460

### Scene ii(e) [The Estates of Blois, continued].

### Argument

*The three orders of France having first, through their deputies, thanked the King for his good will, which was bent on restoring the state to its original form, then presented their remonstrances, the King himself undertakes to preserve the Edict of the Holy Union, which he desires to be acknowledged as the fundamental law of the realm, thereby testifying that he is the inheritor, not only of the royal dignity of the Most Christian monarchs of France, but also of their zeal and affection to the honour of God. And therefore he resolves to give over the indulgence he has hitherto employed, which has served only to increase and harden obstinacy, and to pursue the means of the Holy Union, to which he swore on 18 October 1588, as did also my lords the Cardinals of Bourbon and of Vendôme; the Count of Soissons; the Duke of Montpensier; the Cardinals of Guise, Lenoncourt, and Gondi; the Dukes of Guise, Nemours, Nevers, and Retz; my lord the Keeper of the Seals of France; and many other lords, both those of His Majesty's Council and deputies of the three Estates. This so received the approbation of the people that when the King, with the Princes, departed the assembly to give thanks to God in the church of Saint Sauveur, where a Te Deum was sung, they cried loudly and clearly, "God Save the King, God Save the King." But that exceeding joy was soon converted to sorrow.*

KING

Gentlemen, doubt no further that my utmost wish
Is that the holy unity you show may flourish:
Do not suppose that I harbour the memory,
With vengeful intent, of the wrongs once done to me.
You are my tributary streams, I am your ocean;
I keep and watch over you all.[172] I swore at Rouen
That which my current oath before you ratifies:[173]
I embrace the Union. Who looks with doubting eyes?
I will be the foremost, unshakeable my stance,
To defend it against the attackers' advance.               1470
And as a cedar spreads its proud and lofty crest
Above the ordered ranks of a densely branched forest,
In faith and devotion, I will surpass you all:
Sole vanquisher of Huguenots you shall me call.
I shall permit no one to breach the ordinance
That serves as foundation for the whole state of France.
Touched by the Holy Spirit, by divine love ravished,
I shall see to it that vice from my court is banished:
That ungrateful rabble, traders in degradation,
Who, in tormenting me, tormented my whole nation          1480
With infinite regrets, and whose devious ways
Lead[174] me to lose myself in a bewildering maze—
No longer my royal favour shall they receive.

THE ESTATES

That all of this you may successfully achieve,
May the Almighty aid with strength, and strength of heart,
Your Christian resolution.

KING

                    Only do your part:
I shall follow my God's, my faith's, my law's directing.

THE ESTATES

Long live the King! Always we'll cry, Long live the King!

CHORUS

The sea's high dudgeon does not last,
Swollen by the north wind's blast;                    140
Not forever does frightful lightning
Shake the palace of a king:

Neither does grievous punishment
Always maintain our minds in torment,
Nor misery forever pursue
One who, in flight, finds it anew.[175]

The darkest cloud in anger frowning
Must cease to threaten us with drowning;
Thus grief and trouble in such store
Shall not forever haunt our door.                     150

The King, Church, Nobility,
And People flee the acerbity
Of Schism and Opinion,
Swear agreement to the Union.

The impossible shall we see
With possibility agree,
Before the Union shall be
Without Virtue, Strength, Faith, or Duty.[176]


# Act IV

### Scene i.

## Argument

*All of the accounts of the history of the massacre of our Princes
name some of those who approved of the wrongful resolution of
the King, and who have since so well testified to this. Nevertheless, the poet, so as not to dishonour his poem with their names,*

has gathered them all together under the two letters "N.N."[177]
And this scene is merely a conjecture as to what they might have
alleged, except for the indications we have long had of the reproaches they have directed against the Duke of Guise relating to
ambition, the League, and the taking up of arms. And with these
three darts they so breech the conscience of the King that he agrees
to their cruel and barbarous determination, perfidious and murderous with respect to Justice, on the grounds of these three accusations. For it is well known at what moment the House of Guise
might easily have taken the crown, had it so wished, having had at
that time greater power than it has had since. The League and the
taking up of arms merely reflect the willingness to shed their blood
that they (rather than the state) have displayed in defence of religion, being more concerned not to offend God than to offend the
King — if offence there should be in protecting him so often from
the ambushes and conspiracies of his enemies. Now the hinges on
which all such accusations pivot are attached by a tenuous glue
composed of foreign intelligence and their recourse to arms, even
though the common necessity justifies armed intervention against
those poisonous troublemakers who are ranging throughout this
realm and kindling this widespread sedition against the Catholic
religion. It is the defence of that religion that has stirred them to
this war, having their consciences formed of faith, hope, and fear
of God, not being able to join in or consent to — any more than they
should do — the impieties and blasphemies of the Huguenots, the
plots and adventures of the Politiques,[178] the debaucheries and
irregular expenses of the Minions, and similar evils with which
this wretched kingdom was so burdened that it was groaning and
collapsing under their weight. That was one of the chief motives
for their League. The other was that they did not wish to allow
the various factions of their enemies to grow further to the detriment of the public welfare and to their own ruin, lest they have
their throats cut in the court. This was considered many times,
and they judged the League to be permissible, necessity being ac-
counted the most just and inviolable of all laws. For the protection
of life and liberty against oppression is not only permissible but

*also just, equitable, and sacred. Far from being given or taught to*
*men, that law is imprinted on their hearts and is born with them,*
*being consistent with the safety of the kingdom, the preservation*
*of the state, the tranquillity of the people, and the end of this dan-*
*gerous conflagration. The infelicitous counsel that wrought the*
*death of these two Princes cannot be called otherwise than the*
*enemy of the Catholic religion and the well-being of France. Thus*
*the King, charmed by these evil persuasions, and moved with the*
*impatience he feels at seeing my lord of Guise loved by all for his*
*valour, assisted by so many noble persons for the justness of his*
*cause, resolves to have him massacred.*

*[Enter King and N.N.]*

N.N.

How long will your royal greatness remain on view
As the subject of a madman faithless to you?                    1510
How long are you willing to let your royalty
Languish without power, without authority?
Will you let a bold prince turn the French lily's gleam
Into the tributary of a Spanish stream?[179]
Sire, you let this happen. The people are eager
To follow — don't you see it? — the lead of that Leaguer,
And you are a king only in your fantasy,
Made a serf by ambition, and by jealousy.
What fearful pagan army, by its fierce irruption,
Has ever provoked in France such massive disruption?           1520
What band of rebels within? I ask, can you name
Any quarrel in history more laden with shame?
That blow to the French, the vespers of Sicily,
The brutal shocks of the Scots in full mutiny,
The haughty designs projected by Spanish envy,
The loss at Pavia to Charles's bloody army[180] —
None of these disasters did France so jeopardize
As these outrages of the partisans of Guise.
Cease to tolerate their treacherous arrogance

Or you will gain the name of half a king of France—                    1530
Or a King of Yvetot;[181]  you may simply despair
Of seeing your power preserved—yet keep the care.

KING

*Still, I have hope; no one has ever, I believe,*
*Shunned the ill that heaven ordained him to receive.*
Through the length and breadth of France I see fires flaming,
All too well I foresee the strokes at my head aiming;
I curse my destiny, my courage I accuse,
For failing against my foes my power to use.
I accuse my minions, who, from a warlike hero,
Made me soft and cowardly, a recluse, a zero.[182]                    1540
In my springtime of life, a hopeful expectation
Of my noble qualities sustained the French nation:
On all men's lips was my every accomplishment;
The Duke of Anjou's name soared through the firmament.
But no sooner, in the place of bold enterprise,
Did I take to base pleasure, which dazzled my eyes,
Than I spurned underfoot any higher ambition,
Gave my subjects—alas, and myself—to perdition.
No sooner did I, by a sweet voice overcome,
Let my treasures be fondled by Épernon's thumb,                    1550
Than, of those alluring treasures seeking control,
It pleased him to ruin me both body and soul,[183]
Until without Épernon nothing could content me,
All mixed up, a lone wolf, touchy, solitary.[184]
I saw my friends withdraw far distant from the court;
My enemies I witnessed increasing their effort;
And Guise, who once would not have dared in any mission
Of arms to engage without seeking my permission,
Resolved to enter a League and combat a king
Whom a minion had made a senseless, faithless thing.                    1560
*Profligate pleasures pose, for mighty kings, great dangers;*
*Often they put the realm into the hands of strangers;*
*Then, to sustain such excesses, a heavy tax*

*Weighs upon the innocent people's wretched backs;*
*And the people that sees its king, despised, aspire*
*Merely to wallow pig-like in sensual mire,*
*Deaf, mute, and blind, with wanton fickleness will range*
*Itself on the side of someone who offers change.*
*They will leap up to dance at the first invitation,*
*Eager for justice through violent innovation.*                     1570
*They form leagues, assemble, and resolutely call*
*For the death of those minions who rob them of all.*

N.N.

Kill the minions, did you say, those creatures you cherish,
Who bear along with you the burden of your anguish?
*Ha! It is hardly an ambitious subject's part*
*To measure by his own weight what's in the king's heart:*
*The narrow-minded people must not place confines*
*Upon the pleasure to which royalty inclines.*
*A king who desires alone to keep his state*
*Must choose minions for himself and put down the great.*       1580
When Spring gives consent to the smiling of the earth,
And the meadows to myriad beauties give birth;
When heaven's own breath, diffusing the season's flowers,
With delicious scents applies its enchanting powers,
Our senses are renewed: we are charmed by the sight
Of a fragrant bouquet, whose odour gives delight.
In the same way a prince, replete with love and grace,
Invites his minions at his court to take their place,
To turn their eye on him and him alone accord
Devotion as their sun and light, master and lord.              1590
He lives in assurance, and their fidelity
Shields him from the people's revolt and treachery.
A king's heart is free, and favourites everywhere
Are seen to be special objects of princes' care.
God! — if only you had Épernons infinite
To thwart all those Guisards, who play the hypocrite,
Who seek to steal from you that puissant radiance

Gracing the triple fleurs-de-lys throughout your France.

KING

*All that by human artifice has been erected,*
*By human hands may be demolished and dejected.* 1600
*But the power of kings is established on high;*
*His right hand sustains them; He keeps them in His eye.*

N.N.

The only two examples you need to prove that
Are those of Chilperic the monk and Charles the Fat![185]

KING

Chilperic, a scatter-brain, unworthy to figure
In the ranks of French kings, was shut up in a cloister;
Charles, for consorting with the Viking enemy,
Was deprived by common accord of empery.
Neither one nor the other, as a stately king
I hold the sceptre of the Capets in my keeping. 1610

N.N.

In just the same way as Pepin in France found grace
As monarch, though he was not issued of French race,[186]
Deposing the true king, Sire, the threat is made
That Guise will take your kingdom with the people's aid,
And you, like a useless fool, will be made to dwell,
A second Chilperic, in a monk's holy cell.

KING

Our ample monarchy, everywhere recognized,
Under great kings' foreign sceptres has been aggrandized;
That sovereignty, which the heavens themselves endorse,
Twelve hundred years in France thus far has stayed the 1620
course.[187]
God has never failed to bestow new growth to furnish
The lilies, that with grace immortal they may flourish,
And He shall give me a son, by whose very frown

The slights of those ambitious men will be put down.

N.N.

But as doubts of success grow with so long a wait,
The heartache tormenting your soul does not abate.

KING

*The bitter follows the sweet; always secretly*
*Misery dogs the heels of our felicity.*
*When things are worst, the Almighty does not abandon*
*The king who takes His goodness as a guiding beacon.*                    1630

N.N.

Then you are content that a Leaguer full of gall,
A blood-thirsty baron, a disrupter of all,
Should ravish the flowers that grace your royalty?
Should command at will, and put you to slavery?
Should triumph in Paris over your greatest trophies?
Massacre, murder, beat down, and by the throat seize
Those monsters, those serpents, above whose high heads tower,
In the place of crests, terror, raw hunger for power —
Apes of piety, who claim there is no concern
About who, in France, possesses the right to govern.                    1640
It is time to root out that Spanish race, who drench
The countryside in the true blood of faithful French.

KING

*Shall a bull fear the anger of a tiny mite,*
*An elephant tremble when a fly comes in sight?*
I am the King of the French: what should a king fear?

N.N.

That which he fears the least. They seek to domineer
By making you uphold their right; if you consent,
You will be no longer a king but a lieutenant.[188]

KING

I simply cannot leave the Union in the lurch:

Its aim is the good of my subjects and the Church.                    1650
*A salutary project, which for all makes sense,*
*Cannot be refused, though proposed with insolence.*

N.N.

You will see the League restricting your right to rule;
You'll have a guardian, like a bankrupt or fool.
Sire, remember the lions you dreamt about
At the point when these rebellions first broke out.[189]

KING

Remember yourself that I had them put to death.

N.N.

You didn't kill the one who would crush out your breath
With his heavy paws, trample you into the mud,
And stain his triumphant clan purple with your blood.[190]     1660
When I think of what that rebel prince plans for you,
A horrible fear freezes my soul[191] through and through.

KING

Do you think Guise will murder me?

N.N.

                  Yes. Guise is willing,
If he cannot prevail, to take your crown by killing.
He will be your dream's lion, bristling in his pride,
Which you saw eating you as you lay on your side.
Guise hungers to reign; to become the King of France,
Guise is bound and determined to take any chance.
The hearts of the people and the Church he can claim:
They all take off their hats when they mention his name.     1670

KING

Then shall I lose the title of Most Christian King?
*How wretched to fall from royal greatness to nothing!*

### N.N.

*One who wishes to reign any obstacle leaps;*
*He is never caught napping, since he never sleeps.*
*The man of ambition who aims at a kingdom*
*Will take any risk — mortal danger leaves him numb;*
*To compass his conquest he is ready to die;*
*For the purchase of a realm, no price is too high:*
*Wife and children, justice, places of holiness*
*Are sold at any cost, a sceptre to possess;*       1680
*Honour and obedience are offered as hostage*
*For the sake of being honoured like God's own image.*

### KING

I shall reign alone as my ancestors have done.
*Kingship cannot be cut into two: it is one —*
*A sole and singular power, which cannot bring*
*Together princely partners to make a joint king.*
*My heart, filled with jealousy, will never agree;*
*A king is a king — in life, for eternity.*
*One can't wipe from the soul the royal character,*
*When God has pleased with his finger to carve it there.*     1690
I want to be king alone; I want, from now on,
To have no trouble-making prince as my companion.

### N.N.

Then why do you delay those Guisards' fatal hour?

### KING

*Bloodshed must not be used to constitute one's power.*[192]

### N.N.

Since their ends are cruel, your means may likewise be.

### KING

*A monarch is not rendered safe by cruelty.*

### N.N.

*No prince can rest easy unless he causes fear.*[193]

KING

I prefer my subjects freely to hold me dear.

N.N.

But still you would be feared, if they did not defy
Your Majesty's honour with a disdainful eye.                    1700

KING

They must be killed, then, so that no one can maintain
That I bear a timid heart and a torpid brain.

N.N.

Oh, what a memorable blow! How you shall be
Ravished with contentment, when you claim victory
Over those who, abusing your beneficence,
Desire to throw your France into turbulence!

KING

If I heed your words, I degrade my royalty;
I shall be called perjured, soiled with disloyalty.
When I consider the oath I have sworn, I tremble:
I swore all those princes in safety to assemble.                    1710
What will be said of me?

N.N.

                    It will be said that truly
You can manage your affairs both wisely and duly,
And that you have done what any master would do
With a slave who would seem higher in others' view —
That you have gained the upper hand (or so have done
For an hour or a day). And will anyone
Subject your will to doubt, when it exceeds in force
The power of all who take a contrary course?
The princes of Italy and the King of Spain
Will not take you for a child, or for a lack-brain.                    1720
Then all the world will know that a high-minded prince,
Such as you, on his land authority imprints.

KING

I've got them all here — they are thoroughly ensnared;
By calling the Estates, I lured them unprepared.
What prodigious Estates! No one could fail to see
The righteousness of the anger that seizes me.
Not one of them shall escape: my nets are in place;
The chief Leaguers have entered my deadly embrace.[194]

N.N.

Never have you witnessed such a successful hunt.
Once the Duke of Guise has fallen under the brunt,                    1730
The others in fear will throw themselves at your feet,
And humbly, in silence, to their duty retreat.

KING

That crew of bold Leaguers will find it passing strange
That the château of Blois to a prison can change!

N.N.

Some of them will spend the rest of their lives in chains;
Others will be sentenced to identical pains
As that cursed League's leaders will be made to suffer;
Still others in distant places will run for shelter.
But to assure protection from every ill,
That disloyal duke's brother you must also kill.                     1740

KING

He is prelate of Reims, a cardinal of Rome.

N.N.

*Justice is blind to social rank when she strikes home.*

KING

Execution of two will serve to terrify
All others who have the same mad gleam in their eye.
With three or four heads, I shall count myself content —
The cause of my ills, my victory's monument.

### N.N.

Have them come, therefore, and we shall prepare the net.
Forty-five assassins,[195] daring cut-throats, are set
To despatch him on his journey deep underground
To the darkest caves of hell; there the shades are found          1750
Of the *reîtres* that near Auneau he decimated
Last year,[196] with whose weight Charon's vessel is so
                                        freighted[197]
That Pluto trembles, and his whole fiery troop,
Seeing such an army, with fear begins to droop.
Take just this reason as recompense for your pains:
When the serpent is dead no more poison remains.

### KING

Enough, say no more; I long to have his blood spilt
Today, and my sword soaked in it up to the hilt.

### N.N.[198]

But that is not enough: on the same day take action
To purge all France, with your court, of those          1760
                                    Leaguers' faction.
Lyons, which may restore due awe of royalty,
Which has never been led into disloyalty,[199]
Holds the Duke of Mayenne, and will take any measure
To stop him from escaping to avenge his brother.

### KING

I'll give orders all round, before it is too late;
Mercœur and Aumale shall be sent to the same fate.[200]

### N.N.

Well spoken, Sire — you must crush all his companions.
But when Guise is dead, he shall live on in his sons,[201]
And as long as they remain alive, wretched France
Will be stained with the blood shed by their righteous          1770
                                    vengeance.

KING

And who will avenge him? And who will attack me?
Who will ever dare to rise up in mutiny?
Nothing shall daunt me; I'll be deaf to all I hear
But the unequalled howls, imparting bloody fear,
That shall be hurled at me: but, whatever they say,
Ruthlessness shall rule me; I shall never give way.

CHORUS

Armour of Heaven's assurance,
Used both law and faith to betray —
That is this king's chosen way
With wretched and pitiful France.                    1780

Invoking the high Majesty
Of the Eternal Ruler of all
Serves for the House of Lorraine's fall,
And to cover atrocity.

Though his heart is inhumane,
Yet he shows friendship in his eye;
Bread with one hand does he supply,
And with the other bitter bane.

a    It has pleased God, prince, that you not be
b    Fashioned all out of glass or crystal:
c    Then your stomach's good and evil
d    The naked eye would clearly see.[202]

To hide an unjust vengeance such as
You have secretly decreed,                            1790
To repeat your oath there is no need:
They are all within your clutches.

He who in mind is most secure
Is always first to be caught out,

While he who ever lives in doubt
Is not fetched easily to the lure.

Prince born of race illustrious,
Why do you not to us impart
The fire in your glowing heart,
Which now both burns and freezes us?                          1800

From right and honour you abscond,
So anger does your heart torment;
Is that how such a prince is meant
To keep his faith, our common bond?

Suspicion, disquiet, murmur
All round the Estates are swirling;
They are in the hands of a king,
Who is content his faith to perjure.

The adage Louis Eleventh preferred—
*"He who can't feign a holy show*                             1810
*Does nothing about kingship know"* —
Is also that of Henri the Third.

### Scene ii.

## Argument

*The massacre was not resolved on so secretly but that rumour,
however doubtful, gave some warnings of it to those on whom
the storm was due to fall—so much so that, contrary to all the
becoming and apparent demonstrations of friendship and grace
that the King lavished on them, they were on the point of leaving
the place and removing themselves. But their respect for the Estates, assembled at their request to advise regarding the welfare
of France, held them back, so that they preferred an honourable
and innocent death to a cowardly and suspicious flight. That is
what my lord of Guise says in this scene, trusting in the words,
oaths, and the exceptional kindness of the King, which he man-*

ifested in all sorts of friendly gestures, even in the presence of
the Queen Mother, whom they visited together in her illness. By
these it appears, as fully as one might wish, that the King sought
to show forth the integrity of a soul which has no more within
than without. The Duke likewise trusted to the promise, backed
by many repeated assurances, of the office of Constable, and to the
protestations that the King himself made to the Duke regarding
the scattered rumours renewed at Blois of that murderous design,
in refuting which the King made use of all the oaths he could.
Thus the Duke was unwilling to bow to the salutary counsel of
his friends. At this point he was summoned to the Council on Friday, 23 December 1588, scarcely having the time to dress himself,
whither he went freely and openly out of obedience to the King —
but rather to the sacrifice of his blood, which he vows to God for
the liberty of the people and the Church, and to maintain the truth
of the Catholic, Apostolic, and Roman religion.


DUKE OF GUISE [alone]

We are assured: the King has thoroughly disclosed
His will and his heart; the passage lies unopposed
To a holy war, and some day decrepit France
Shall recover her health and youthful countenance.
The devastated people, poor people — alas! —
For their afflictions will receive the longed-for solace.
The vessel of the Church waves shall not overwhelm.
We have heaven's blessing; the King is at the helm.[203]          1820
Yet it is told me that the favour of the King,
His faith and oath, are aimed at me, part of his plotting —
That they wish to root out the whole race of Lorraine,
Intend my own murder; that a death inhumane
Awaits me in the private study of the King, where
He summons me this morning to close some affair.[204]
All that is mere wind, a frivolous misconception.
I am not daunted, for I suspect no deception.
The other day he balked at doubts he was sincere,

Saying, "Good Cousin, for God's sake, who is more dear    1830
To me than you? I could turn the world upside-down
And find none who loves more the honour of the crown."[205]

Shall I then let others tell me that I resist,
With cowardly distrust, despite what he has promised?
That, because of the vain report of someone who
Aims at my public disgrace, I simply withdrew?
Shall I be charged with quitting, without courage or heed,
Clergy, Nobility, and Commons in their need?

Shall I deceive the hopes of this ample assembly,
Animated, filled to the brim with joy, by me?    1840
Shall I forfeit the end of what I set afoot,
Which promises our troubles wholly to uproot?
No, no, I fear nothing; my holy state of conscience
Towards my God, my King, purges fear with innocence:[206]
God truly weighs my heart. I could not justify
Letting down so many because I fear to die.
Our days are measured. I pray only that God wills
At once my life to take away and France's ills!
Ah, I shall die content, sure that along with me,
As Faith is reborn, shall perish Heresy —    1850
Faith, the gate-keeper of heaven, alone possessing
That great radiance's every grace and blessing.
I will gladly die for her sake; she will inspire
Me to pass with noble courage through pikes and fire.
For her I shall be witnessed, with right hand robust,
Blasting our enemies' schemes and smashing to dust
All their armies, and in full strength, as in full view,
Piercing the bodies of Huguenots through and through.
For I count myself so sure of the sacred vow
Of the King, that no misgivings trouble me now;    1860
To stake my faith on that, would I were not alone,
But had here with me wife, children, all that I own!
*He who is duly armed with the rugged cuirass*

*Of holy virtue need not fear either the menace*
*Or the paltry anger of a Prince who opposes*
*Against truth and right all the vain things he supposes.*
I well know that Heaven destroys, to ashes burning,
That man of haughty pride who would usurp a king,
And I recall the Titans' gruesome destinies,
When they rose up against the puissant deities.          1870
Do not countenance, my God, that such an offence,
Even in mere thought, should harbour within my conscience.

The Council is meeting; only for me they stay.
The journey the king intends we must not delay:
At Cléry he will spend that day which is the sign,
Nourishing token, of marriage with the divine.[207]
But I feel regret at departing from this place
Without, as is my custom, asking for God's grace.[208]

CHORUS

Ah, Prince, who are the hope of France,
Whither goest thou?[209]  Turn back!          1880
Your noble mind's assurance
Invites death's dastardly attack.

Greatness of spirit, blood, or place,
Abounding wealth, cannot delay
Our falling on the fatal day
When death at last takes us in chase.[210]

When, in Heaven's ruling sight,
It is time to pluck life's flower,
No caution, admonition, flight
Can save us from that woeful hour.          1890

But the soul without duplicity,
Upright under virtue's standard,
Exposes fearlessly

His breast to death's dart sharp and hard.

Death has its common stratagems
Against us all, its cunning ruses,
But when it takes aim at diadems[211]
A different style it uses.

Death, which had no power to seize
Guise in fearful combat, alas,                           1900
Now forces him by treacheries
To a king's murderous palace.

By perfidious death are conjured
Of brutal cut-throats forty-five;
The word of a king who is perjured
Of brilliance two torches will deprive—

Two torches, by whose dazzling gleams
Such splendour on the French is shed,
The first and primal light it seems,
By which the months and years are led.                   1910

## Scene iii.

### Argument

*The King, letting himself be guided by pernicious and desperately unjust advice, feels remorse, which seizes him by the throat and gives him an alarm of fear, horror, anguish, which he finally manages to master, giving the victory in the struggle to his perfidious and unexampled vengeance. And he deems no evidence admissible[212] but the fear he has that the Duke of Guise—beloved by all for the cause he is defending, respected by all as the father of his country, swaying the majority of Frenchmen by the motions of his high-minded initiatives—should take the sovereign reins of the French state. And he recalls that kings wish to have only kings as their companions, and that while the Roman empire, for all its great and wide extent, encompassing under its sceptre Eu-*

rope, Asia, and Africa, had merited a government by several, yet
it could not tolerate Caesar and Pompey, who were father and
son-in-law,[213] any more than in earlier times Romulus and Remus, just as Thebes was unwilling to accede to the rule of two
brothers. Thus, impelled by a vain jealousy telling him that the
merit of Guise was unequal to his reward — and lest the history of
Chilperic should be repeated in his own time[214] — the King makes
up his mind to have him killed, thereby violating all the ordinances
respecting liberty in France — liberty especially recognized in the
Estates, the assembly of which is sacred and inviolable, being indeed authorized by the will of him who has the power to summon
them. And in despite of human rights as universally observed,
he breaks his publicly given faith, drawing that wicked doctrine
from Machiavelli, who in his book of The Prince sets bounds to a
prince's faith by conceding him free recourse to perfidy when he
desires to take vengeance and to reign in security.

*[Enter King and Murderers.]*[215]

KING

The tigers, lions, dragons, snakes, however savage,
Which the sandy African wilderness ravage —
All the fearful monsters, the lynx, the bear, the panther —
Cannot equal in their rage my terrible anger.
Relinquishing the simple mildness of my nature,
I must be cruel if I wish to be secure.
By no one else's eyes can my fury be spied;
Myself from myself, in others' sight, I divide.
Oh, my cares are bullet-wounds; the pangs never cease:
Not even an hour's respite to eat in peace!                    1920
Would that heaven had given me at birth no vaster
Station than a lowly ploughman's place! Then, as master,
Though not of a palace, at least of a poor hovel,
Slave-like to my servants I would not have to grovel.

But I am your King, you tell me? O fickle France,
Have royalty, duty, lost all significance?
If I am your father, if your lord I remain,
Why do you afflict me with suffering and pain?
If you rid your eyes of this persistent disease,
You will then see yourselves as your own enemies,                    1930
Realize that your revolt, which aims at innovation,
Entails of love, respect, and feeling your privation.
In the towering waves, that star is lost to view
Which, when you had no lantern or sail, shone for you
In the Louvre; and your recreant imbeciles,
Who call themselves your heart, shall now become your heels.[216]

Ah, Henri, brimful of pity, prince overkind,
If you had a heart of steel, a bloodthirsty mind,
You would reign all alone, and no plot of revolt
Would cause you to wake in the morning with a jolt.                  1940
Your complexion would not be so white, pale, and pasty,
If your people honoured your royal majesty.
I must cease to be a child:[217] it is now high time
To slaughter that Leaguer raging from crime to crime.
It must be cut off in its tracks, the uncorrected
Audacity of that prince, whose soul is infected
With ambition's foul air, before his influence
Corrupts France's humours,[218] destroys obedience.

A vessel on the waves, drifting out of control,
Is like the troubled thoughts in my wandering soul.                  1950
Two strong contrary impulses my mind attack:
By one I'm pushed forward, by the other held back.
The cold remorse of conscience accuses my will;
    Desire to reign alone excuses me still:[219]
I yearn to devise a mad horror of confusion
To crush that head filled with ambition in profusion.
    I shall but hurl at myself my destructive power:
He and France itself shall die in a single hour.

*I have sworn to preserve the public faith.  One must*
*Violate an oath that tramples right into the dust.*    1960
*A monarch's promise should never be disavowed.*
I want to destroy those to my destruction vowed.
*It is lawful to take up arms in faith's own cause.*
*Without the king's consent, to do so breaks the laws.*

I have granted him the Union, which will increase
The welfare of all the state, and whose goal is peace.
He forced the Union on me, which impedes the growing
Of the very dearest seeds of my royal sowing.[220]
*A monarch is obliged to rate at their true value*
*Those princes who have always come to France's rescue.*    1970
Their prowess fills me with hatred and jealous pain:
All the honour is grabbed by Henri of Lorraine.
*Heaven ordains all things that happen here below.*
On stubborn Guisards no care would Heaven bestow.
*By a noble prince all offences are excused;*
*No potent king could stomach being so abused.*

These rebellions are too strong for me to resist,
Unless the men who lead them no longer exist;
To end these troubles, in which so much blood is spilled,
The only hope is to have the chief Leaguer killed.    1980
If I have him murdered, his whole faction will tremble;
But the people in armed rebellion will assemble.
If I let him live, I face my elimination
And consign the French lily to a foreign nation.[221]
If I have him killed, my faith will be deemed a wile,
The law, the Estates, and the Union to beguile.
If longer I live in this state of burning envy,
My spirit will languish forever in its frenzy.
If I have him killed, nobody shall ever see
A king less feared, revered, obeyed than I shall be.    1990
If he lives longer, he will claim my rule by right;
He must be killed, then—I could be in no worse plight.

[*He turns to address the murderers.*]

The moment he enters, fall on him, all of you;
Be ready: this is the day he must not live through.

### CHORUS

    Why, O heavens in justice lacking,
    Do your sword, scourge, fire not smite
    This palace, these murderers, this King,
    Dragging to death a Duke upright?

    Why, O lamp of diurnal beauty,
    Do you not eclipse with darkness         2000
    This court, which into obscurity
    Today casts faith, peace, righteousness?

    France, you see your dearest offspring
    Massacred, Herculean twins,
    For all their feats of daring,
    Now at the mercy of assassins.

    The most abominated tyrants,
    Renowned for their unequalled fury,
    Were never such fierce termagants
    As to do to faith this injury.         2010

    Faith, once to our kings so precious,[222]
    Their bulwark, their rampart, their guide,
    By the last Valois[223] — perfidious,
    Cruel, and disloyal — has died.

# Act V

## Argument

*This last act represents the pitiful and unhappy end of the Estates of Blois and the just lament of Madame de Nemours,*[224] *seeing her son the Duke of Guise wretchedly slaughtered in the King's chamber on Friday, 23 December 1588, at about nine o'clock in the morning. At that time, when he arrived, against the advice of those most devoted to his service, at the place where the execrable plot of the murderers was prepared, holding his hat in one hand and the tapestry of the doorway in the other, half stooping to enter (it was so low), the cut-throats threw themselves on him, and, as the King looked on, they struck down, tortured, and murdered the man who, living, they dared not look upon without trembling. And when that noble martyr was in his death agony, yielding his soul to God amidst a great flood of blood and sobs, he raised his head and moved his lips, upon which the King ran forward and finished his treacherous vengeance upon him by stabbing him in the heart, as he placed his foot on his throat and cried out, "We are two no longer; now I am the King!"*[225]

*[Enter Madame de Nemours, Messenger.]*

MESSENGER

O France violated! Detestable slaughter-man!
O horrible tyrant, hateful barbarian!

MADAME DE NEMOURS

What frightening deed, what outlandish accident
So resounds with outcry?

MESSENGER

             O prince too negligent!
Your faith, your loyalty, your purity of conscience
Have tricked you, murdered you, in righteous innocence.    2020
O sorrow, O anguish, O dire cruelty!
O woeful spectacle of death, O treachery!

Poor prince abused!

MADAME DE NEMOURS

O God, tell us the news at once!

What word from the château? What grief has come upon us?

MESSENGER

Madame, can you endure with constancy to hear
The story told, or I to voice it to your ear?

MADAME DE NEMOURS

My son — has he been killed?

MESSENGER

Alas, your son heroic,

The Duke of Guise, despite the faith affirmed in public,
Traitorously slaughtered, lies stretched out on the ground.

MADAME DE NEMOURS

O fierce traitor! God, all's lost, never to be found!           2030

MESSENGER

But hear yet, Madame, in what execrable fashion
That great Duke was murdered. His virtue still lives on;
His name cannot perish; he receives as his bier
The whole heart of France, which wails with tear after tear!
The King, who long disguised[226] his vengeful purposes
With shows of love and kindness, faithful promises,
Today when he awakened, as his morning greeting,
Ordered that great Duke summoned to the Council meeting.
The latter rose at once, and scarcely had the leisure
To dress his valiant person in a proper manner,           2040
Being all too ready to obey the command
Of that inhuman prince, whose sword was in his hand.
In the deadly chamber the thugs by him were told
To murder that blameless man as he crossed the threshold.
The whole pack of cut-throats entrusted with that crime,
Armed to the teeth, there awaited the fatal time.

The Duke was given warning, even as he went
To Council, of the King's nefarious intent.
One said in his ear, "They all seek your death," well knowing;
The other said, "My Lord, alas, where are you going?"[227]        2050
But feeling armed with faith and virtue from above,
He trusted in his duty, and in the King's love.
He was called, he went alone, walking with assurance;
He held his head high — O sorrow! — in his advance.
Then a qualm dimmed the gleaming lilies[228] of his face;
Suspicion struck him, seized his heart in its embrace.
He greeted them, and all of them — brimming with fury —
Raising up and turning the doorway tapestry,
Attacked him — O the cowards! At once, he is stabbed
In the breast, his feet are held tight, his hand is grabbed.        2060
One, whom his face's lofty mien would have dismayed,
Gives him a blow from behind with a coward's blade;
Another seizes his sword — that which formerly
Had so served so well to combat France's enemy.[229]
Briareus[230] could not have resisted the rampage
Of those butchers so prepared for that cruel outrage.

The Prince, kicking and flailing, strove with might and main
To get out of their hands: alas, it was in vain.
His body was all wounded, and the bloody river
That burst forth shall his murderers to God deliver.[231]        2070
He cried, "Is faith no more? O traitor! O treachery!
Is it for my sins? Then I pray God may have mercy!
True, I have greatly offended You, but my conscience
Concerning King and duty shines with innocence.[232]
Receive my soul, O God!"[233] At once, this having said,
With sighs and prayers he fell at the foot of the bed
Of that inhuman monarch, whose gaze, despicable,
Follows with half-closed eyes that appalling spectacle.
Seeing that the lofty spirit within his frame
Displayed a brave reluctance to renounce its claim,        2080
He approached, all over trembling with violent rage;

He set his foot down hard upon that pallid visage;
He cried, "All alone, all alone I wish to reign.
I am the King henceforth; we are no longer twain."
The Duke struggled mightily, when that voice was heard,
To lift his bare head a little; his lips he stirred.
The other, fearing he had strength while he had breath,
Gave him a dagger-blow, and completed his death.
That was the end of my lord: thus perished Atrides;
Thus fell Caesar once; in the same way died Alcides.[234]      2090
Thus died by the hand of a traitor, a perjurer,
A great prince, a great Duke, a great peer, a great master.

### MADAME DE NEMOURS[235]

And have you from me, then, with your thirst for blood, ravished
Him whom I carried in my womb, him whom I nourished?
O Lestrigon, barbarian, Sarmat![236] You cloaked
Beneath your vow a soul with vicious rancour choked!
Have you thus faithlessly, with feigning love, decoyed
My child to the court, so that he could be destroyed?
O breach of faith, whose like was never known in France!
O miserable fraud! O God, what evil chance      2100
Has struck the faith of the Union? Were the Estates
Called to witness a crime nature abominates?
Have you, then, murdered him? Then also murder me:
The mother would keep son and father company —
Those guardians of France: for without them, the sceptre
Would hardly be yours that adorns our kings with honour.
Your heart is more prompt unjust vengeance to dispense,
Than for a benefit to grant just recompense.

O my son, my son! Why were not my words believed?
By your own faith, truth, and duty you were deceived.      2110
O perjurer! Of such falseness were you capable
When you favoured his rise to the rank of Constable?
Is this the fit reward your great bounty determines
For his last years of victories over the Germans?

Yes — you fully purposed that their rage inhumane
Should swallow in an instant the House of Lorraine.
Brute, you threw your subjects to those wolves so reviled,
Who hungered above all for the skin of my child.
O my son, my son, now you do abandon me
To despair, to weeping, to sorrow's agony!                              2120
The crescent moon beneath your feet, you live on high;[237]
You leave France to languish without your watchful eye.
You have left everywhere your name's memorial;
But always in my heart I'll keep your funeral.
Alas, will those murderers let me, in my woe,
The last offices to your mangled body show,
That I may place you on your bier, and in my arms:
So two may die in one day from our mingled harms.
O loss deplorable! Did my ancestor kings
Build Blois to be the scene of such murderous things?[238]         2130

O Heaven, O just Heaven![239]  But what good is it —
Your justice, anger, lightning-bolts — if you permit
Such evil to spawn its horrors? And will you thrive,
O Faith-Breaker, Tyrant, while I in pain survive,
Condemned to outlive those who should exceed my date?
No, no, and since your throat you must inebriate
With blood of innocents, let me have no reprieve:
My welcome death far greater torments will relieve.

Time, which diminishes the harshest agonies,
The bitterness of my just wrath shall not appease.                     2140
Your heart — your coward's heart — in the most peaceful nights
Shall be overwhelmed with anguish, horrors, and frights,
For my God, dispenser of justice, will not fail
Your fury, your livid tyranny, to assail:
Like a second Cain, you shall be dogged at your heels
By the ghost of my child, as you sit at your meals;
The blood of that noble Duke shall swell up your veins;
You shall be flayed alive, put to the utmost pains

Of relentless remorse; panic-terrors your head
Shall fill to overflowing with horror and dread — 2150
And if, though a coward, you feign yourself undaunted,
Your pale conscience shall ever by vengeance be haunted.
The pricking of remorse will drive you forth to stand
And beg pardon of the people with torch in hand.[240]

## Notice to the Reader
### Concerning the Continuation of This Tragedy

The unfruitful pursuit and unpleasant exertions of Poesy owing
to the malice of the present age could not deter the will of the poet,
the author of this *Guisiade*, when this catastrophe occurred, from
excavating the quarry of a second subject, in order to construct
another tragedy as grave, moral, and ingenious as the first with a
plot taken from what remains. Hence, he set himself the project
of treating the death of Cardinal Louis de Lorraine and the imprisonment of the Princes and other lords, with a continuation of
the history and all that happened from the cruel treatment of the
dead bodies until the death of the Queen Mother, honouring this
second tragic poem with the title of *Sacrilege*, being determined to
leave to posterity such testimonies of the prodigious marvels of
our time. To these laborious designs he was spurred by nothing
more conducive to a cheerful readiness than your good will, accompanied by a solid and pure judgement in weighing the first
wares of his merchandise. This you will easily do if, in embarking
on your reading, you cease to struggle against the passions that
cause you to picture the most feigning things in the sacred and
innocent livery of truth. Adieu.

*Notes to*
# The Guisiade

1 See below, n. 16.

2 Matthieu's use of tenses in the Discourse and the Arguments is inconsistent, as he switches between describing the action of the play and narrating historical events. The confusion is compounded by the obtrusion of the historical present (*présent historique* or *présent de narration*). In the interest of readability, my translation reduces, though it does not entirely eliminate, this effect. I have also divided some of Matthieu's long and complicated sentences, but by no means all of them, since this would obscure his tortuous prose style.

3 The expression "most Christian" ("treschrestienne") is ironic, since the formula traditionally belongs to the French king, and this one clearly does not deserve it. Cf. below, ll. 373–74 and 629–30.

4 The Union was the political agreement severely curtailing the royal power which was forced upon Henri III by the League after the Paris "barricades," and which the Estates of Blois were called in order to ratify. By the terms of the Union, the king pardoned previous acts of rebellion by the League and undertook to use force to eliminate "heresy" (i.e., Protestantism) from the realm of France, while his subjects declared that they would never accept a heretic as king (thereby excluding the heir apparent, Henri of Navarre). On the details of the agreement, and the historical context, see *Histoire et dictionnaire des Guerres de Religion*, ed. Jouanna et al., pp. 1353–54.

5 The site, in Val-de-Marne, near Paris, of one of the royal châteaux.

6 See below, l. 618 and n. 83.

7 Presumably on the occasion of his funeral oration for Julius Caesar, victim of the conspiracy led by his erstwhile friend, Marcus Brutus.

8   "To a faith-breaker, let faith be broken likewise."

9   The comparison between Henri III and Edward II was a staple of League attacks, which also parallelled Épernon and Piers Gaveston. Matthieu's account distorts events to this end. See my *Shakespeare, Marlowe and the Politics of France*, pp. 106–07 and 215, n. 81. Cf. Matthieu's *Pompe funèbre*, where the English element becomes a real political influence (though rather obscurely), while the minions are added to the picture by way of an ingenious image of yeast ("levain" also means agitation) that causes bread to fall rather than rise:

> Quelque race de Machiauel, vray esclaue de la tyranie, quelques colonies d'Angleterre, disons plutost vray leuain des mignons en le Royaume, qui despuis quelques annees ont [maigri?] vostre paste, veulent icy lascher le nerf de la loy, & briser son authorité.

> [Some offspring of Machavelli, a thorough slave of tyranny, some dependents of England, let us say rather the stirring-up of the minions in the realm, who for several years have shrunk your dough, here seek to strip the sinews of the law and break its authority.]                                                      (pp. 18–19)

10  The negative example is that of Theodotos of Chios, counsellor of Ptolemy XIV of Egypt, who advised his king treacherously to murder Pompey on the grounds that "a dead body does not bite" (Plutarch, *Life of Pompey*, 77.3–7). It is to the point that Marcus Brutus later took a terrible revenge on Theodotos (see also *Life of Pompey*, 80.7–9; *Life of Brutus*, 33.3–6; *Life of Caesar*, 48.2).

11  This assassination occurred in 1407; the consequent war between the Burgundians and the so-called Armagnacs was of great benefit to the invading English.

12  See Judges 19–20.

13  Jean-Louis de Nogaret de La Valette, duc d'Épernon, as the chief minion of Henri III, was the *bête noire* of Leaguers at this period and the object of innumerable slanderous attacks accusing him of crimes including sodomy and sorcery. A concerted campaign of propaganda, of which Marlowe was certainly cognizant, compared him to Gaveston, the minion of Edward II. See Hillman, *Shakespeare, Marlowe and the Politics of France*, esp. pp. 97–104. For an even-handed biography, see Maria Chaintron, *Le duc d'Épernon 1554–1642. L'ascension prodigieuse d'un cadet de Gascogne* (Paris: Éditions Publisud, 1988).

14  See below, n. 177.

15  The Arguments, as well a considerable amount of dialogue (includ-

ing the first fourteen lines of Guise's opening speech), comprise additions to the third edition of the play, which post-dates the assassination of Henri III. In general, as Lobbes points out (n. to ll. 1–14), these additions suggest an understandable concern posthumously to exonerate the hero (hence his successors in the League) for implication in the latter event. Even cruder League propaganda, which less guardedly anticipated Henri III's "punishment" for the Guises' death, prudently kept its distance from Jacques Clément's regicide by representing him as acting alone, though inspired by God. The standard Protestant line, by contrast (reflected, for example, in Marlowe's *Massacre*), insisted on the League's active complicity. There is also a broader context for Matthieu's rhetoric of justification: supporters of the House of Lorraine had always been on the defensive, to some extent, with regard to both their motives and their methods; cf. Fronton Du Duc, *La Pucelle*, trans. and ed. Hillman: "we give no ear to those who dare to write, / Savaging that House's honour, and in despite / Of truth" (Pro. 25–27).

16 On 12 May 1588, the supporters of the League, responding to Guise's triumphal return to Paris contrary to the express royal command, created such disorder in the capital that the King was forced to flee, and subsequently to concede the holding of the Estates General at Blois; see *Histoire et dictionnaire des Guerres de Religion*, ed. Jouanna et al., pp. 336–39. Matthieu's allusion to this event obviously plays up the king's pusillanimity and plays down Guise's responsibility.

17 Cf. *Coligny*, l. 206 and n. 42.

18 Presumably, the Pope.

19 Lines 27–34 comprise another justificatory supplement to the third edition.

20 The laurel, of course, is the symbol of conquest; cypress is associated with mourning and thus adds the dimension of death in battle.

21 After receiving a serious facial wound at Dormans in 1575, Henri, duc de Guise, become commonly known as Le Balafré ("the scarred one"). See Introduction, p. 28–29 and n. 52.

22 Dirae (Fr. *Dires*): i.e., the Furies.

23 The so-called *reîtres*, German mercenary cavalry usually sent by Protestant princes to the aid of their French coreligionists (though not always — cf. *Coligny*, n. 20), were notorious for their pillaging and atrocities. See the article in *Histoire et dictionnaire des Guerres de Religion*, ed. Jouanna et al., pp. 1237–38.

24  The reference enfolds Guise's past heroism into recent events, very much at the king's expense. Guise had recently defeated the *reîtres* again at Vimory (near Montargis) in October 1587, then devastatingly at Auneau (Eure-et-Loir) in November. The king was thereby enabled to negotiate their withdrawal (hence his own overblown claims of victory, bolstered by a triumphant royal entry into Paris and mass of thanksgiving); to Guise's angry consternation, they received a cash payment and were escorted by Épernon. See *Histoire et dictionnaire des Guerres de Religion*, ed. Jouanna et al., pp. 327–28, and Constant, pp. 160–61.

25  Lines 89–104 comprise an addition to the third edition.

26  Caesar: the Holy Roman Emperor; particularly intended is Charles V, whose wars with François I and Henri II extended over forty years until his abdication in 1558.

27  In 1558, François, 2nd duc de Guise, father of the current duke, recaptured Calais, thereby finally completing the expulsion of the English from France initiated by Jeanne d'Arc. The exploit was celebrated by Joachim Du Bellay in a poem echoed here, though Matthieu's Guise re-appropriates the glory that Du Bellay had attributed to the French king, Henri II; see Lobbes, ed., n. to l. 93, and Hillman, *Shakespeare, Marlowe and the Politics of France*, p. 219, n. 43. The same Guise had won great acclaim for his heroic defence of Metz against the forces of Charles V in 1552.

28  On the image of the Giants, cf. *Coligny*, l. 470 and n. 71. Lobbes, n. to l. 98, identifies the fifth Evangelist as Calvin, but the German origins of Protestantism are stressed in *The Guisiade* (ll. 311–15, 1340–40), and the Huguenots were regularly termed "luthériens," so the reference may be more particularly to Luther.

29  This is not mere metaphor, as the subsequent conjuring of Épernon confirms, together with much crude League propaganda. A popular belief that Épernon had supernatural powers is attested by Brantôme (see Pierre de Bourdeille, abbé de Brantôme, *Œuvres complètes*, ed. Ludovic Lalanne [Paris: La Société de l'Histoire de France, 1864–82], 6: 97). Cf. Hillman, *Shakespeare, Marlowe and the Politics of France*, pp. 108–09.

30  Lines 109–16 were added in the third edition.

31  Lines 123–26: the first of many marked by *guillemets* in the early editions.

32  Henri II died at the Palace of Tournelles in Paris after being accidentally struck in the eye with a lance by Gabriel de Lorges, comte de

Montgomery, during a festive tournament in 1559. Cf. the representation of Montgomery in *Coligny*.

33  The repetition of "triumph" as the rhyming word in ll. 158 and 160 is present in the original.

34  The accusation in the Chorus's final quatrain, scarcely tenable as stated, was added in the third edition; although it reflected the League's anger at the king's buying off of the *reîtres*, evidently to deny Guise the further glory of annihilating them, the claim might have seemed excessive even to Matthieu during the king's lifetime.

35  "Princes" broadly suggests the leadership of the House of Lorraine (including Charles de Lorraine, duc de Mayenne; Charles de Lorraine, duc d'Aumale; Charles III, duc de Lorraine; Philippe-Emmanuel de Lorraine, duc de Mercœur; and Charles de Lorraine, duc d'Elbeuf), as well, of course, as the play's two victims: Henri, duc de Guise, and his brother Louis de Lorraine, cardinal de Guise.

36  As Lobbes, ed., points out (n. to l. 177), the distinction between this pejorative term and the neutral "Guisiens" (used by the Queen Mother [l. 316]) was current at the time. It was not, however universal, as is clear, for instance, from Belyard's *Le Guysien* (see Lobbes, "L'exécution des Guises, prétexte à tragédie," p. 572, n. 4) and from the anonymous poetical evocation of the same events entitled *La Guisiade. A Monseigneur Charles de Lorraine, duc de Mayenne, pair et lieutenant général de l'Estat royal et Couronne de France* ([n.p.: n.pub], 1589). Not surprisingly, the latter work has been attributed to Matthieu (see BnF catalogue, RES-YE-4380), but, despite its overlap with the tragedy in ideology and basic narrative, I find it difficult to accept the attribution; there are few substantial verbal parallels, and the verse is markedly inferior. (Incidentally, confusion should also be avoided with *La double tragédie du Duc et Cardinal de Guyse jouée à Bloys le 23 et 24 Décembre dernier, envoyée à Mgr. le Duc du Mayne et autres Princes catholiques, qui tiennent le party de la saincte union* [Paris: Fleurant des Monceaux, 1589], an even slighter anonymous poem [BnF YE-2603].)

37  Lines 183–92, echoing the usual League accusations against Henri, including that of sexual impropriety, were a further addition to the third edition.

38  Henri, while his brother ruled France as Charles IX, had been elected to the throne of Poland; at his brother's death, he returned hastily to France to claim the French crown. League propaganda often referred to him as King of Poland to reinforce the erroneous claim that he had

renounced his royal inheritance in France.

39  With Henri's vainglorious (and petulant) address to Paris here, cf. Caesar's to Rome in Garnier, *Cornélie*, ed. Ternaux, ll. 1303ff. Both "tyrants" associate themselves with the pride that is conventionally associated with Babel-like towers doomed to be cast down—see, e.g., *Porcie*, ed. Lebègue, ll. 175ff. This motif makes a contrast with the harmony between outward and spiritual richness evoked by Jupiter in *Coligny*, ll. 645–60.

40  Pallas Athena, divine patroness of the arts: the reference is to Henri's active promotion of intellectual culture in Paris, where he instituted an Academy. Astraea was the goddess of justice, who dwelt on earth during the Golden Age. Cf. *Coligny*, l. 412.

41  The French plays on the double sense of "conjurer" ("conjure" and "conspire"), when Henri plans to "conjurer" the death of the "conjurez" ("conspirators"). The pun is important, given Henri's association with the black arts of magic in League propaganda and the subsequent conjuring of Épernon.

42  The Scythians and Sarmatae were related nomadic tribes of eastern Europe renowned in ancient times for their fierce warrior culture. Herodotus reports that the Sarmatae were descended from Scythian men and Amazons. But there is a more specific reference to Henri, given his Polish connection: see below, ll. 471 and 2095; cf. Introduction, pp. 30–31].

43  The original's "rameaux" seems to glance at the triumphal entry into Jerusalem of Jesus and the disciples on Palm Sunday ("Dimanche des Rameaux") and thus to evoke the crusading tradition claimed especially by the House of Lorraine. See Introduction, pp. 24–25, 26–27, 58], and cf. Fronton Du Duc, *La Pucelle*, trans. and ed. Hillman, ll. 31–32). Consistently opposed to the true religious zeal of the Guises, in League propaganda as in the discourse of the Queen Mother here, was the king's ostentatious religiosity, widely dismissed as "hypocrisy" (l. 277); cf. below, ll. 393ff. Opinions as to Henri's sincerity in religious matters varied according to political orientation; see Hillman, *Shakespeare, Marlowe and the Politics of France*, pp. 160–61.

44  The imagery is a rather strained evocation of the Erinyes (or Eumenides, or Furies); cf. Lobbes, ed., n. to ll. 285–86.

45  The imperfect rhyme "ambition"/"fiction" is in the original.

46  Again, in the context of League propaganda, this was not a mere metaphor.

47  "Two noble-minded brothers": François, duc de Guise, and Charles, cardinal de Lorraine, respectively the father and uncle of the present duke.

48  The first words of this sententious line ("Bien-heureux le malheur") accentuate the paradox and lend it spiritual authority by echoing the Beatitudes ("Blessed are . . ." [Matt. 5:3ff.]).

49  It will emerge that a particular heretic is meant: Henri of Navarre. In the *Pompe funèbre*, Matthieu, with reference to the king, combines spiritual with sexual dissolution in speaking of "l'heresie, secrette concubine de son ame [heresy, the secret concubine of his soul]" (p. 14).

50  Given the charged political climate and the ascendency of the Guises, Épernon had thought it prudent to retire from court for the time being.

51  Lines 365–72, which imply the king's breaking of an Erasmian contract with God and with his subjects, were added for the third, postregicidal edition. The prophetic accusation in ll. 367–68 would particularly suit the king's alliance with Henri de Navarre against the League after the assassination of the Guises.

52  The insinuation, frequently echoed in League propaganda, is that Henri was unworthy of the title earned for French monarchs by the sainted Louis IX, whose crusading exploits are implicitly contrasted here with Henri's unholy alliances.

53  Alcoran: metonymic for Muslim.

54  "Le Machiaveliste, et l'homme de fortune." Lobbes, ed., n. to 379, sees "l'homme de fortune" as a separate reference to an adventurer; it seems at least as likely that Matthieu is evoking the notorious "religion" of the Machiavel. Cf. *Coligny*, ll. 63ff.

55  Prince: from 1580, the Catholic Charles Emmanuel I, Duke of Savoy, son of Emmanuel Philibert, a close ally of Philip II of Spain. The legal status of Calvin's Geneva was a perennial source of political and military contention.

56  Geneva was known as the Protestant Rome. Like the coming of Antichrist, the apocalyptic image of the Great Whore of Babylon (Apoc. 17:1) served to symbolize the adversary for both Protestants and Catholics.

57  Antoine de Bourbon, King of Navarre and father of Henri IV, also had close ties with Calvin's Geneva, although he reverted to Catholicism towards the end of his life.

58  Henri III received the Order of the Garter from Elizabeth in 1575 (a highly strategic move on her part), three years after the Treaty of Blois allied the two countries militarily. Apart from the English support for the Huguenot cause, the 1587 execution of Mary Queen of Scots, allied by blood with the family of Guise, particularly rankled Leaguers when *The Guisiade* was composed. On the Guises, Mary Stuart, and Henri III, see also Fronton Du Duc, *La Pucelle*, trans. and ed. Hillman, Introduction, pp. 24–51.

59  The animal comparisons are recognizable, pejoratively, as Machiavellian.

60  Again, that this is not mere bluster will be abundantly confirmed.

61  During the very brief reign of François II (1599–60), the Guises exercised enormous influence. He was succeeded by Charles IX, then ten years old, initially with his mother as regent.

62  Lines 409–16 were added in the third edition.

63  In fact, the League entertained the idea of shutting away the deposed Henri in a monastery, as had been the fate of several French monarchs of earlier times. Cf. below, n. 144.

64  "[L]e sceptre Sarmatique": the crown of Poland. Henri is blind to the connotation of inhuman barbarity. Cf. below, ll. 471 and 2095.

65  Matthieu pointedly rhymes "royal" and "desloyal" in echoing the League propaganda that played up Henri's breaking of faith with his Polish subjects. Lines 477–84 appear only in the third edition.

66  "Anatomie": i.e., a skeleton (a common Renaissance usage in French and English).

67  Lines 489–90 read, in the original: "Je vis tes chers enfans à tes pieds massacrez, / Les temples prophanez, et les autels sacrez." Matthieu pointedly employs the loaded word "massacre" consistently for Henri's assassination of the Guises. Henri, amongst other false claims, is here appropriating the anti-heretical heroism of his royal predecessor, to judge from Ronsard: "Il a veu de Jesus abbatre les Maisons, / Prophaner les Autels, les Messes sans usage, / Et la Religion n'estre qu'un brigandage [He saw the houses of Jesus knocked down, the altars prophanes, the masses abandoned, and religion become nothing but thievery]" ("Le Tombeau du feu Roy tres-chrestien Charles Neufiesme," ed. Céard et al., ll. 40–42).

68  The references to making an "entry" here and in l. 503 have reference to the often-elaborate ceremonies with which the walled cities of the time welcomed their rulers and demonstrated their willing

submission to authority.

69 "Déguise": the original's rhyme with "convoitise" ("ambition"), adds a dimension to the pun on "Guise."

70 The full irony of these lines cannot be intentional, since they evidently predate Henri's assassination, but the general situation would have been clear enough to the author well before. There was no question of the king's returning to Paris after the assassination of the Guises: the city was in open revolt, and recapturing it was an essential objective of the joint military manoeuvres undertaken by Henri and his new ally, Henri de Navarre, from May 1589 until his own murder in August, while the city was under siege.

71 A devastating irony is produced by the contrast between Henri's heroic bluster here and the underhanded means by which he overcame his enemies.

72 The quintessentially Senecan revenge (see *Thyestes*), with overtones of civil war.

73 Matthieu must have counted on his audience to see this common accusation against the House of Lorraine (on the grounds of its Germanic origins) as part of the perverted thinking of the king, and so as patently discredited. Cf. Hillman, *Shakespeare, Marlowe and the Politics of France*, p. 91.

74 For the impious Henri to associate his unfounded and petty vindictiveness with divine retribution is presumptuous, indeed blasphemous; the situation is far otherwise in *Coligny*, where Jupiter intervenes on behalf of a genuinely pious and merciful Charles.

75 "Head" and "father" are commonplace political metaphors in the period.

76 "[D]echevestrez"; the term evokes animals who have broken free of their "chevêtre" or restraint. The elaboration of Henri's thought in ll. 543–46 was added in the third edition.

77 "[T]wo foes": Épernon and Henri de Navarre.

78 "[D]esguiser": again, a pun is surely intended.

79 As a sign of his righteous wisdom, Guise is well stocked with *sententiae* in this stichomythic debate: all his lines from this point to l. 614 are so distinguished.

80 Cf. *Coligny*, ll. 1081–83, where this indeed proves effective political medicine.

81 Here begins the first instance in the play of the stock debate between

mildness and harshness (see Introduction, pp. 14, 36–37, and n. 15).
The reprise of this device later, in the scene between Henri and his
counsellors (ll. 1694ff.), makes it ironically clear that Henri is mild
and merciful where he should be harsh and just, and *vice-versa*.

82    "À un cœur généreux toute chose est facile." Lobbes, ed., p. 188,
n. to l. 600, plausibly suggests that the line's aphoristic power is
reinforced by echoing the motto of Jacques Cœur (1400–1456): "À
vaillant cœur rien d'impossible." The allusion would gain ironic
point if the audience saw a parallel between Guise and that extraordinary man of genius and energy who was finally turned on by the
envious Valois king he served (Charles VII). Cœur escaped death
at the king's hands, however, and, having entered the service of the
Pope, died fighting for the faith against the Turks, thereby enacting
the crusading model which the House of Lorraine claimed as its
inheritance and destiny.

83    "[R]ompt les coups" — literally, "softens the blows." But the point
of Guise's reply is the same grim play on words the translation
attempts to convey, since "rompt les cous," pronounced identically,
would mean "breaks their necks," and wholesale hangings indeed
followed the Protestant rebellions of Amboise (1560) and Meaux
(1567), during the reigns of François II and Charles IX, respectively,
when the influence of the Guises was in the ascendant. Lobbes, ed.,
strangely, appears to miss the primary meaning, proposing merely
that "coups" must be a bad spelling of "cous" (p. 188, n. to l. 617);
just as strangely, Olivier Millet fails to see the secondary one (rev. of
Lobbes, ed., *Bulletin de la Société de l'Histoire du Protestantisme Français*
138 [1992]: 313).

84    The Hydra, slain by Hercules, was a common metaphor for the
Huguenots. The traditional figuration of Hercules as an heroic type
of Christ is evoked at a number of points in the play. See below, l. 888
and n. 112, l. 1169 and n. 145, l. 1446 and n. 170. Cf. Garnier, "Au Roy
de France et de Pologne," who reminded Henri in 1585 that Hercules
earned immortal fame when "la terre purgea de ses monstres desfaits
[he purged the earth of its monsters, which he defeated]" ( *Œuvres
complètes*, ed. Lebègue, l. 24). As with other commonplaces of League
rhetoric (the motifs of martyrdom and vengeance, the condemnation
of tyranny, atheism, Machiavelism, and foreign influence), this image
also (and earlier) served the Protestant cause; cf. "*Souhait* pour la
France [Wish for France]" in the 1576 edition of the *Anti-Machiavel*
by Innocent Gentillet (ed. C. Edward Rathé, Les Classiques de la
Pensée Politique, 5 [Geneva: Droz, 1968], p. 635):

Qu'il estaigne aux champs et aux villes
Les feux de nos guerres civiles:
Et comme un Hercules gaulois
Couppe les testes de ce monstre,
Qui encor aujourd'huy se monstre
Ennemi juré de nos loix.

[May he (our prince) extinguish in fields and towns the fires of
our civil wars, and, like a Gallic Hercules, cut off the heads of
that monster, which still today shows itself the sworn enemy of
our laws.]

Grévin, in *César*, makes Cassius use the image (and the word "massacre") in gloating over the successful assassination (Ginsberg, ed.,
ll. 1041–44).

85 Guise significantly echoes the rebuke of Catherine de Medici in l. 374,
but he is respectfully diplomatic.

86 "Aux extremes tourmens le remede est extreme": a variant of the
still-current proverb, "Aux grands maux les grands remèdes." Cf.
*Coligny*, ll. 1075–77.

87 Wenceslas IV (1361–1419) — whose sister was Anne, first wife of
Richard II of England — had at first backed the religious reform
movement led by Jan Hus. Hus was finally burnt at the stake for
heresy in 1415, but when the king subsequently acted against Hus's
followers, there was massive unrest, which developed into civil war.
Hus was inspired by John Wycliffe, so Guise's allusion to foreign
intervention in l. 648 may specifically evoke the Huguenots' backing
by the English.

88 "Qu'il ne veut que la paix, qu'il combat de la parole." Lobbes, ed., n.
to l. 659, considers the second "qu'il" to contain a relative pronoun
referring to "paix," syntax which would give the sense, "claims to
seek only peace, which he fights against with his words." This is
squarely at odds with the next line, which is unambiguous and, in
my view, imposes a reading of l. 659 as composed of two parallel
clauses, each introduced by a conjunction.

89 "[L]'Huguenot . . . / Qui brave vos subjects asseuré de vostre aisle."
Cf. Marlowe, *Massacre*, where, in a parallel dialogue in the sequence
leading up to Guise's assassination, the latter assures the king that
he "need not fear mine army's force: / 'Tis for your safety, and
your enemy's wrack" (xix.53–54), but threatens the Huguenots and
"Navarre, that cloaks them underneath his wings" (51).

90 Guise is referring, of course, to Épernon.

91   The reference is to the substantial concessions obtained from Henri on behalf of the church and the League after the Day of the Barricades. For details, see Lobbes, ed., n. to l. 701.

92   Avernus: i.e., the underworld.

93   "[E]n Solime": Jerusalem (Lobbes, ed., n. to l. 725), with reference to the House of Lorraine's crusading heritage.

94   The final two stanzas of the Chorus, which anticipate the exercise of divine grace that, in the League's view, produced the assassination of Henri III, were added after that event.

95   Jean de la Valette was a member of the minor nobility who indeed seems to have been an upright and widely respected royal officer.

96   "[D]egenerate / As I am": "car trop je degenere"; cf. *Coligny*, where the Chorus reproaches "Châtillon, wicked wretch" (l. 247), for his criminality despite having "Come from blood most thoroughly bred / And [being] issued of most noble race" (ll. 253–54). Marlowe, in *Massacre*, has Guise stamping on the body of Coligny with the words, "Ah, base Shatillian and degenerate, / Chief standard-bearer to the Lutherans" (v. 38–39). Protestants generally saw divine retribution in the equivalent stamping of Henri on the body of Guise — see below, l. 2082.

97   Lines 773–80 were added in the third edition.

98   With Épernon's invocation, including its comic self-consciousness and exaggeration, cf. the opening soliloquy of the diabolical Admiral in *Coligny*. Senecan and Neo-Senecan precedents, of course, abound.

99   "Fils de confusion": biblical (Prov. 10:5).

100  The Duke of Guise, with reference to the Day of the Barricades.

101  Styx, Phlegethon, Cocytus, Acheron: rivers in the lower world; cf. *Coligny*, l. 20.

102  The ambiguity of the pronoun references is present in the original.

103  This is recognizably the rhetoric of Protestant martyrdom. It is an outright lie (though it was a common one) to present Épernon as a Huguenot. There is reliable testimony that he considered Navarre a heretic — see Hillman, *Shakespeare, Marlowe and the Politics of France*, pp. 99–100.

104  Probably in the campaigns of 1575 and 1587, though perhaps in the two battles during the latter. See above, n. 24, and Introduction, p. 29.

105  "[I]l pourra quelque jour / Sur le ventre marcher du Roy et de la Cour": an ironic anticipation of the king's shameful treatment of

Guise's dead body; see below, ll. 2079–82.

106 Cataline: the Roman epitome of seditious conspiracy, defeated thanks to Cicero (63 B.C.E.).

107 Henri de Navarre became a prime candidate, of course, for identification with the emperor Julian. Cf. Introduction, pp. 52.

108 One of the Eumenides — the one who presides over the civil strife in Garnier's *Porcie*; the other two, Alecto and Tisiphone, will shortly be added to the invocation.

109 The notorious punishments of Tantalus ("Tantal") in the underworld would make him a virtual embodiment of the horrors of hell. Still, the other names in the line are geographical, and this seems a possible printer's error for "Tartarus" ("Tartare").

110 Minos, King of Crete, sacrificed Athenians to the Minotaur; Rhadamanthus was his brother. Both became dispensers of justice in the underworld. Cf. *Coligny*, l. 871.

111 "[G]aping" ("beante") is the reading of the third edition, followed here throughout; Lobbes, ed., n. to l. 872, observes that the reading of the first two editions, "relante," appears to be an adjectival neologism based on the noun "relent" ("bad odour"). Matthieu has already used this coinage in l. 777 ("putrid").

112 The analogy with Caesar was also widely used against Guise: cf. Marlowe, *Massacre*, ii.95, xxi.67, 87. Coupling it with comparison to the Maccabees, heroic warriors for religion's sake, confirms that Épernon cannot withhold his admiration.

113 The point is not, as supposed by Lobbes, ed., n. to l. 888, the far-fetched notion that Hercules was a dissembler, but rather that Henri will ingeniously attempt to present himself as a hero for having defeated the formidable Guises. This does in fact match the royal propaganda following the assassination, according to which the king had managed to foil a dangerous conspiracy. There is also an ironic twisting of the idea that the true route to Herculean status would be to slay the monster of Huguenot heresy — see above, ll. 623–24 and n. 84, and below, ll. 1169, 1446, and n. 171.

114 Busiris, the King of Egypt finally killed by Hercules, was notorious for slaughtering strangers; the monstrous guard-dog of Hades, Cerberus, was mastered by Hercules in another of his labours (cf. *Coligny*, ll. 878–81). In general, Hercules' role as a killer of monsters and purger of the earth is suggestively prominent in Catholic texts of the period; cf. Antoine's catalogue of his ancestor's feats

in *Porcie*, ll. 1085–112, esp. ll. 1110–12: "Qui Buisire inhumain, Tyran Egyptien, / Massacra de ses mains [Who killed with his own hands the inhuman/inhumane Buisiris, the Egyptian tyrant]." Agrigentum (Greek Acragas) was the Sicilian city where the tyrant Phalaris (reigned 570–554 B.C.E.) roasted his victims alive in a bull (Matthieu's text makes it an ox ["boeuf"]) fashioned of brass.

115  A *toise* (the equivalent of the English fathom) consisted of six feet, roughly two metres.

116  Matthieu obviously signals the symbolic importance of this suggestive position.

117  "[B]y the grace of God": because he too would have been killed; Guise's successor as head of the League was, of course, the dedicatee of Matthieu's tragedy.

118  Henri refers to the realms of France and Poland.

119  The orc ("orque") is specifically a sea-monster, with evident reference to the biblical Leviathan, so the maritime metaphor of the following lines is introduced.

120  There seems to be an undertone of irony at Henri's expense in having him identify Heresy's death with his own.

121  It has been already made clear that Guise's recent heroic triumphs over the *reîtres* are a particular sore point for Henri, who here takes credit for preventing them from crossing the Loire and presents his preference for negotiating with them as an act of Christian charity. He is also implicitly assimilating to his less-than-brilliant present position the "trophies" of his youth, when he vanquished at Jarnac and Montcontour, the theme also of ll. 1541–44 below. See *Histoire et dictionnaire des Guerres de Religion*, ed. Jouanna et al., pp. 182–84, 327–28, 1238.

122  Alcides: Hercules; cf. l. 888 and n. 113. The irony is blatant.

123  I take "Ou'il" at the beginning of this line in Lobbes, ed., as a misprint for "Qu'il." In the reference to Poitou, Lobbes (n. to l. 992) perceives an allusion to unsuccessful League operations currently underway. Far more probably intended, in my view, is the king's campaign of the previous year against Henri de Navarre and the Prince de Condé, who were in fact joined by a number of prominent Catholic supporters of the House of Bourbon; the culmination was the disastrous loss, for the royal forces, of the battle of Coutras (20 October 1587), at which the duc de Joyeuse, Épernon's predecessor as chief *mignon*, was killed. This loss dealt Henri "un grand coup

politique et affectif [a great political and emotional blow]" (*Histoire et dictionnaire des Guerres de Religion*, ed. Jouanna et al., p. 966; see also pp. 323–24).

124 The "apostate" in question, of course, is Henri de Navarre.

125 Lobbes, ed., n. to ll. 1021–22, here detects an echo of Ronsard, "Les Parques," without precedent in Henri's actual speech:

> L'Aigle de l'Aigle naist: le Lyon genereux
> Engendre le Lyon: d'un pere valeureux
> (Valeureux comme luy) tu a pris ta naissance,
> Et d'un Roy tu prendras ta gloire et ta puissance.

[The eagle is born of the eagle; the noble lion engenders the lion: of a valorous father you have been born, valorous like him, and you will obtain your glory and your power from a king.]
(*Œuvres complètes*, ed. Céard et al., vol. 1, ll. 35–37)

It is indeed ironic, as Lobbes points out, that Ronsard's poem (1584) was dedicated to the Duke of Épernon, and it seems likely that the irony was deliberate on Matthieu's part: having the king echo a paean to Épernon surreptitiously (or involuntarily, as if under a spell) is not far from having him hint at his heretical leanings and his sexual relation with Épernon by ventriloquizing Du Bartas (see ll. 1549–54 and n. 184). Moreover, Matthieu's Épernon has already (ll. 773–75) undercut Ronsard's claim that he resembles his noble father.

126 "[Q]ui du profound Tenare / Sont sortis conjurez." For Taenarus, see *Coligny*, l. 857 and n. 120. The line is highly ironic in the light of Épernon's conjuring, and again there is a pun on "conjurez" (see above, l. 248 and n. 41).

127 Henri is at once falsely appropriating Guise's discourse of heroic devotion (cf. above, ll. 47–52) and exacerbating his future breech of faith.

128 "[P]uisque c'est à bon jeu": Lobbes, ed., n. to l. 1030, takes this expression to mean that the goal is worth the effort, but Millet (p. 313) points out that it refers to doing the honest thing.

129 The nearly bathetic undercutting of Henri's lofty rhetoric here goes beyond an attack on his personal hypocrisy, profligacy, and immorality to evoke a systemic political issue. The Estates General of 1588–89 may have been held in a specific and highly charged political context, but the monarch's need for funds was a constant factor, and source of conflict, in his periodic recourse to that consultative body.

See *Histoire et dictionnaire des Guerres de Religion*, ed. Jouanna et al., p. 901 ("États Généraux").

130 A daringly graphic (indeed melodramatic) evocation of Henri's wounding by Jacques Clément; the addition of ll. 1069–72 to the third edition is conclusive evidence that the latter postdates his death on 2 August 1589.

131 This makes a remarkably theatrical touch for a play not necessarily intended for performance: Henri is clearly referring to his physical position in the hall (see the Argument to the scene) as analogous to his God-given authority.

132 The abbey of Saint Denis, outside Paris, was the traditional burial place of French kings.

133 "Qui n'endure ny fard, ny simulation." This seems a barbed irony; Henri's penchant for dressing effeminately and wearing make-up ("fard") — as he evidently did regularly at least during the First Estates General in Blois in 1577 — was often cited in attacks on his sexuality. Aubigné evokes in particularly acid terms the king's appearance in public as a "putain fardée [made-up whore]" (*Les tragiques*, ed. Lestringant, 2.784).

134 "Je me plains du trespas de la Religion": there seems to be in this wording an indirect refutation of French Protestantism, which had termed itself "la Religion."

135 The figuration of the union between Christ and the Church as a mystic marriage is a theological commonplace, derived exegetically from the Song of Songs. Cf. *Coligny*, l. 287 and n. 54.

136 Presumably a reference to the Christianizing mission associated with contemporary, and especially Spanish, conquest and colonization of the New World.

137 Such terms were often applied to Luther, as they presumably are here.

138 Belial: the devil. Cf. 2 Cor. 6:15: "And what concord hath Christ with Belial? or what part hath he that believeth with an infidel?"; 2 Cor. 14:17 is more generally echoed in this speech. The story recounted in 1 Sam. 5:1–4 of the collapse of the idol of Dagon (god of the Philistines) in the presence of the Ark of the Covenant was widespread in the Renaissance. More broadly relevant is the sequel recounting God's punishment of the infidels for purloining the Ark. The Archbishop's rhetoric works to deflect onto the Huguenots the king's previous accusations of divisive factionalism and "leagues."

139 "[L]a Gaule . . . en cent pars divisée": An ironic allusion, implying

a return to paganism, with overtones of foreign conquest, to the famous opening of Caesar's commentary on the Gallic wars: "Gallia omnis in tres partes divisa est [The whole of Gaul is divided into three parts]."

140 Although this claim may be explained by the constant Catholic exhortations to Protestants to return to the fold, Lobbes, ed., n. to l. 1145, may be right in detecting a specific reference to the conference held at Poissy in 1561 in a vain attempt to reconcile the Catholic and reformed doctrines.

141 Just prior to the Saint Bartholomew massacre in August 1572, the future Henri IV had married the king's sister Marguerite — an event prominent in *Coligny* (see ll. 457–58, 817–20, and n. 70). She was often termed the "pearl of France" ("marguerite" is both a pearl and a flower).

142 According to legend, the fleur-de-lys was indeed a gift of heaven. Lines 1153–60 comprise the first of several passages in this speech, including two sections signalled for special attention typographically, that Matthieu adapted (sometimes repeating himself word for word) from his *Stances svr l'hevreuse publication de la paix et saincte vnion* (1588); cf. p. 7 of that work. (Nero is also evoked in the *Pompe funèbre*, p. 18.) It is especially suggestive that the *Stances* express the same refusal to accept a "tyrant" or a heretic as king and the same willingness to abrogate the Salic law if necessary. The ostensible premise of the poem is that Henri is no tyrant because he accepts the Union, but the term resonates with League propaganda dating back to the mid-1570s and points to his potential for relapsing. (On the likelihood that Chantelouve's *Pharaon* so characterized Henri in 1576, see Introduction, pp. 28–31.)

As for the previously sacrosanct Salic law (cf. Fronton Du Duc, *La Pucelle*, trans. and ed. Hillman, ll. 93ff.), it had been questioned by at least some Leaguers, as the succession of Henri IV loomed larger with the death of the king's brother François, duc d'Anjou (formerly d'Alençon), in 1584. Lines 1157–60 are found only in the third edition of the play, as is noted by Ernst ("Des deux *Guisiade*," p. 374), though not indicated by Lobbes; their derivation from the poem, however, shows (*pace* Ernst, pp. 374–75) that the issue was in the air before the assassination of Henri III.

With the cosmic impossibilities in ll. 1157–58, which amount to saying that creation would have to be undone, cf. *Coligny*, ll. 705–12. It is implied that abrogating the Salic law would be as radical an alteration, but in the cause of realigning the human order with the divine.

143  This reference to the first Frankish dynasty appears less than wholly complimentary, since the last Merovingian king, Childeric III, who was stripped of power and confined to a monastery, was often used in League propaganda as a model of what might be done to a "fainéant" ("do-nothing," "idle") king such as Henri III. Cf. ll. 428 and 1663ff.

144  The early editions all read "Marcel" — an obvious error, also found in the passage from *Stances svr l'hevreuse publication de la paix et saincte vnion* (p. 7) from which ll. 1163–66 are derived. The reference, which in the new context is laden with irony, is to the heroic Charles Martel, whose triumph in 732 at the Battle of Poitiers (or of Tours, since the precise location is uncertain) halted the advance of the Saracens into France.

145  Cf. above, l. 888 and n. 113.

146  Lines 1171–75 (but not 1176) are adapted from *Stances svr l'hevreuse publication de la paix et saincte vnion*, pp. 7–8. The celebratory poem does not make reference to the vices of the court or to the minions. Lines 1177–78 come, word for word, from a later passage in the same text (p. 9).

147  Latona (Greek Leto) was the mother of Diana (the moon) and Apollo (the sun).

148  Lines 1183–84 adapt *Stances svr l'hevreuse publication de la paix et saincte vnion*, p. 9.

149  "Opinion" in this period was often applied to deviant notions of purely human origin, as opposed to divinely guided "reason," and thereby served Catholics as a means of denigrating Protestantism; see Lobbes, ed., n. to l. 1189.

150  "Grand Panetier": an important officer of the royal household, whose functions included serving and tasting the king's dishes. At this period, the Count of Brissac had become disaffected from the king, who he felt undervalued his military abilities, and was a notable partisan of the Guises; see *Histoire et dictionnaire des Guerres de Religion*, p. 827 ("Cossé, famille de").

151  The relation between formal royalty and entitlement is indirectly problematized here, since Charles Martel, an obvious heroic Christian precursor of the Duke of Guise, was never crowned king but effectively wielded royal power.

152  This string of negative formulations, ending in a reference to masculine virtue and appearance, may well be ironic. Lobbes, n. to l. 1214,

remarks that the allusion to Alexander may be particularly so, given that Henri had been christened "Édouard-Alexandre." One might add that Alexander the Great, however commonplace his mention in royal compliments, was also an ambiguous model, whose lack of personal self-control and predilection for tyranny were often condemned. These famously extended to his drunken murder of his companion Clytus — cf. Shakespeare, *H5*, IV.vii.44ff.

153 Nemean lions: such as that slain by Hercules.

154 A bizarre passage to modern sensibilities, but the "Princes of the Faith" ("Princes de la Foy") are being celebrated for their violent repression of religious dissent; Chantelouve's tragedy puts the attitude in perspective. Cf. Jamyn, who in his "Epitaphe du feu roy Chrales IX," claims that "les Princes Chrestiens / Qui iadis ont voulu leur braue sang espandre / Pour sauuer leur païs, & l'Eglise defendre [the Christian princes who in former times were willing to shed their brave blood to save their country and defend the Church]" (sig. Bii$^v$) are keeping Charles company in heaven. Part of the same discursive space, to the point of anticipating Matthieu's language ("Prodigues de leur sang"), is the praise by Garnier's Porcie of the heroic virtue of "Ces vieux pères Romains" (Lebègue, ed., l. 1702) who with so many foreign conquests glorified their country, "pour lequel leur sang il prodiguerent [for which they were prodigal with their blood]" (l. 1712) — a country now fallen into tyranny.

155 "Greece": an allusion to the taking of Constantinople in 1202 during the fourth crusade; see Lobbes, ed., n. to l. 1264.

156 "Vandals" here seems to conflate, deliberately or not, the Germanic tribe that sacked Rome in 455 C.E. with the Waldenses (or Valdenses, or Vaudois), who, as the target of anti-heretical "crusades" during the Middle Ages, would be more likely to figure alongside the Arians and Albigensians. Cf. *La Pucelle*, trans. and ed. Hillman, l. 650 and n. 77.

157 The crusades in the Holy Lands are obviously being invoked — a long-standing paradigm for the crusade against infidels at home; cf., e.g., Du Rosier, sigs. C$^r$–Ciii$^r$.

158 Again, irony is clearly intended, given the extreme accusations and comparisons deployed against Henri. It is nevertheless significant that, in the play's terms, Henri could still theoretically change his ways. Thus the speech goes on to offer the prospect of a blessing in the form of a son, harking back to Henri's hope of producing one, God willing (ll. 1015ff.). This corresponds to the two-part structure

of the most influential piece of contemporary anti-Épernon propaganda, *Histoire tragique et memorable de Pierre de Gaverston* [sic] *Gentilhomme Gascon jadis le mignon d'Edoüard 2. Roi d'Angletere, tirée des Chroniques de Thomas Walsinghan* [sic] *& tournée de Latin en François Dédiée à Monseigneur le duc d'Espernon*, attributed to Jean Boucher ([n.p.]: [n.pub.], 1588). In this barbed history lesson, Edward II's abusive association with his minion, who is finally eliminated by the barons, is followed by a happy interlude featuring the birth of a son; Edward relapses into vice, however, this time with Hugh Le Despenser, and is finally himself punished by death. See my discussion of this text in *Shakespeare, Marlowe and the Politics of France*, passim, esp. p. 107.

159  The expression, "possession par prescription du temps," and the concept are legal ones; the speaker is a lawyer, as was Matthieu.

160  See l. 98 and n. 28. In this passage, the German origins of the heresy (ll. 1347–48) particularly evoke Luther.

161  See *Coligny*, l. 260 and n. 50.

162  Medea: like Circe (l. 1379), an archetypal witch.

163  The language ("voute astree") specifically evokes the myth of Astraea.

164  Lobbes, ed., n. to l. 1399, points to the prominent position of Lombard bankers in France; beyond this allusion lies the more general perception of Italian economic, cultural, religious, and political influence, which League propaganda exploited in attacking the Valois court. See *Histoire et dictionnaire des Guerres de Religion*, ed. Jouanna et al., pp. 992–94 ("Italiens").

165  Again, there is an insinuation of literal spell-casting.

166  This is seemingly an allusion to a hearth-tax (Lobbes, ed., n. to l. 1410).

167  The reference is to the legendary Sardanapalus, a well-known model for ill-fated effeminate debauchery also applied to Henri III by Aubigné (*Les tragiques*, ed. Lestringant, 2.776).

168  "Il devient faixneant" — lit., "he becomes idle." "Faixneant" (or "fainéant") — i.e., "do-nothing" — had become a League buzzword for Henri's kingship, although it seems to have been satirically applied first by Ronsard during the reign of Charles IX; "idle" was the standard contemporary translation (see Hillman, *Shakespeare, Marlowe and the Politics of France*, p. 161 and n. 62).

169  In the original, the same rhyme is similarly repeated, with the effect of making ll. 1427–30 a coherent unit.

170  Particularly in the massacre of Saint Bartholomew's day, viewed in

the familiar apocalyptic light. One of the commemorative medals struck for this occasion did indeed portray Charles as Hercules, slaying the many-headed Hydra (Capefigue, vol. 3: 241), and the image was further diffused poetically — by Ronsard, among others, in terms that Matthieu seems to echo throughout the play on behalf of Guise:

> Il se vit au berceau des serpens assailli,
> Comme un jeune Herculin, dont il rompit la force:
> . . . . . . . . .
>
> Il eut le cœur si ferme et si digne d'un Roy,
> Que combatant pour Dieu, pour l'Eglise, et la Foy,
> Pour autels, pour fouyers, contre les Heretiques,
> Et rompant par conseil leurs secrettes pratiques,
> Telle langueur extréme en son corps il en prist,
> Qu'il mourut en sa fleur martyr de Jesus-Christ.
> ("Le Tombeau du feu Roy tres-chrestien Charles Neufiesme," ed. Céard et al., ll. 44–56)

As the last of the play's Herculean allusions, that in l. 1446 pointedly confirms that Henri is not cut out for the role. Cf. above, ll. 623, 888, 1169 and nn. 84, 113.

171 Lobbes, ed., n. to 1453–54, aptly compares the prophetic rhetoric of Ezekiel, with its monstrous threats and transcendent promises regarding the divided people of Israel, esp. 11:19: "And I will give them one heart, and I will put a new spirit within you; and I will take the stony heart out of their flesh, and will give them an heart of flesh." The reference to Hercules in l. 1446 fits the messianic pattern.

172 The French seems straightforward — "Je vous conserve tous" (lit. "I preserve you all") — but "conserver," in this context, may carry overtones of its naval sense: to escort a ship by keeping it within sight. Henri's rhetoric, then, would work to reappropriate the standard image of the ship of state just invoked against him in ll. 1437–40.

173 A reference to the Treaty of Rouen, imposed on Henri by the League on 15 July 1588; the Edict of Union was recorded in Parlement a few days later (Lobbes, ed., n. to l. 1466).

174 The verb, in the original, is pointedly present.

175 This paradoxical view of the human relation to misfortune was a commonplace, represented in emblem books.

176 There is an ironic ambiguity to these lines, which overtly celebrate the permanence of the Union and indirectly call attention to its contingency on the qualities which Henri will shortly be shown spec-

tacularly to lack.

177   The Argument (supplied only, one should recall, for the third edition) attaches to these unnamed advisors of the king what the dramatic text clearly presents, regardless of the precise staging originally
envisaged, as a diabolical function exteriorizing the inner voice of
temptation to evil (the equivalent of the Bad Angel in Marlowe's
*Faustus*), which Henri at first resists—as if, indeed, speaking to
himself.   There is continuity, then, with Épernon's earlier conjuration. Lobbes, ed., pp. 23–24, simply takes "N.N." to be the devil
himself, in keeping with medieval dramatic convention, but this may
be to undervalue Matthieu's innovative adaptation of that tradition.
The initials themselves carry an air of mystery, even if they may orig-
inate merely in Latin "nonnulli" ("certain persons") or the plural of
"nomen" ("name")—i.e., "fill in the blanks"; another possibility is
"Nogaret" (as if Épernon's name stood for several such), but it is
also suggestive that, in the *Pompe funèbre*, p. 18, Matthieu opines that
Henri's extreme wickedness (especially in having the bodies burnt)
must have been learnt from devils and "Necromantiens" ("Necro-
mancers").

178   "Politiques": the moderates, mainly Catholic, who put the peace
and stability of the kingdom before religious interests; see *Histoire et
dictionnaire des Guerres de Religion*, ed. Jouanna et al., pp.   1210–13
("Politiques").

179   "Rende le lis François à l'Ebre tributaire"—lit., "Render the French
lily tributary to the Ebro" (the river that flows through Sargasso
in Spain).

180   In the so-called "Sicilian vespers" of 1282, the French rulers of Sicily
(under Charles I of Anjou) were surprised and massacred by an
uprising sponsored by the House of Aragon.  The parallel with the
current situation, then, extends to Spanish enmity, as in the reference
to Pavia, where in 1525 François I was defeated and taken prisoner
by the forces of Charles V.  The Scottish mutiny referred to, on the
other hand, must be that of 1559–60, when French troops sought to
defend the queen regent, Mary of Guise, then governing on behalf of
her daughter, Mary Stuart, against Protestant (and English-backed)
rebels.

181   "King of Yvetot": a mocking expression, derived from an ancient
feudal privilege of that Norman town, for a ridiculous application
of the royal title.

182   If "zero" seems strong as a translation of "vaunéant" (lit. "worth-

less"), it is worth recalling that one of the abusive anagrams made of Henri's name was "H. Rien" (i.e., "H. Nothing"); see Hillman, *Shakespeare, Marlowe and the Politics of France*, p. 160. The following lines nostalgically evoke his youthful triumphs as commander of the royal army at Jarnac (13 March 1569) and Montcontour (3 October 1569) during the third civil war; see *Histoire et dictionnaire des Guerres de Religion*, ed. Jouanna et al., pp. 182–84.

183 *Pace* Lobbes, ed., n. to l. 1550, I find ll. 1549–52 heavy with sexual double-entendre, although "à son pouce" (lit. "with his thumb") has a primarily figurative sense ("as he liked").

184 Matthieu here seems to load the dice doubly against the king — in the very midst of his struggle with conscience — by having him unmistakably echo the portrayal by the Protestant Du Bartas (in his epic of creation) of what man would be like in the absence of woman:

> ... qu'un Loup garou du soleil ennemi,
> Qu'un animal sauvage, ombrageux, solitaire,
> Bigarre, frenetique, à qui rien ne peut plaire
> Que le seul desplaisir.

> [. . . a mere were-wolf, enemy of the sun, a mere savage beast, quarrelsome, solitary, mixed-up, frenzied, capable of being pleased only by what is unpleasant.]   (*La Semaine [texte de 1581]*, ed. Yvonne Bellenger, 2 vols., Société des Textes Français Modernes [Paris: Librairie Nizet, 1981], 6.950–53)

Cf. Hillman, *Shakespeare, Marlowe, and the Politics of France*, p. 108). Du Bartas, in fact, exerted a formative influence on Matthieu as a dramatist, as has been pointed out by Louis Lobbes, "Du Bartas et Matthieu: genèse d'une vocation de dramaturge," in *L'Art du théâtre. Mélanges en hommage à Robert Garapon*, ed. Yvonne Bellenger, Gabriel Conesa, Jean Garapon et al. (Paris: Presses Universitaires de France, 1992), 61–66; see also below, n. 219.

185 Chilperic: seemingly intended is Childeric III (son of Chilperic II), the last of the Merovingians, deposed and shut up in a monastery by Pepin the Short in 751; cf. above n. 143. (If there is such confusion, it appears to have been widespread in League propaganda, given the existence of a tragedy of Chilperic II in 1590 — see Introduction, p. 64).

Charles III ("the Fat") was deposed in 887 — in part, as stated below (l. 1607), because of his feeble resistance to Norse invaders; the reference thus accords with what the League saw as Henri III's collaboration with German and English Protestants.

186 Pepin, the first of the Carolingians, was of Germanic origin; the House
of Lorraine, branded as similarly foreign by its opponents, traced its
origin to Charlemagne, whose line was deposed by Hugues Capet
in 987.

187 The argument that God has sanctioned transfers of royal power, even
by usurpation, is obviously double-edged.

188 A "lieutenant," etymologically, is one who takes the place, hence
transmits the orders, of another.

189 Henri had dreamt of being devoured by a lion, whereupon he ordered
those in the royal menagerie to be slaughtered (Lobbes, ed., n. to
l. 1655). His dream, then, and his superstitious inclination were
hardly a secret, but the way in which N.N. uses both to play on
his fears hints at supernatural access to the inner self—an inverted
version of the heaven-derived knowledge of the Dauphin's prayer
attributed to Jeanne d'Arc in some versions of her legend; see, e.g.,
Fronton Du Duc, *La Pucelle*, trans. and ed. Hillman, ll. 220ff. and 508ff.

190 The verb "empourprer" ("empurple") may also mean "invested in
purple clothing"—the garb of royalty.

191 The word "soul" ("âme"), though used in a general sense, also draws
attention, with subtle irony, to the complex and elusive function of
N.N., who seems to embody at once Henri's wicked counsellors, his
inner voice, and the devil himself. The last of these, of course, is in
the business of ensnaring souls.

192 Cf. above, l. 595 and n. 81.

193 Like other arguments of the N.N., this point is recognizably Machiavellian; see Lobbes, ed., n. to ll. 1697 et passim, and (in the context of
the conventional debate between mildness and harshness) Jondorf,
*Robert Garnier*, pp. 106–07.

194 Henri's gloating anticipation of revenge is recognizably Senecan,
stopping just short of the hubris of the sadistic Atreus at the analogous moment in *Thyestes*: "Mine is the kingdom and the glory
now, / Mine the ancestral throne. I need no gods" (Watling, trans.
and ed., ll. 887–88). Indeed, that play closely models Henri's para-
noid jealousy and projection of ambition upon the innocent Guise, as
well as the curse on the House of Valois. Cf. especially Atreus' discussion with his Minister, as he plots his horrible vengeance against
his brother:

> *Minister.*                    By what device
> Will he be lured to walk into our net?
> He looks for danger everywhere.

| *Atreus.* | We could not |
| | Catch him, were he not hoping to catch us. |
| | Already he aspires to win my throne; |
| | To gain this end he would stand up to Jove |
| | Armed with his thunderbolts; to gain this end |
| | He is about to brave the angry sea, |
| | To cross the dangerous shoals of Libyan Syrtis; |
| | For this, he will endure what he most hates — |
| | His brother's sight. |
| *Minister.* | How will he be persuaded |
| | That peace is made? Whom will he trust for that? |
| *Atreus.* | Dishonest hope is always credulous. . . .    (ll. 286–98) |

195 The best historical account of these forty-five Gascon "coupe-jarret" ("hamstringers"), and indeed of the details of the assassination, is by Pierre Chevallier, *Henri III: roi shakespearien*. (Paris: Fayard, 1985), pp. 662–73.

196 See above, n. 24.

197 Charon ferried souls across the river Styx in Hades.

198 Lines 1759–76 were added for the third edition. By now, in the view of the League, a supernatural answer had been provided to the question Henri hubristically poses in ll. 1771–72.

199 More irony on Matthieu's part, given his vigorous promotion of the League cause, not to mention the publication of *La Guisiade*, in Lyons.

200 In fact, Henri failed in his designs against both Philippe-Emmanuel de Lorraine, duc de Mercœur, who was the half-brother of the Queen, and Charles de Lorraine, duc d'Aumale, Guise's cousin, whom the League made Governor of Paris. Both survived to become re-doubtable enemies of Henri IV.

201 It is tempting to consider that Marlowe might have taken this point as encouragement to stage the invented episode, found in only once source in the surviving propaganda, in which Henri uses the sight of the slain Guise to admonish Guise's son (*Massacre*, xxi.117ff.).

202 This elliptical stanza was suppressed in the third edition — hence its omission from the regular line numbering. The suppression may be due to aesthetic considerations, as supposed by Lobbes, ed., n. to ll. 1788[a–d]. On the other hand, the anticipation of Henri's wound in the abdomen is remarkable, if fortuitous (indeed, Matthieu is recycling the image from a previous play of his own), and it seems possible (despite l. 1072 above) that he sought to avoid any suspicion

that his work had provided Jacques Clément with a blueprint for assassination. As for the literal sense, Lobbes takes 1788[a] to mean, "Would that you had not been . . .", in which case, as he says, it flatly contradicts what follows. On the other hand, the opening words, "Pleut à Dieu," when, as usual, they express a wish, are normally followed by the subjunctive (as in ll. 1847–48 below); here the indicative follows ("que vous n'estes"). If "Pleut à Dieu" is taken as being also in the indicative (modern French "[il] plut" rather than "plût"), the expression may be translated as I have done, and the contradiction disappears. The parallel passage cited by Lobbes seems to me to support this reading.

203 "Le Roy tient l'aviron" (lit. "holds the oar"). Given the definite article, I take this to mean the so-called "aviron-de-queue" or steering oar. (*Le Trésor de la langue française* cites a similar usage, though from the early nineteenth century, with reference to the Ship of State.) The point may seem trivial, but if Guise instead means, "the king bears an oar," he is approving of the king's support rather than welcoming his leadership—specifically of the Union; the latter seems more in keeping with the respectful humility Matthieu attributes to him.

204 The irony is obvious, but Guise's innocence prevents him from seeing it. Behind this scene clearly lies the model of Caesar's rejection of misgivings to attend the Senate; cf. Grévin, *César*, ed. Ginsberg, 779ff., whose protagonist courageously overcomes his fears. In Marlowe's *Massacre*, on the other hand, Guise's Caesarism is pure arrogance: "Yet Caesar shall go forth. / Let mean conceits and baser men fear death. / Tut, they are peasants; I am Duke of Guise" (xxi.67–69).

205 Again, Guise is innocently blind to the double meaning of the king's words; cf. the inversion of this technique in Marlowe, *Massacre*, where at the corresponding moment the king's deceives Guise with an ambiguous assurance ("Cousin, assure you I am resolute— / Whatsoever any whisper in my ears— / Not to suspect disloyalty in thee" [xxi.44–46]), but the latter's proud self-assurance presents his access to the hidden sense. In Marlowe, by the way, the "whisperer" in the king's ear, who thus corresponds to the N.N., is none other than Epernoun, who, however, is no instrument of the devil.

206 Regarding Guise's doubly clear conscience here, cf. below, ll. 2073–74 and n. 232.

207 " . . . l'alme journee / Qui de Dieu et de nous rapporte l'Hymenee." The representation of Christmas as marking the marriage, such as the Union would have confirmed, of God and man is especially barbed in this context. The king's announced journey to Cléry-Saint-André,

site of the tomb of Louis IX, was part of his ruse.

208 Apparently, the Duke intended to go to the chapel but found it closed and settled for saying a brief prayer at the door (Chevallier, p. 669). (This detail was rather more compatible with the League's image of the Duke than the fact that he had spent part of the night with his mistress [p. 667].) Inclusion of the detail may be due to Grévin's *César*, where the Messenger reports that Caesar went to the Senate without having made sacrifice—an element otherwise found only in obscure sources (see Ginsberg, ed., ll. 900 and n. 111).

209 In the French, too ("Où vas tu"), the Biblical allusion is pointed and presents Guise (as in much League propaganda) as a figure of the betrayed and crucified Christ. Cf. John 13:36: "Simon Peter said unto him, Lord, whither goest thou? Jesus answered him, Whither I go, thou canst not follow me now; but thou shalt follow me afterwards." The extended context—Christ's betrayal by Judas at the instigation of the devil (13:2)—is obviously relevant. Cf. also John 16:5–6: "But now I go my way to him that sent me; and none of you asketh me, Whither goest thou? But because I have said these things unto you, sorrow hath filled your heart."

210 This is the only stanza in this Chorus to rhyme *abba*.

211 Since the immediate reference is to Guise, "diadems" ("diadèmes") must here be metonymic for nobility in general, rather than royalty in particular.

212 "[N]'allegue rien de recevable": in keeping with his juridical training, Matthieu uses legal language to represent the king's trial by conscience.

213 With the futile aim of cementing a short-lived political alliance, Caesar gave his daughter Julia in marriage to Pompey.

214 Again, Childeric III is presumably meant (see above, n. 185).

215 The most effective staging of this scene would call for the Gascon guardsmen, whom the King addresses in l. 1992, to be menacingly present in the background throughout the opening soliloquy.

216 The last two lines, here translated literally, are not without ambiguity, but they seem simply to mean that the most forward and outwardly courageous rebels will be the quickest to take to flight, once the king has eliminated the Duke of Guise. Henri has thus internalized the argument of the N.N. at ll. 1730–32.

217 Lobbes, ed., n. to 1943, takes "sortir de page" to mean "turn the page." More probably, "page" here is the word meaning a young

servant-apprentice in the feudal system: "sortir de page" meant, in older French, to advance beyond the status of a page, and that idea extended figuratively to gaining one's independence, as is attested by a number of expressions; see *Le Grand Robert*.

218   According to Renaissance medical ideas, the image is of the body politic distempered, through contagion, because of Guise's own disease of ambition.

219   I indent and emphasize lines as in the original, which obviously aims by this means to render Henri's self-struggle more dramatic, although the pattern is not perfectly consistent. Behind this passage lies the hesitation of the heroine in Du Bartas's *La Judit* (Lobbes, ed., pp. 46–50); cf. above, n. 184.

220   The expression "royale semence" (lit. "royal seed") would normally be applied to a monarch's descendants, and this might be the meaning here, but it seems more likely that Henri is thinking, in revealingly twisted fashion, of his minions, whom the Union directly aimed at putting down.

221   Henri alludes again to the Spanish sponsorship of the League.

222   "Precious": "mignonne," which (unlike English "minion") can still be used positively. There is an ironic contrast with the perverse "mignons" precious to this king.

223   "[L]e dernier de Valois": even in the editions preceding Henri's assassination, the eradication of his line seems a foregone conclusion.

224   Anne d'Este (of the formidable family of Ferrare) had married the Duke of Nemours after the murder of her first husband François, Duke of Guise (see below, 2104–05) — an event for which she persisted in seeking vengeance against the Protestants, and Gaspard de Coligny in particular. She is well placed, then, to incarnate for Matthieu the victimization of the House of Lorraine, and her mingling of mourning for her son with calls for retribution are true to life. In fact, like several of the prominent women associated with the House of Lorraine, the Duchess of Nemours was militantly active in the cause of the League, and she continued so after her brief imprisonment at Blois on the occasion of the murder. See *Histoire et dictionnaire des Guerres de Religion*, ed. Jouanna et al., under "Lorraine," "Nemours," and "Este," esp. p. 894.

225   This is among the most melodramatic of the many and various accounts of the king's behaviour at the murder scene.

226   "[D]éguisoit" — again, Matthieu could not have been unconscious

of the pun.

227 "[O]ù allez vous?" Cf. above, ll. 1880 and n. 209. The scriptural echo makes itself heard despite the necessity of using the formal "vous" in the place of "tu."

228 The gleaming lilies ("lis") of Guise's faith associate him at once with heavenly purity and with the heaven-bestowed fleur-de-lys of French royalty.

229 I keep "enemy" in the singular of the original: for Matthieu, the Huguenot enemy is at once a single entity and a many-headed monster.

230 A monster in Greek mythology (also known as Aegaeon), who had a hundred arms and fifty heads, as would obviously have been an asset to Guise in this situation. It may also be to the point that, according to some legends, Briareus and his brothers, the sons of Uranus (Heaven), defeated the Titans on behalf of Zeus. See above, ll. 98, 1869–70, and n. 28; cf. *Coligny*, n. 71.

231 "[S]es meurtriers devant son Dieu appelle" (lit. "calls his murderers before his God"); cf. Apoc. 6:10, Gen. 4:10, and the Duchess's renewal of the curse of Cain in ll. 2145ff.

232 One might almost suspect the contradiction between Guise's consciousness of his sins here and his earlier doubly clear conscience (ll. 1843–44) to have engendered the ambiguity in Marlowe's corresponding lines:

> *Guise.* O, I have my death's wound! Give me leave to speak.
> *Second Murderer.* Then pray to God, and ask forgiveness of the King.
> *Guise.* Trouble me not, I ne'er offended Him,
> Nor will I ask forgiveness of the King.        (*Massacre*, xxi.75–78)

See Introduction, p. 67.

233 Cf. Luke 23:46.

234 Atrides: i.e., Agamemnon, son of Atreus, treacherously murdered by his wife Clytemnestra; the death of Hercules (Alcides) was also due to his spouse, Deianira, who unknowingly had given him a poisoned garment. The classical instances, then — famous subjects of tragedy on a grand scale, (Matthieu had himself produced one on Agamemnon) — are all stories of betrayal, although it was the parallel with Caesar that was most widely applied to Guise's death by both supporters and detractors. Matthieu seems again particularly to have recalled the version of Grévin. Lines 2090–91 ("Ainsi mourut

Cesar, ainsi mourut Alcide, / Ainsi meurt par la main d'un perjure, d'un traistre, / Un grand Prince . . .") redeploy to contrary effect the vaunt of Decime Brute:

> Ainsi, ainsi mourront, non de mort naturelle,
> Ceux qui voudront bastir leur puissance nouvelle
> Dessus la liberté, car ainsi les tirans
> Finent le plus souvent le dessein de leurs ans.

> [Thus, thus shall die, not with a natural death, those who would build their new power higher than liberty, for thus do tyrants most often complete the plan of their years.]
>
> (*César*, ed. Ginsberg, ll. 1051–54)

See also the Messenger's recital of César's death to Calpurnie (ll. 875–916) and the latter's lament, which includes an apostrophe urging the murderers to kill her too: "Venez doncques à moi, venez, faux homicides, / Destramper vostre rage en mes veines humides [Come, then, to me, come, false murderers and drench your rage in my moist veins]" (ll. 929–30).

235 Despite its highly political content and its classicism, which reinforces the invocation of retribution upon the House of Valois, this speech also gains emotional force by tapping into the tradition of the *planctus Mariae*, the lament of Mary standing before the cross of the crucified Christ.

236 "Lestrigon": from a savage and cannibalistic people mentioned by Homer (*Odyssey*, Bk. 10); "Sarmat": see above, l. 251 and n. 42 cf. l. 471.

237 The "crescent" ("croissant") must be the moon (not the earth, *pace* Lobbes, ed., n. to l. 2121), with the meaning that the spirit of Guise has passed beyond its sphere, the boundary between the mutable and immutable realms. Thus, too, in Matthieu's *Pompe funèbre*, pp. 23–24, the dead princes are raised to the stars. Such apotheosis was the fate of Hercules.

238 The château of Blois had been enlarged by Louis XII, the grandfather of Madame de Nemours (Lobbes, ed., n. to 2130).

239 Having delivered a virtual *planctus Mariae* in aid of her son's assimilation to the crucified Christ, Guise's mother here shifts into the apocalyptic rhetoric of martyrdom and vengeance often appropriated by both Catholics and Protestants in the period; cf. Apoc. 6:9–17, esp. 6:11. With her vision of divine punishment by way of "remorse" ("remors" [l. 2149]), cf. the peroration of Matthieu's *Pompe funèbre*, where he assumes much the same prophetic tone with an

even sharper political edge:

> En quelle saulse mangez vous vos delices? à quel traits humez vous vos plaisirs, par force retranchez, ayant à vos flancs l'ombre de ces deux Princes, et dernier [*sic*, for "derrière"] vous le victorieux Duc du Mayne? Vous voyez l'espée nue, pendu à vn poil de cheual au dessus de vostre teste.

> [With what sauce do you eat your delicacies? With what draughts do you moisten your pleasures, of necessity curtailed, having at your side the shades of those two princes, and at your back the victorious Duke of Mayenne? You see the naked sword hanging by a horse-hair over your head.]                    (p. 22)

Cf. also *Coligny*, ll. 193ff., esp. 235–40, where the blood of the previous Duke of Guise similarly torments the Admiral. Obviously to the point, as well, is César's anticipation of the destiny of his murderer in Grévin's tragedy:

> Quel honneur, quel proffit, quel plaisir, quel bienfaict
> Suyvra l'auteur premier d'un si cruel mesfaict?
> Mais plustost un remors, un remors miserable
> De la mort desireux talonnant ce coupable
> Viendra ramentevoir un antique desir,
> Allonguissant ses jours, lorsqu'il vouldra mourir,
> Se sentant trop heureux, si pour mieux luy complaire,
> On avance sa mort ainsi qu'il me veult faire.

> [What honour, what profit, what pleasure, what benefit shall come to the first author of such a cruel crime? Rather, remorse, wretched remorse, desirous of death, dogging the heels of the guilty one shall bring to his mind a long-past desire, prolonging his days when he wishes to die, counting himself only too happy if someone would oblige him by advancing his death, as he seeks to do to me.]                    (Ginsberg, ed., 109–16)

240 The last two lines, which were dropped from the third, post-regicide edition, refer to so-called *amende honorable*, the public ritual whereby criminals, including heretics, were compelled to ask pardon of God, the king, and justice, often prior to execution; see Nicholls, esp. pp. 49–50 and 58. In fact, Henri was shaken when the Pope threatened him with excommunication if he did not perform *amende honorable* for the death of the Cardinal of Guise (*Histoire et dictionnaire des Guerres de Religion*, ed. Jouanna et al., p. 967).

# Bibliography

## Early Texts and Editions

*Arrest de la covrt de parlement contre Gaspart de Colligny, qui fut Admiral de France, mis en huict langues, à sçavoir, François, Latin, Italien, Espagno, Allemant, Flament, Anglois et Escoçois* (1569). *Archives curieuses de l'histoire de France.* Ed. Cimber L. and C. Danjou. Ser. 1, vol. 6. Paris: Beauvais, Membre de l'Institut Historique, 1835. 375–93.

Aubigné, Agrippa d'. *Les tragiques.* Ed. Frank Lestringant. Paris: Gallimard, 1995.

Barnaud, Nicolas (attrib.). *Le Reveille-Matin des François et de levrs voisins: Composé par Eusebe Philadelphe Cosmopolite, en forme de Dialogues.* 1574; fac. sim. Paris: Éditions d'Histoire Sociale, 1977.

Belleforest, François de. *Les grandes Annales et histoire générale de France, dès la venue des Francs en Gaule jusques au règne du Roy très-chrestien Henry III.* 2 vols. Paris: G. Buon, 1579.

Belyard, Simon. *Le Guysien, ou perfidie tyrannique commise par Henry de Valois es personnes Princes Loys de Loraine Cardinal & Archevesque de Rheims, & Henry de Loraine Duc de Guyse, grand Maistre de France.* Troyes: Jean Moreau, 1592.

Bèze, Théodore de. *A Tragedie of Abrahams Sacrifice, Written in French by Theodore Beza and Translated into English by Arthur Golding.* Ed. Malcolm W. Wallace. English version trans. Arthur Golding. Toronto: University of Toronto Library, 1906.

Boucher, Jean (attrib.). *Histoire tragique et memorable de Pierre de Gaverston [sic] Gentil-homme Gascon jadis le mignon d'Edoüard 2. Roi d'Angletere, tirée des Chroniques de Thomas Walsinghan [sic] & tournée de Latin en François Dédiée à Monseigneur le duc d'Espernon.* [n.p.]: [n.pub.], 1588.

Brantôme, Pierre de Bourdeille, abbé de. *Œuvres complètes.* Ed. Ludovic Lalanne. 11 vols. Paris: La Société de l'Histoire de France, 1864–82.

Capilupi, Camillo. *Le stratagème, ou la ruse de Charles IX, Roy de France, contre les Huguenots rebelles à Dieu et à luy. Archives curieuses de l'histoire de France.* Ed. L. Cimber and C. Danjou. Ser. 1, vol. 7. Paris: Beauvais, Membre de l'Institut Historique, 1835. 401–71.

Chantelouve, François de, seigneur de Grossombre. *Pharaon.* Ed. Marian Meijer. *La tragédie à l'époque d'Henri III,* vol. 1 (1574–1579). Théâtre français de la Renaissance, ser. 2. Florence: Leo S. Olschki; Paris: Presses Universitaires de France, 1999.

——. *La tragédie de feu Gaspar de Colligni, Jadis Admiral de France, contenant ce qui advint à Paris le 24 Aoust 1572, avec le nom des Personnages.* Ed. N. Lenglet du Fresnoy. Paris: P. Gandouin, 1744.

——. *La tragédie de feu Gaspar de Colligni, Jadis Admiral de France, contenant ce qui advint à Paris le 24 Aoust 1572, avec le nom des Personnages. Journal de Henri III, Roy de France et de Pologne, par Pierre de L'Estoile. Nouvelle édition. Accompagnée de remarques historiques, et des pièces manuscrites les plus curieuses de ce règne.* Ed. J. Le Duchat, D. Godefroy, and N. Lenglet de Fresnoy. 5 vols. La Haye: P. Grosse; Paris: P. Gandouin, 1744. 1: 549–98.

——. *La tragédie de fev Gaspard de Colligny iadis Admiral de France, contenant ce qui aduint à Paris le 24. d'Aoust 1572, auec le nom des personnages.* [Paris]: [N. Bonfons], 1575.

——. *La tragédie de feu Gaspard de Colligny.* Ed. Keith Cameron. Exeter: University of Exeter Press, 1971.

——. *La tragédie de feu Gaspard de Coligny.* Ed. Lisa Wollfe. *La tragédie à l'époque d'Henri III,* vol. 1 (1574–1579). Théâtre français de la Renaissance, ser. 2. Florence: Leo S. Olschki; Paris: Presses Universitaires de France, 1999.

——. *Tragédie de Pharaon et autres œuvres poétiques, contenant hymnes, divers sonnets et chansons.* Paris: N. Bonfons, 1577.

Chapman, George. *The Tragedy of Caesar and Pompey. The Plays of George Chapman: The Tragedies.* Ed. Thomas Marc Parrott. 2 vols. Vol. 2. New York: Russell and Russell, 1961.

Chréstien, Florent. *Jephté, tragédie traduicte du latin de George Buchanan, escossais.* Paris: R. Estienne, 1573.

Claudian [Claudius Claudianus]. *In Rufinum [Against Rufinus]. Claudian.* Ed. and trans. Maurice Platnauer. 2 vols. Vol. 1. Loeb Classical Library. Cambridge, MA: Harvard University Press; London: Heinemann, 1976.

Cotgrave, Randall. *A Dictionarie of the French and English Tongues*. Anglistica and Americana, 77. 1611. Fac. rpt. Hildesheim: Georg Holms, 1970.

*La double tragédie du Duc et Cardinal de Guyse jouée à Bloys le 23 et 24 Décembre dernier, envoyée à Mgr. le Duc du Mayne et autres Princes catholiques, qui tiennent le party de la saincte union* [anonymous poem]. Paris: Fleurant des Monceaux, 1589.

Du Bartas, Guillaume de Salluste, seigneur. *La Judit*. Ed. André Baïche. Publications de la Faculté des Lettres et Sciences Humaines de Toulouse, ser. A, vol. 12. Toulouse: Association des Publications de la Faculté des Lettres et Sciences Humaines de Toulouse, 1971.

———. *La sepmaine (texte de 1581)*. Ed. Yvonne Bellenger. Société des Textes Français Modernes. Paris: Librairie Nizet, 1981.

Du Rosier, Pierre. *Déploration de la France sur la calamité des dernieres guerres ciuilles aduenues en icelle, l'an 1568*. Paris: Denis du Pré, 1568.

Estienne, Henri (attrib.). *Discours merveilleux de la vie, action et deportements de Catherine de Medicis, royne-mere*. Ed. Nicole Cazauran et al. Les Classiques de la Pensée Politique, 15. Geneva: Droz, 1995.

Fleury, Antoine. *Responce à un certain escrit, publié par l'Admiral et ses adherans, prentendans couvrir et excuser la rupture qu'ils on faite de l'Edict de Pacification, et leurs nouveaux remuemens et entreprinses contre l'Estat du Roi, et le bien et repos de ses subjectz*. Paris: Claude Fremy, 1568.

Fronton Du Duc. *The Tragic History of La Pucelle of Domrémy, Otherwise Known as The Maid of Orléans*. Trans. with Introduction and Notes by Richard Hillman. Carleton Renaissance Plays in Translation, 39. Ottawa: Dovehouse Editions, 2005.

Garnier, Robert. *Antonius*. Trans. Mary Sidney Herbert, Countess of Pembroke. London: William Ponsonby, 1592.

———. *Cornelia*. Trans. Thomas Kyd. *The Works of Thomas Kyd*. Ed. Frederick S. Boas. Oxford: Clarendon Press, 1901.

———. *Cornélie*. Ed. Jean-Claude Ternaux. Textes de la Renaissance, 53. Paris: H. Champion, 2002.

———. *"Hymne de la Monarchie." Robert Garnier. Sa vie, ses poésies inédites avec son véritable portrait et un facsimile de sa signature*. By Henri Chardon. 1905. Rpt. Geneva: Slatkine Reprints, 1970. 249–70.

———. *Œuvres complètes de Robert Garnier: Porcie, Cornélie*. Ed. Raymond Lebègue. Les Textes Français. Paris: Les Belles Lettres, 1973.

Gentillet, Innocent. *Anti-Machiavel. Édition de 1576 avec commentaires et notes*. Ed. C. Edward Rathé. Les Classiques de la Pensée Politique, 5. Geneva: Droz, 1968.

Grévin, Jacques. *César.* Ed. Ellen S. Ginsberg. Textes littéraires français. Geneva: Droz, 1971.

*La Guisiade. A Monseigneur Charles de Lorraine, duc de Mayenne, pair et lieutenant général de l'Estat royal et Couronne de France* [anonymous poem]. [n.p.: n.pub], 1589.

Horace [Quintus Horatius Flaccus]. *Odes and Epodes (Q. Horatii Flacci Carminum Libri IV, Epodon Liber).* Ed. T.E. Page. London: Macmillan, 1967.

Hotman, François (attrib.). *The lyfe of the most godly, valeant and noble capteine and maintener of the trew Christian religion in Fraunce, Iasper Colignie Shatilion, sometyme greate admirall of Fraunce.* Trans. Arthur Golding. London: Thomas Vautrollier, 1576.

——. *La vie de Messire Gaspar de Colligny Admiral de France (c. 1577).* Ed. Émile-V. Telle. 1643. Fac. rpt. Geneva: Droz, 1987.

Jamyn, Amadis. "Epitaphe du feu roy Charles IX." *Le Tombeau du feu Roy Tres-Chrestien Charles IX, Prince tres-debonnaire, tres-vertueux & treseloquant, par Pierre de Ronsard Aumosnier ordinaire de sa Majesté & autres excellents Poëtes de ce temps.* Paris: F. Morel, 1574.

Jodelle, Etienne. *Cléopâtre captive.* Ed. Françoise Charpentier, Jean-Dominique Beaudin, and José Sanchez. Mugron: J. Feijóo, 1990.

Languet, Hubert (?), Philippe de Mornay (?) (pseud. Stephanus Junius Brutus). *Vindiciae contra tyrannos: sive, De principis in populum, populique in principes, legitima potestae.* "Edinburgh" (Basel (?)): [n. pub.], 1579.

*La magicienne étrangère, tragédie en laquelle on voit les tiranniques comportemens, origines, entreprises, desseigns, sortilleges, arest, mort et supplice, tant du marquis d'Ancre que de Leonor Galligay, sa femme, etc.* Rouen: D. Geuffroy et J. Besongne, 1617.

Marlowe, Christopher. *The Massacre at Paris. Dido Queen of Carthage and the Massacre at Paris.* Ed. H.J. Oliver. The Revels Plays. London: Methuen, 1968.

——. *The Tragical History of the Life and Death of Doctor Faustus.* Ed. John D. Jump. The Revels Plays. London: Methuen, 1962.

Matthieu, Pierre. *Aelius Sejanus, histoire recueillie de divers auteurs.* Paris: R. Estienne, 1617.

——. *Clytemnestre. De la vengeance des injures perdurable à la postérité des offencez, et des malheureuses fins de la volupté.* Ed. Gilles Ernst. Textes Littéraires Français. Geneva: Droz, 1984.

——. *Discours veritable, et sans passion. Sur la prinse des armes & changemens aduenus en la ville de Lyon, pour la conseruation d'icelle, sous l'obéissance de la S. Vnion & de la Coronne de France, le 18 septembre 1593.* Lyons: [n.pub.], 1593.

——. *L'entree de très-grand, très-chrestien très-magnanime et victorieux prince Henri IIII. Roy de France & de Nauarre en sa bonne ville de Lyon, le IIII septembre l'an MDXXXXV. de son regne le VII. de son aage le XLII. Contenant l'ordre & la description.* Lyons: P. Michel, 1595.

——. *La Guisiade.* Ed. Louis Lobbes. Textes Littéraires Français. Geneva: Droz, 1990.

——. *Pompe funèbre des pénitens de Lyon, en déploration du massacre faict à Blois sur les illustres et genereuses personnes de Louys et Henry de Lorraine, avec l'oraison sur les mesme suject, prononcée par M. Pierre Matthieu, Docteur és Droicts & Aduocat.* Lyons: J. Roussin, 1589.

——. *Stances svr l'hevreuse publication de la paix et saincte vnion. Avec un Hymne de même argument prins de l'Erinophile du sieur Germain d'Apchon, Chevalier de l'ordre du Roy.* Lyons: B. Rigaud, 1588.

*Miracles de Nostre Dame par personnages.* Ed. Gaston Paris and Ulysse Robert. Paris: Firmin Didot, 1876–83.

Montaigne, Michel de. *Les Essais de Michel de Montaigne. Édition conforme au texte de l'exemplaire de Bordeaux avec les additions de l'édition posthume, etc.* Ed. Pierre Villey. Rev. V.-L. Saulnier. Paris: Presses Universitaires de France, 1965.

Nashe, Thomas. *The Unfortunate Traveller. The Works of Thomas Nashe.* Ed. Ronald B. McKerrow. Rev. F.P. Wilson. 5 vols. Oxford: Blackwell, 1958. 2: 187–328.

*Opuscula et moralia carmina sciliet: de Nuce, de Philomena et de Pulice.* Rouen: R. Goupil, [1500–21?].

Peele, George. *David and Bethsabe. The Dramatic Works of George Peele.* Ed. Elmer Blistein, *Life and Works of George Peele,* vol. 3. New Haven, CT: Yale University Press, 1970.

Plutarch. *Plutarch's Lives.* Ed. and trans. Bernadotte Perrin. 11 vols. Loeb Classical Library. Cambridge, MA: Harvard University Press; London: Heinemann, 1914–26.

Rabelais, François. *Le Quart Livre.* Ed. Robert Marichal. Textes Littéraires Français. Lille: Giard; Geneva: Droz, 1947.

Rivaudeau, André. *Aman. Tragédie sainte.* Ed. Keith Cameron. Geneva: Droz, 1969.

Ronsard, Pierre de. *Œuvres complètes.* Ed. Jean Céard, Daniel Ménager, and Michel Simonin. 2 vols. Bibliothèque de la Pléiade. Paris: Gallimard, 1993–94.

——, Amadis Jamyn, and Robert Garnier. *Le Tombeau du feu Roy Tres-Chrestien Charles IX, Prince tres-debonnaire, tres-vertueux & tres-eloquant, par Pierre de Ronsard Aumosnier ordinaire de sa Majesté & autres excellent Poëtes de ce temps.* Paris: F. Morel, 1574.

Seneca, Lucius Annaeus. *Four Tragedies and Octavia*. Trans. and ed. E.F. Watling. Harmondsworth, Middlesex: Penguin Books, 1966.

——. *Les tragédies très-éloquentes du grant Philosophe Seneque diligentement traduictes de Latin en Françoy. Avec plusieurs épitaphes, épigrammes, dictz moraulx et aultres choses mémorables nouvellement adjoustées.* Ed. and trans. Pierre Grognet. Lyons: [n.pub.], 1539.

Shakespeare, William. *Hamlet*. Ed. Harold Jenkins. The Arden Shakespeare. London: Methuen, 1982.

——. *The Riverside Shakespeare*. Gen. eds. G. Blakemore Evans and J.J.M. Tobin. 2nd ed. Boston: Houghton Mifflin, 1997.

Sidney, Philip, and Hubert Languet. *The Correspondence of Sir Philip Sidney and Hubert Languet*. Ed. and trans. Steuart A. Pears. Westmead, Farnborough, Hants: Gregg, 1971.

Spenser, Edmund. *The Complete Poetical Works of Spenser*. Ed. R.E. Neil Dodge. Cambridge edition. Boston: Houghton Mifflin, 1908.

Virgil [Publius Virgilius Maro]. *The Aeneid of Virgil*. Ed. T.E. Page. 2 vols. London: Macmillan; New York: St. Martin's, 1967.

*Le Vray Discovrs de la deffaicte des Reistres par Monsieur le Duc de Guyse, le lundy dixiesme d'octobre, 1575. Ensemble la poursuyte, qui a esté faicte à l'encontre d'iceux.* Paris: J. de Lastre, [1576].

Whetstone, George. *Promos and Cassandra. Narrative and Dramatic Sources of Shakespeare*. Ed. Geoffrey Bullough. 8 vols. Vol. 2. London: Routledge and Kegan Paul; New York: Columbia University Press, 1963. 442–513.

## Critical and Historical Scholarship

Brereton, Geoffrey. *French Tragic Drama in the Sixteenth and Seventeenth Centuries*. London: Methuen, 1973.

Buisseret, David. *Henry IV, King of France*. London: Routledge, 1984.

Capefigue, Jean-Baptiste-Honoré-Raymond. *Histoire de la Réforme, de la Ligue, et du règne de Henri IV*. 8 vols. Paris: Duféy, 1834–35.

Cazaux, Yves. *Jeanne d'Albret*. Paris: Éditions Albin Michel, 1973.

Chaintron, Maria. *Le duc d'épernon 1554–1642. L'ascension prodigieuse d'un cadet de Gascogne*. Paris: Éditions Publisud, 1988.

Chardon, Henri. *Robert Garnier. Sa vie, ses poésies inédites avec son véritable portrait et un facsimile de sa signature*. 1905. Rpt. Geneva: Slatkine Reprints, 1970.

Chevallier, Pierre. *Henri III: roi shakespearien*. Paris: Fayard, 1985.

Chocheyras, J. "La Tragédie politique d'actualité sous les régnes de Henri III et de Henri IV." *Études sur Étienne Dolet: le théâtre au XVIe siècle: le Forez, le Lyonnais et l'histoire du livre. Publiées à la mémoire de Claude Longeon.* Ed. Gabriel-André Pérouse. Travaux d'Humanisme et Renaissance, 270. Geneva: Droz, 1993. 161–73.

Constant, Jean-Marie. *Les Guise.* Paris: Hachette, 1984.

Crouzet, Denis. *Les guerriers de Dieu. La violence au temps des troubles de religion (vers 1525–vers 1610).* 2 vols. Seyssel: Champ Vallon, 1990.

——. *La nuit de la Saint-Barthélemy. Un rêve perdu de la Renaissance.* Paris: Fayard, 1994.

Ebert, Adolf. *Entwicklungs-Geschichte der Französischen Tragödie vornehmlich im XVI. Jahrhundert.* 1865. Rpt. Geneva: Slatkine Reprints, 1970.

Ernst, Gilles. "Des deux *Guisiade* de Pierre Matthieu." *Bibliothèque d'Humanisme et Renaissance* 47 (1985): 367–78.

Faguet, Émile. *La tragédie française au XVIe siècle (1550–1600).* Paris: Hachette, 1883.

——. *La tragédie française au XVIe siècle (1550–1600).* 2nd ed. Paris: Fontemoing, 1912.

Forsyth, Elliott. *La tragédie française de Jodelle à Corneille (1533–1640). Le thème de la vengeance.* Études et Essais sur la Renaissance, 5. 1962. Rpt. Paris: H. Champion, 1994.

Freeman, Arthur. *Thomas Kyd: Facts and Problems.* Oxford: Clarendon Press, 1967.

Gofflot, L.-V. *Le théâtre au college du moyen âge à nos jours.* Introd. Jules Claretie. Le cercle français de l'Union Harvard. Paris: H. Champion, 1907.

Hillman, Richard. "Richard II, *La Guisiade* of Pierre Matthiieu and the Invention of Tragic Heroes." *Richard II de William Shakespeare. Un œuvre en contexte.* Ed. Eisabelle Schwartz-Gastine. *Cahiers de la Maison de la Recherche en Sciences Humaines,* numéro spécial, février 2005. Caen: Équipe Littéraire et Sociétés Anglophones, Cahiers de la Maison de la Recherche en Sciences Humaines de Caen. 87–98.

——. *Shakespeare, Marlowe and the Politics of France.* Houndmills, Basingstoke, Hampshire: Palgrave, 2002.

Huchon, Mireille. "Vie de Sainte Catherine ou Discours merveilleux: les avatars d'un pamphlet." *Cahiers V.-L. Saulnier* 2 (1984): 55–67.

Hutton, James. *Themes of Peace in Renaissance Poetry.* Ed. Rita Guerlac. Ithaca, NY: Cornell University Press, 1984.

Jondorf, Gillian. *French Renaissance Tragedy: The Dramatic Word.* Cambridge Studies in French. Cambridge: Cambridge University Press, 1990.

———. *Robert Garnier and the Themes of Political Tragedy in the Sixteenth Century.* Cambridge: Cambridge University Press, 1969.

Jouanna, Arlette, Jacqueline Boucher, Dominique Biloghi, and Guy Le Thiec, eds. *Histoire et dictionnaire des Guerres de Religion.* Paris: Robert Laffont, 1998.

Kingdon, Robert M. *Myths About the St. Bartholomew's Day Massacres 1572–1576.* Cambridge, MA: Harvard University Press, 1988.

Lacroix, Paul (pseud. "P.-L. Jacob, bibliophile") et al. *Bibliothèque dramatique de M. De Soleinne.* 9 vols. in 6. Paris: Administration de l'Alliance des Arts, 1843–45.

Lamb, Mary Ellen. *Gender and Authorship in the Sidney Circle.* Madison: University of Wisconsin Press, 1990.

Lazard, Madeleine. *Le théâtre en France au XVIe siècle.* Littératures Modernes. Paris: Presses Universitaires de France, 1980.

Lebègue, Raymond. "La Renaissance: théâtre et politique religieuse." *Études sur le théâtre français.* 2 vols. Vol. 1: Moyen Âge, Rennaissance, Baroque. Paris: Nizet, 1977. 195–206.

———. "La Renaissance: les tragédies de Sénèque et le théâtre de la Renaissance." *Études sur le théâtre français.* 2 vols. Vol. 1: Moyen Âge, Rennaissance, Baroque. Paris: Nizet, 1977. 180–94.

———. "Tableau de la tragédie française de 1575 à 1610." *Bibliothèque d'Humanisme et Renaissance* 5 (1944): 373–93.

———. *La tragédie française de la Renaissance.* 2nd ed. Collections Lebègue et Nationale, 4th ser., no. 46. Bruxelles: Office de Publicité, 1954.

———. *La tragédie religieuse en France: les débuts (1514–1573).* Bibliothèque Littéraire de la Renaissance, n.s., vol. 17. Paris: H. Champion, 1929.

———. "La tragédie 'shakespearienne' en France au temps de Shakespeare." *Études sur le théâtre français.* 2 vols. Vol. 1: Moyen Âge, Renaissance, Baroque. Paris: Nizet, 1977. 298–339.

Lobbes, Louis. "Du Bartas et Matthieu: genèse d'une vocation de dramaturge." *L'art du théâtre. Mélanges en hommage à Robert Garapon.* Ed. Yvonne Bellenger, Gabriel Conesa, Jean Garapon et al. Paris: Presses Universitaires de France, 1992. 61–66.

———. "L'exécution des Guises, prétexte à tragédie." *Le mécénat et l'influence des Guises. Actes du colloque organisé par le Centre de Recherche sur la Littérature de la Renaissance de l'Université de Reims et tenu à Joinville du 31 mai au 4 juin 1994 (et à Reims pour la journée du 2 juin).* Ed. Yvonne Bellenger. Colloques, Congrès et Conférences sur la Renaissance, 9. Paris: H. Champion, 1997. 567–79.

———. "Pierre Matthieu, dramaturge phénix (1563–1621)." *Revue d'histoire du théâtre* 50 (1998): 207–36.

Mazouer, Charles. "Chantelouve et la Saint-Barthélemy: *La tragédie de feu Gaspard de Colligny* (1575)." *Les écrivains et la politique dans le sud-ouest de la France autour des années 1580. Actes du Colloque de Bordeaux 6–7 novembre 1981.* Ed. Claude-Gilbert Dubois et al. Bordeaux: Presses Universitaires de Bordeaux, 1982. 129–40.

———. *Le théâtre français de la Renaissance.* Paris: H Champion, 2002.

McGowan, Margaret M. *The Vision of Rome in Late Renaissance France.* New Haven, CT: Yale University Press, 2000.

Millet, Olivier. Review of Louis Lobbes, ed., *La Guisiade,* by Pierre Matthieu (Geneva: Droz, 1990). *Bulletin de la Société de l'Histoire du Protestantisme Français* 138 (1992): 312–13.

Nicholls, David. "The Theatre of Martyrdom in the French Reformation." *Past and Present* 121 (1988): 49–73.

Noguères, Henri. *The Massacre of Saint Bartholomew.* Trans. Claire-Éliane Engel. London: Allen and Unwin, 1962.

Pallier, Denis. *Recherches sur l'imprimerie à Paris pendant la Ligue (1585–1594).* Centre de Recherches d'Histoire et de Philologie, 4^e Section de l'École Pratique des Hautes Études, 6; Histoire et Civilisation du Livre, 9. Geneva: Droz, 1975.

Parmelee, Lisa Ferraro. *Good Newes from Fraunce: French Anti-League Propaganda in Late Elizabethan England.* Rochester, NY: University of Rochester Press, 1996.

Peach, Trevor, and Jean Brunel, comps. *Le "Fonds Goujet" de la Bibliothèque Municipale de Versailles: Textes littéraires des XVI^e, XVII^e et XVIII^e siècles: Catalogue alphabétique.* Geneva: Slatkine, 1992.

Pernot, Michel. "Le cardinal de Lorraine et la fondation de l'université de Pont-à-Mousson." *L'Université de Pont-à-Mousson et les problèmes de son temps. Actes du colloque organisé par l'Institut de Recherche Régionale en Sciences Sociales, Humaines et Économiques de l'Université de Nancy II (Nancy 16–19 October 1972).* Nancy: Université de Nancy II, 1974. 45–66.

Postel, Claude. *Traité des invectives au temps de la Réforme.* Paris: Les Belles Lettres, 2004.

Romier, Lucien. *Les Origines politiques des Geurres de religion.* 2 vols. 1913–14. Rpt. Geneva: Slatkine-Megariotis, 1974.

Stone, Donald, Jr. *French Humanist Tragedy: A Reassessment.* Manchester: Manchester University Press, 1974.

Street, J.S. *French Sacred Drama from Bèze to Corneille: Dramatic Forms and the Purposes in the Early Modern Theatre.* Cambridge: Cambridge University Press, 1983.

Sutherland, Nicola Mary. *The Massacre of St Bartholomew and the European Conflict 1559–1572*. London: Macmillan, 1973.

Taveneaux, René. "L'Esprit de croisade en Lorraine aux XVI<sup>e</sup> et XVII<sup>e</sup> siècles." *L'Europe, l'Alsace et la France, problèmes intérieurs et réactions internationales à l'epoque modern. Études réunies en l'honneur du Doyen Georges Livet pour son 70<sup>e</sup> anniversaire*. Publications de la Société Savante d'Alsace et des Régions de l'Est, Collection "Grandes Publications." Colmar: Les Éditions d'Alsace, 1986. 256–63.

Tissier de Mallerais, Martine. "La propagande par le texte et l'image." *La tragédie de Blois. Quatre siècles de polémique autour de l'assassinat du duc de Guise. Catalogue de l'exposition au Château de Blois 17 décembre 1988–19 février 1989*. Ed. Martine Tissier de Mallerais et al. Blois: Ville de Blois, Conservation du Château et des Musées, 1988. 29–38.

Tricomi, Albert H. "Joan la Pucelle and the Inverted Saints Play in *1 Henry VI*." *Renaissance and Reformation/Renaissance et Réforme* 25.2 (2001): 5–31.

Yates, Frances. *The French Academies of the Sixteenth Century*. Studies of the Warburg Institute, vol. 15. London: Warburg Institute, University of London, 1947.

**Carleton Renaissance Plays in Translation**

This volume of the Carleton Renaissance Plays in Translation was produced using the T<sub>E</sub>X typesetting system, with Adobe Palatino PostScript fonts and in-house critical edition macros.

Printed and bound
in Boucherville, Quebec, Canada by
MARC VEILLEUX IMPRIMEUR INC.
in August, 2005